"You want e~~noug~~ get a good seal."

"Like this?" She put the instrument to her mouth, her lips tingling at the smooth feel of metal still warm from his mouth.

"Right." He drew her hands up and cupped them around the mouth harp. His heat curled around her; leather, and the dark richness of his own scent, played havoc with her senses. Her hands trembled and she forced herself to concentrate on his voice, his instructions.

"There are ten holes. Feel each hole with your tongue." Startled at his words as much as at the intimacy of his voice, she jerked her gaze to him. Was he joking? A corner of his lips tugged up in a half grin. He stared at her, waiting.

"Okay." Her voice was soft, breathless with anticipation, and she berated herself. He was giving her a mouth harp lesson, nothing more.

"No, no. Imagine you're kissing someone." He gave a short laugh. "A lover—not the pope's hand."

Her gaze was riveted on him. Was he really teaching her to play the instrument or was he up to something else entirely?

High Praise for *A Secret Yearning*

"AN EXCITING AND MOVING WESTERN RO-
MANCE starring two superb lead characters who
have the complexity to make the audience believe in
them."

—Harriet Klausner, *Affaire de Coeur*

"A GREAT READ! Debra Cowan paints such vivid
scenes with words that you'd think she had a paint-
brush and canvas in hand!"

—Carol Finch, author of *River Moon*

"EXCITING, VIVID AND TOUCHING. Debra
Cowan is pure gold."

—Janis Reams Hudson, author of *Apache Flame*

"DEBRA COWAN HAS PENNED A MARVEL-
OUS TALE. This is what romance is all about. She
writes from the heart and it shows. *A Secret Yearning*
will leave you wanting more."

—Kristina Wright, *The Literary Times*

"A GREAT READ! *A SECRET YEARNING* is a
fast-paced, fabulous love story. This emotional page-
turner by a multitalented author will captivate the
reader."

—Sara Orwig, author of *Comanche Temptation*

A
SECRET
YEARNING

Debra Cowan

A Dell Book

Published by
Dell Publishing
a division of
Bantam Doubleday Dell Publishing Group, Inc.
1540 Broadway
New York, New York 10036

ISBN: 0-440-22195-1

Printed in the United States of America

Published simultaneously in Canada

September 1996

10 9 8 7 6 5 4 3 2 1

OPM

To the memory of Mike McQuay
(1949–1995)

Teacher extraordinaire, peer, friend

ACKNOWLEDGMENTS

Very special thanks to Barbara Stoll of the Missouri Historical Society Library for the maps, the recommended reference material, and the generous gift of her time.

Veiled by night, secret passion flickers
And flares into yearning.
It hungers,
It bares,
It nurtures.
Embrace the yearning
For it shall come no more.

                              D.S.C.

CHAPTER ONE

August 1873
Calcutta, Missouri

She was an angel sent to comfort him and he intended to take full advantage.

"Let me go," Regina whispered. The man in the alley intimidated her like the devil himself. She'd been drawn to Cole Wellington since her arrival six months earlier, but had managed to keep a distance. Until now.

Her demand echoed along the alleyway of the town orphanage, shattering the stillness of the clammy night. Cole blinked, trying to focus on the woman in front of him.

The small building, the alley backing onto the north edge of town, told Cole where he was, but who was she? Fixing his gaze on her face, he tried to steady his wobbling world. Though her features were blurred due to darkness and too much whiskey, he knew she was beautiful. Oddly, a faint sense of the forbidden surfaced, but the liquor washed it away.

She smelled of fresh soap and sultry heat. The heavy tang of his whiskey hovered on the edge. Darkness shrouded her hair. He couldn't see her eyes, but somehow knew he'd seen them before and they were as green as the verdant Missouri hills behind his home. Something about her nagged at him, though his fuzzy brain couldn't grasp it.

In the midnight shadows, her eyes were deep, mesmerizing, afraid. He focused on her face as much to steady himself as to satisfy the hunger growing inside him. She *was* an angel—his angel. Ignoring the fear in her eyes, he leaned closer. Clumsy with drink, he stumbled and braced his body against hers.

Regina shuddered with both awareness and apprehension. She wanted to lean into his hard body, steal some of his strength, but her caution of the last months prevailed. Her nun's robes had provided the perfect disguise in her attempt to hide from her father's murderer. She couldn't jeopardize her disguise, not for a moment that would certainly lead to regret.

"Please. Don't." Her soft voice was strained.

The night, thick and hot, was made for cool water and dark secrets. And Cole wanted to plumb the depths of this woman's secrets, all of them. He reached for her.

Frightened by the sharp tug of desire in her belly, she bucked against him and her breasts brushed his chest. "You don't want to do this."

"You're right." He pinned her against the rough boards of the wooden building and stilled both of her hands against his chest with one of his. The alcohol burned through his veins, firing his lust. With his free hand he traced the starched whiteness of her collar. "I want to do much, much more."

"Let me go," she hissed. She struggled again, landing an elbow to one of his ribs. He grunted and shifted slowly, his reflexes dulled by the liquor.

Anger burned behind the whiskey. She was resisting, playing with him, taunting him with a game he had never understood. Sarah always did that. His brain clicked at the reference to his wife. No, the woman with him wasn't Sarah. But Sarah was the reason he was hurting so damn bad.

Though the woman in front of him struggled, he knew she wanted him, but something about her pricked his conscience, nagged like a long-forgotten prayer. Trying to connect with what he knew, he shook his head. The movement spurred rivets of pain through his skull and down his neck.

"Be still," he growled. The words sounded slurred even to his own numbed ears.

Tired of being denied what he knew they both wanted, Cole kissed her. Roughly at first, then gentling as her tense surprise gave way to surrender.

The warm, insistent pressure of his lips thawed her defenses. She relaxed against him and opened her mouth. He made a sound of satisfaction deep in his throat and stroked her tongue with his.

Desire stabbed down low, and she ached to give herself to him. *Give herself to him?* She hadn't successfully escaped Wendell Cross by boarding that boat in St. Louis only to lose all ground now, when Abe Grand's detectives were so close to finding her father's murderer. Alarmed at the heat stealing through her body, she shoved at Cole's chest—hard—and pushed past him.

He staggered back, grabbing for her arm and getting only air. "Damn!"

He whirled to see her disappear into the night. Pain swelled in his head as the flowing black of her dress fused with darkness. A flash of white. The hollow clack of wooden bead against wooden bead. A spark of memory.

Cole blinked, realization widening his eyes. He remembered, at last, what had bothered him about the woman.

"Holy hell!"

He'd just accosted a nun.

In the last six months Cole had spent more time drunk than sober. And look what he'd done because of it. Shame and revulsion tugged at him. He'd pawed a nun, an innocent. A woman sheltered from men. Until now.

"Hell." He leaned against the wall and slid to the ground, his boot clanking against the empty whiskey bottle he'd dropped when she'd come down the alleyway.

Since Sarah's betrayal and death, he'd surrendered to the numbing peace of alcohol. But now even an entire bottle couldn't staunch the reality of how squalid and meaningless his life had become. Tortured by guilt and anger, Cole had become a man mired in helplessness, a man with no pride. A man who stooped to accosting nuns.

If only he hadn't turned on Sarah. If only he hadn't lost his temper, perhaps she wouldn't have run from him.

But his guilt held an edge of rage. He'd had a right

to his anger. After all he'd found his wife with another man. Not just any man but a man he considered as close as a brother. A man he'd thought dead. A man he would kill.

Cole hated what he'd become, hated that he couldn't crawl out of a shot of whiskey long enough to know his own name, much less find Sutter. And now he'd tried to seduce a woman of the cloth.

He rested his head against the rough wood of the wall at his back. For the first time since the night Sarah and the baby had died, Cole forced himself to remember, to *feel*. He let the memories razor through him.

The winter thunderstorm abated and clouds scudded away from the moon, leaving a steady glow. He stood in the doorway of the barn as shock rippled into pain.

A couple nestled in the hay, kissing, stroking, fondling. The man was big with shaggy dark hair and wide shoulders. The woman was blond with china blue eyes, still slender despite her eight-month pregnancy.

Cole's wife. And his best friend.

When Sarah had left the house that night, he'd followed her, intent on discovering the reason for her increasing sleeplessness of the last several months. He'd never expected to find her with a man, certainly not the man who was his best friend, a man he thought dead.

"You bastard!" Cole charged into the barn, pushing Sarah out of the way and punching Sutter in the face. "I'll kill you, you son of a bitch."

"Stop it!" Sarah screamed, rushing to stand in front of Luke. "Stop it, Cole! I want to be with Luke. I'm going to be with him!"

Luke swung at him and Cole ducked then stumbled. He fell onto the hay, then rose snatching up the pitchfork on a reflex. Sarah screamed again and moved clumsily in front of him.

Rage swallowed him up and he gripped the pitchfork until his knuckles burned. "Whore! Have you been giving yourself to him all this time? All those nights that I'd wake up and find you gone?"

"No!" Luke yelled, dodging Cole's wicked swipe at his middle with the pitchfork.

Sarah gripped Cole's arm, her nails digging into his flesh. "I want to be with him! You can't stop me."

"You're not taking my baby!" He shook her off, lunging again for Luke.

"This baby isn't yours!"

Her words slammed into him, locked him in place for an instant. Rage bubbled up, churning, overpowering all reason. He dropped the pitchfork and lunged for her. Sutter barreled into him from behind, taking him to the ground and only then did Cole realize he'd nearly struck Sarah with his fist.

"Luke, come on!" Sarah urged. "Now."

"Sarah, we're not going. We can't." Luke grunted with the effort to control Cole.

Cole thrashed beneath his one-time friend, managing to roll to his back and land a severe punch to Sutter's ribs. He freed his hands completely and struck a staggering blow to Luke's jaw.

Sutter's head snapped back, but he leaped up, fists

clenched. Suddenly his shoulders sagged and his face crumpled in sadness. "I haven't been with her, Cole."

"Damn liar." Cole swiped at his bloody nose. "Come on. Let's finish it."

"No!" Sarah screamed, trying to move around Cole and get to Luke. Cole caught her by the upper arms and held tight.

"No, Luke, please!"

Sarah's cries tore at Cole's heart. Luke's features were pinched with regret and sorrow. His gaze moved from Sarah to Cole then he shook his head and walked out the back door.

"Nooo!" Sarah turned on Cole, pummeling his chest with her fists. "I don't love you! I love him!"

"Well, you're married to me and you're carrying my baby." He wanted her to reinforce that, but she said nothing.

She'd always loved Luke. From the age of fifteen, the two of them had planned to marry, but the War Between the States had intervened. At the end of the war, everyone, including Cole, had thought Luke dead. About a year later, Cole had fallen in love with Sarah. And he'd thought Sarah had fallen in love with him.

He gripped her wrist. "It *is* my baby, isn't it?"

She pulled away from him, hate firing her blue eyes. Placing a protective hand over her stomach, she darted out the front door of the barn, into the rain-slicked night.

"Sarah, damn it!" He strode to the doorway, his nerves jangled and raw. "How long have you been meeting Sutter? Tell me that's not his baby."

He couldn't see her, couldn't hear her. Dread clenched Cole's muscles and for a moment he stood motionless. His side ached; blood oozed from numerous cuts on his face. Then he heard the thunder of hoofbeats.

"Sarah, no!" He bolted out the door, slipping in the mud, searching through the chill haze of the night. She rode pell-mell across the flat meadow on Gracie, her black mare.

Horse and rider flew across the muddy earth, silhouetted against a clearing midnight sky. Sarah's blond hair streamed out behind her like platinum ribbons. Frigid February air bit through Cole's damp clothes. "Sarah, no! Don't take the gully!"

She didn't slow and panic edged in. He began to run. "Sarah, no! Don't jump! It's too slick. You'll never—"

Sarah, a consummate horsewoman, urged her mount toward the gully at the edge of Luke's property. The horse leaped into the air and cleared the muddy water-filled hole.

But before Cole could catch a breath, the horse slipped. Powerful front legs flailed; the mare screamed and went down. Sarah screamed, too, the horrible sound piercing the night.

Chills slid under Cole's skin and he raced for the gully, sliding into it on his hands and backside.

He managed to get her to Doc Warren's office, but exactly how was a tangled blur of guilt and shame and rage.

The image of Luke and Sarah burned into his brain and the knowledge of what he'd seen ate at him. Sarah and Luke. Luke and Sarah. His best friend with his wife.

He stood in Doc Warren's office, waiting to hear if his wife and baby would live or die.

"Cole?"

Doc Warren's voice penetrated his dark thoughts and he turned, dread pounding at him. "Sarah? Is she . . . ?"

Compassion darkened the doctor's blue eyes. "I'm so sorry."

His legs went weak and he gripped the wall for support. "The baby?"

Doc Warren glanced down then placed a hand on Cole's shoulder. "She didn't make it either."

A girl . . . a daughter. He went numb, his mind capable of only one thought: Sutter would pay.

Something thudded against the wall behind him and roused Cole out of his dark memories. Sutter *would* pay. But not as long as Cole sat here in the alleyway like the town drunk.

Disgust rolled through him and this time it somehow became determination. He crawled to his feet, steadying himself against the wall as he kicked the bottle viciously into the shadows.

Had Sarah lied about the child she carried? Was the baby Cole's as she'd always said? Or did the child belong to Luke, as she'd screamed that night?

Cole would find out. Either way, Sutter had caused two deaths. And he would pay.

CHAPTER TWO

August 1874
Calcutta, Missouri

"We've caught him. At the Texas-Mexico border."

Whispered voices filled the tiny lean-to behind Calcutta's orphanage. Thin reeds of moonlight filtered through the crack at the open door.

"You're sure?"

"Absolutely." Lance Spradling's tone brooked no doubt. "Even now Wendell Cross is on his way to St. Louis, guarded by five armed men."

"I can't believe it. After eighteen months . . ." Regina Suzanne Harrison, alias Sister Regina, closed her eyes and took a deep breath of the stifling summer air that rolled off the Mississippi River.

She'd never made it to New Orleans. The *Lorilei*'s boiler had exploded in Calcutta's harbor and the ship's emergency docking had forced her to continue with the disguise. Automatically, her hands folded in a prayer as she released her pent-up breath. "Finally."

"Regina?" Lance laid a hand on her shoulder and squeezed. "You must still be extremely careful. Cross and his brothers know what you look like."

"But you said he was on his way to St. Louis." Regina turned toward the undercover detective, searching his dark eyes for the blunt truth she always found there.

"He is. But he has two brothers. I saw only one of them in Texas."

Fear, the same she'd carried for all these months of hiding, stabbed at her. "Were you followed?"

"It's possible, not probable," Lance answered in his usual clipped tones. The older man stared over her head, his gaze distantly focused on some unseen problem. "You should be safe enough in the disguise."

"I hope so. He did realize it was me once I boarded the steamboat in St. Louis." Regina touched the light wool of her habit, thankful once again for the Sisters of Charity, but sadly reminded of Alfred Poindexter, the detective who had helped her escape, and whom she'd learned from Abe had indeed been killed by Wendell Cross.

Lance removed his travel-limp black hat and ran a hand through his dark hair. "Good. It should still work in your favor. Just be careful. Especially now."

"I can't believe it." After all the sleepless nights, the anger and frustration, finally it would be over. Her father's murder would be avenged. "And the trial will be in less than a month?"

"Yes. Get to St. Louis around the first of September. Don't change your schedule or tell anyone. Not *anyone*."

"But what about Leah? And the children at the orphanage?" Regina whispered, careful to stay away from the slightly open door where moonlight twined into the small room.

Even after all this time, Regina could not rid herself of the guilt of lying to the people who had become her friends. Especially Leah Montgomery, the woman who helped occasionally at the orphanage and who'd befriended Regina soon after she'd arrived here. "I've got to tell them something before I leave."

Lance was quiet for a moment, then returned her whisper. "Maybe the woman. She can watch the children while you're gone. But no one else." He shook his head, the shadows of the room merging with his gray-streaked beard.

She nodded, the paranoid caution of the last eighteen months easing somewhat. Still, there was the lie she lived. Frustration at her prolonged secrecy nagged her, but now she could see the end. "Thank you, Lance."

"Thank *you*." He touched her arm, holding it for a moment. "Not just for keeping the cover, but for the safe stopping place." He indicated the lean-to with a sweep of his hand.

Gardening tools, a sack of potatoes, and a blanket in the corner occupied the small shed that had served as a safe house for traveling agents since her arrival last year. She'd contacted Abe soon after.

Her throat stung with tears and her whisper was fervent. "I had to do something. It was hard not to follow you on your search for Cross, but I knew I'd be useless out there. I can handle a gun and that's about all."

"I hope you know how important your help has been. Mr. Grand considers you part of the agency."

"Thanks." Affection mingled with resentment at

the thought of Abe Grand, first her father's employer, now her protector. She patted Lance's hand and stepped around him. "I know you're hungry. I'll be right back with some food."

"And coffee?"

"Yes. I haven't forgotten how you like it." She reached the door then turned back. On impulse, she brushed a kiss across his dusty cheek. "Thank you, Lance."

"Well, I didn't know nuns were allowed to kiss men," he teased, his eyes glinting in the moonlight.

She grinned. "In special cases, the Church grants dispensation."

They smiled at their shared secret and she turned again for the door. Lance moved to the corner and allowed the shadows to swallow him. Regina used no candle, never had. To do so would invite attention she could not afford.

She stepped outside, closing the well-oiled door behind her with only a whisper of sound and walked to the kitchen door of the orphanage. In less than a month, she would give the testimony to convict her father's killer, then she would be free to live a life without secrets. At last.

Inside the dim kitchen, she hurriedly fixed coffee and grabbed a half-loaf of bread from the bin along with the remaining roast from supper. Careful not to wake the children, she padded out the back door and made her way to the lean-to.

Pushing the door open with her hip, she noticed at once a raw, sweet odor. "Lance?"

She turned, looking for her friend, and stifled a

scream. A wedge of moonlight illuminated him. He lay faceup, eyes open, blood streaming from a slit throat. The sandwich and coffee fell from her fingers. The sting of the hot liquid on her hand barely registered.

She dropped to her knees beside him, whimpering as she pressed a hand to his face. She didn't need her frequent experience helping Doc Warren to tell her Lance was dead. All the fear of being discovered, doggedly hovering for months, erupted. Her whole body shook. Someone knew about the lean-to. Did they also know of her connection to Lance?

Whoever had killed Lance could still be lurking. Waiting for her? Driven by cold fear, she lunged for the door.

Who had done it? Could it be one of Wendell Cross's brothers? Where were they?

"Sister Regina?"

Elliot, the oldest boy from the orphanage and one of her closest friends, stepped in front of her. A scream caught in her throat and her heart clenched painfully.

"Elliot." She sagged with relief. Instinct kept her voice at a whisper and she stayed stubbornly in the doorway, shielding Lance from Elliot's eyes.

"If it's okay, I'm going over to Doc Warren's." The fifteen-year-old frowned and peered closer at her. "Is everything all right? You look funny."

"Everything's fine," she choked out, her mind whirling. What was she going to do with Lance? She couldn't let Elliot see him.

The boy stared at her, concern creasing his features, then shrugged. "If you need me . . ."

"I'll be fine."

He turned to walk away and Regina spun, hurrying to grab up the blanket that was usually stuffed in the corner and throw it over Lance.

"Oh, my gosh!"

Elliot! A startled scream escaped her. She tried to roll Lance up in the blanket, but his body, limp and heavy, lay across one edge. "Go away, Elliot! Go on."

The boy walked inside and looked over her shoulder. "What's going on?" Horror pinched his face and his gaze slanted to Regina. "He's dead. Did you kill him?"

"No. Help me."

"I'll go get Marshal Sanders."

"No!" She clutched at his arm, panic clawing through her. "You can't do that."

"What? Are you kidding? He's *dead*, Sister."

"I know that. Help me wrap him in the blanket." She shoved at Lance's body, biting back tears. Fear pounded at her as well as worry about Elliot and what he'd seen.

"You're not going to tell anyone?" The boy stared hard at her. "How come you don't want me to get the marshal? Or even Doc Warren? If you didn't kill him, shouldn't we find out who did?" He turned for the door again.

"No!" She couldn't let Elliot go. The first rule she'd learned was if an agent died, leave him on his own so as not to jeopardize anyone else. Regina's eyes filled with tears, torn at wanting to properly bury Lance and keeping herself, and now Elliot, safe. "I have to hide him."

"That's crazy." Elliot stood unmoving by the door, suspicion and horror flashing across his features. His words tumbled out as he searched for an explanation. "You did kill him, didn't you? No one will blame you. You're a nun. You were just protecting yourself."

"No, Elliot. I'm not a nun." Panicked and desperate, she barely registered the words. "This man was trying to warn me and we can't let anyone know he was here." She turned back to Lance, managing to draw the blanket from under his bulk and shove him further into the corner.

For an instant, there was only the sound of Regina's labored breathing and the faintest hint of music from the Blue China Saloon. Then Elliot's voice came, hurt and accusing. "What do you mean, you're not a nun?"

Regina started, realizing for the first time what she had blurted out in her panic. Inwardly she flailed herself, but she would have to trust him. The bond between them went deeper than friendship. It was a bond forged by forced independence and shared trials. "I can't explain right now. I need your help."

"You *are* a nun," he said, confusion underlining his words. His voice rose. "You are."

"Shhh!" Regina stood and turned, whispering fervently. "You go on. I'll take care of this."

"You're not a nun?" The boy stared at her, horror and betrayal creasing his young face.

She reached out to touch him and he stumbled back. All she had to do was tell him she was a nun, add another lie to the ones she already lived, and yet it choked her, lodged in her throat along with tears and panic and bitter regret.

"You told me you were a nun. You told *everyone!*" His voice rose, sharp with hysteria.

"I had no choice." She kept her voice low, wishing he would do the same. "I can explain later, but for now, please help me."

"You lied!" He backed toward the door and stepped over the threshold. "What else have you lied about?"

"Elliot, come back," Regina whispered in a rush. She took the two steps to the door. "Please, I can explain."

"You always told us to never lie."

"Elliot—"

"No." The word shook with pain. The boy turned and disappeared into the shadows beyond the orphanage.

Regina gripped the edge of the door frame, wanting to go after him and knowing she must take care of Lance. Tears burned her eyes and an ache settled in her chest.

She turned back to the detective, a man who'd become a good friend during these long months. Lance was one of the several men who had helped her rein in her impatience about the long search for her father's killer and helped her accept that her lying would be beneficial in the end.

She knelt and drew the blanket over him. Who had killed him? There could be several people who wanted him dead. After all, he had been a detective eleven years, almost as long as her father had.

But she couldn't shake the fear that one of the Cross brothers might have killed Lance. The possibility spurred a cold chill across Regina's shoulders. She must finish here and find Elliot.

A shuffle sounded at the door and a shadow cut across the stream of moonlight. She sucked in a breath of relief and turned. "Oh, Elliot, I'm so glad you came back—"

"Hello, Sister." The rough unfamiliar voice pierced her heart like a bullet. "Or should I address you by your given name? Regina Suzanne Harrison."

Her breath clotted in her lungs and swelled. Slowly, she raised her gaze past the dull shine of a knife blade to a pair of vengeful glittering eyes. Her fingers tightened on Lance's limp arm as her every nightmare crowded in a panicked rush through her memory.

A stocky boulder of a man stepped inside, his lips thinning in a feral grin. He closed the door behind him. "*My* given name is James Bartlett Cross and I've come to kill you."

He craved whiskey, but a woman would do just fine. One who was sleek and hot and all over him like smoke on fire. Tonight of all nights, he needed to forget. He'd lost Sutter's trail. Again.

Cole Wellington climbed off his dun mare and looped the reins over the hitching post in front of the Blue China Saloon. Next door, Doc Warren's house sat in quiet darkness. Thick August air swelled the night, the moon a thin silver thumbnail in a metal-gray sky.

Main Street was deserted. Across from the saloon, the church and smithy stood empty. Lamplight fluttered in an undulating pattern in the windows of Clemma's Restaurant and Boardinghouse.

The hazy night shadowed Horse's nugget-gold coat and deepened the black of her tail and mane. Cole ran a hand over the mare's muzzle, grinning at her name. Gage, his younger brother, had wanted to name her Russia. Cole thought that too prissy for the sturdy mountain animal and had named her Horse instead. Partly out of orneriness and partly because, at the time, he had been drunk too often to remember his own name, much less that of a horse.

Hot thick air tightened Cole's throat and he swallowed, pushing away the mental image of a cool shot of liquor. After last year, he'd gone light on whiskey.

The incident with The Nun had scared some caution into him. Except for the Christmas party at the orphanage, when his cousin Jack had roped him into taking a tree to the orphans, Cole hadn't been within fifty yards of the woman. And intended to keep it that way.

Last summer, he had kissed her. He tried not to think of The Nun as a woman, but as a sort of institution. It had been then he had realized his drinking was out of control. Kissing her was the only thing he'd ever done that he couldn't explain away.

It had excited him when it should have shamed him. No man he'd ever known had kissed a nun or at least admitted to it. He'd been drunk and therefore had made a severe error in judgment—he doubted she would call it that—and that chafed.

Over the last year, his search for Luke Sutter had taken him frequently away from home, but when Cole was in Calcutta, he stayed completely away from liquor. Because of that kiss. Anger at the incident rose and he shoved the thoughts away, concentrating instead on the night to come with Shell Owen.

He stepped onto the planked walk and hesitated outside the swinging double doors of the saloon. "Oh! Susannah" jangled from the piano inside. A low roar of voices swelled and ebbed under the chirpy notes. Cigar smoke swirled into a thin vapor at the height of the polished oak ceiling. He scanned the crowded room for Shell's blond hair.

Tension eased from his shoulders as he soaked in the freedom beckoning just beyond the doors. Here in the Blue China, he owed no explanations or apologies. And nobody wanted anything from him—except Shell, and he was more than willing to oblige her.

He saw her next to the bar, picking up a tray of drinks. She turned and her hazel eyes sparkled at him. With his head, he motioned to the alley in a silent message. She nodded. After delivering the drinks to a nearby table, she threaded her way through the crowd to the back of the room and the other door.

The petite saloon girl was the prettiest, cleanest girl the saloon had to offer. When Cole was in town, she treated him like a king. A man could use pampering like that every once in a while.

Cole gave Shell a few minutes, then strolled down the planked walk and stepped into the alley.

"Co-ole." Her teasing voice carried through the darkness. Shell always said his name as if it were two syllables instead of one. "Back here."

In the moonlight, he could see the pale gold of her hair and a flash of alabaster skin. She stood at the rear of the alley between the saloon and Doc Warren's house, crooking her index finger at him in invitation.

Anticipation flickered in his belly and his blood heated. He chuckled. "Whatcha doin' down there, Shell?"

"Waitin' for a big bad man. You comin'?" She melted into the shadows, giggling softly.

Cole grinned, teased with thoughts of her hot mouth and full white breasts. He kept a slow, lazy pace down the wall of the saloon, savoring the want as it built.

Her eyes shone like polished stones through the shadows; a creamy bare shoulder taunted him. He reached for her. She darted deeper into the darkness and turned to face him, backing away as she motioned him closer.

He chuckled, his heart quickening at the game between them. He was already hard, ready to lose himself in her, but the anticipation made it better. In three long strides, he caught her and pinned her against the wall. The light scent of rose toilet water mingled with the smell of his own sweat. The weathered wood vibrated, the rattle drowned by the noise from inside.

Cole could barely hear the piano over the rush of blood in his ears. He'd been a long time without a woman and he wanted to savor every minute. In a rapid flash, the memory of his kiss shared with The Nun tripped through his mind.

Startled and annoyed, he slammed his mouth against Shell's and she opened for him. Her tongue stroked his, drawing a groan from him. Leaning his full weight against her, he thrust his tongue deep into her mouth, one thigh between hers.

She curled her arms around his neck and pressed herself against him. The neckline of her satin and taffeta dress slashed low over her full white breasts, nearly exposing them completely. With one hand, Cole cupped a breast, rubbing his thumb across her nipple and bringing it to a tight bud. She moaned into his mouth and moved against him.

He strained poker-stiff against his britches. Running his other hand under her skirt, he stroked the back of her thigh, skipped over her garter belt, and kneaded one bare cheek. She gasped and shifted against him, opening her legs wider.

"Missed me, did ya?" He smiled against her mouth.

He sensed a presence the same time a hand descended on his shoulder.

His heartbeat skipped. With a muttered curse, he tore himself from Shell and whirled, pulling out his Smith & Wesson and thumbing down the hammer in one smooth motion. Shell squeaked and grabbed his arm.

He shook her off then eased the hammer forward as he recognized the intruder. "Gage. Hell!"

"Sorry. Thought I saw you come back here." Cole's younger brother grinned and peered around him. "Hey, Shell."

"You scared me to death, Gage," she huffed with a twitch of her skirts.

"Sorry, but I need to talk to Cole." His blue eyes hard and obsidian dark in the shadows, he leveled a gaze at his brother. "Got a minute?"

Immediately, Cole's shoulders tensed. He tried to shrug off the remnants of halted passion and the beginnings of anger at his brother. He narrowed his eyes, asking in a tight voice, "Can't it wait?"

"Nope."

Cole could see Gage wasn't going anywhere. He turned to Shell. "I'll only be a minute."

Shell glanced at Gage, stood on tiptoe, and dipped her tongue in Cole's ear. "Meet me upstairs."

She walked past him and he slapped her bottom. Giving him a wink over her shoulder, she skipped down the alley, onto the saloon's walk, and disappeared around the corner.

He took a steadying breath, wondering what Gage wanted, hoping it had nothing to do with his search for Sutter. Cole knew what his younger brother thought of that and it needled.

Gage didn't waste time with pleasantries, though Cole had been home this time only a day. "I need to know how long you're staying."

Cole shrugged, fighting down resentment. He had not answered to anyone, even family, in a long time. "The usual. A day, maybe three."

Gage was silent for a moment, giving the impression that he, too, was weighing his response. "Do you think you could stay a little longer?"

"Is something wrong?" Cole's gaze narrowed. "Leah? Mama?"

"No, not them."

"Then what?" He refrained from saying he had a job to do. Gage knew that all too well. And didn't like it. "I don't really see how I can."

Gage let out a deep sigh. Cole knew Gage was struggling to hold his temper, but he didn't know why. His younger brother usually let loose, no matter what. Gage's words, when they came, were controlled and stiff. "With all the coming and going you've done in the last year and a half, you'd think you could at least stay two weeks."

"What for?" Cole waited, his hand curling tightly at his side. They were tiptoeing around the issue of Sutter and both knew it. He and Gage didn't agree, never had, and never would.

Gage scratched his head and pulled his hat down. "I'm leaving tonight on a horse-buying trip to Kentucky. Emmett's going with me so he can't watch the horses and Pa's bringing in the last of the hay."

"I don't know, Gage. In a couple of days, I'll be ready to go."

"It's only two dang weeks, Cole. I'm not askin' you to settle in and start a family. Besides, you haven't caught him in all this time. Two weeks isn't going to make that much difference."

Cole took a step forward, fury flashing to a quick boil. Gage stood toe to toe with him, his own eyes sparking fire. For one split second, Cole considered slamming his fist into Gage's face, but his brother was right. Two weeks wouldn't make much difference.

Since he'd sobered up a year ago, he had been trailing one step behind Luke Sutter. Two months ago, Cole had learned that his one-time friend worked for the Abe Grand Detective Agency in St. Louis. However, once there, Cole found no Sutter and no further information. But Gage wouldn't ask about that. And Cole wouldn't tell him. "I'll stay."

"You will?" Gage's voice was rough with surprise.

"I said I would." Intent on heading to the saloon, he stepped around Gage, his body still throbbing from the feel of Shell. He held thoughts of Luke Sutter and Sarah at bay. Forever, his wife's memory would be inextricably entwined with Sutter's. Tonight, he would forget, regardless of Gage.

"Your word, Cole. I need your word." His brother's voice stopped Cole in mid-stride.

Not sure he'd heard correctly, he turned his head and looked over his shoulder. Gage, a good three inches shorter than Cole's six foot four, seemed to tower in the shadows. His gaze pierced Cole through the haze of the night.

Pain cinched his gut. He'd known Gage, and Emmett, too, thought him half-crazy with hatred. They had since the day he'd started after Luke Sutter. But less than trustworthy? He never thought he'd have to give his word to his own brother.

Gage's voice lashed across the alley. "Your word."

"You have it," Cole bit out. He could remember when a simple nod would have served as bond between him and his family. Refusing to acknowledge the flicker of sadness he felt, he watched Gage walk past him, around Doc Warren's house, and disappear into the night.

His brother's muffled footsteps faded away, leaving memories in their wake. Images tumbled through Cole's head, each one nicking a raw place inside him. Luke and Sarah in each other's arms. Sarah's fall from the panicked horse. Blood soaking the ground, her clothes. Doc Warren's pronouncement that Sarah and the child were dead.

As always when he thought of the baby girl, Cole's breath ached in his chest and doubts crept in.

He cursed under his breath. He needed no memories or responsibilities heaped on him tonight. Just the company of a willing woman.

With a ruthlessness born of practice, Cole dismissed thoughts of his brothers, his wife, and Luke Sutter from his mind and started for the saloon.

Too late, he heard a rush of wind behind him, grabbed his gun and whirled. A body hurtled into his. As Cole drew, he registered softness and curves and layers of clothes.

Automatically, his arm shot out, grabbing a slight shoulder to steady the woman. She rocked back on her feet and went stone-still. Taller than most women, her gaze met his squarely.

For an instant, the two stared at each other. Cole saw the black habit and white coif before he understood the picture. He shoved his gun back into the holster and bit off a curse. *The Nun!*

Harsh breathing peppered the still night. A fine mist of sweat covered her face. He recognized fear and the fringes of desperation in her eyes.

"Sorry," she panted in a whisper and hurried around him. She tripped and once again, his hand shot out. He clamped on to her arm and she steadied herself then pulled away.

She darted a glance over her shoulder and Cole mimed her movement, seeing nothing and no one in the shadows.

Curious about who she was running from, his grip tightened. "You all right?"

"Let me go. Please." She kept her voice at a whisper, tugging frantically to free her arm from his grasp. For her height, she was slight. There was a fragile but wiry strength in her arms. Yet even through the layers of her robe, he could feel her tremble. Her gaze, wild with the beginnings of hysteria, shot again to the end of the alley and her eyes widened.

It was then Cole became aware of footsteps—rushing, heavy, and coming down the alley behind Doc Warren's. Toward them.

The nun jerked her arm from his hold and turned to run. The footsteps grew louder and Cole knew she'd be seen if she tried to make it around the front of the saloon. "You'll never make it."

Her gaze sliced to Main Street then back to him. Indecision crossed her features. "Help me. Please."

His brain was already clicking for a plan. Automatically, his hand covered his gun.

"No." She touched his arm, hesitated for a moment then backed against the wall. Before he could react, she grabbed his shirtfront and tugged him toward her.

Stunned, Cole stared, but felt a reluctant spark of admiration as he understood her plan. Pretending to be lovers was not an idea he would expect from a woman of the cloth. He pressed hard against her, taking perverse delight as she tensed against the feel of his body. When desire knifed through him, sharp and lethal, he attributed it to Shell.

The white coif around her face flashed in the darkness like a guiding star and his hands tightened on her arms. Leaning close enough to brush his whisker-stubbled cheek against her smooth one, he mouthed in her ear, "Put your head down and don't move."

CHAPTER THREE

Regina wanted to push Cole Wellington away and run, but right now, she needed him. So she held on and prayed.

Seconds crawled by. She knew James Cross was at the opposite end of the alley and she had to escape him. She had to get to St. Louis for the trial.

Her knees had turned to jelly and Cole's iron-hard grip held her up rather than any strength of her own. She barely breathed, fleetingly aware that she depended on Cole Wellington more than she should—or had ever wanted to.

Through his sister and her friend, Leah, Regina knew of Cole's frequent absences from Calcutta. He intrigued and threatened her at the same time, as he had since that kiss behind the orphanage last year.

She tried to concentrate on her breathing, knowing the slightest sound could alert Cross and cause him to investigate further. A distant part of her mind was vaguely aware of Cole's hard body pressed against hers, the blistering heat of his chest against her forehead where it rested on him. Listening intently, she focused on the noise around her.

Cole's breath in her ear sounded like a hostile wind though she knew Cross probably couldn't hear. The music from the saloon faded for a moment then climbed with a rush. The scrape of chairs and booted feet across the saloon floor was muffled. In her nostrils lingered the scent of Lance's blood.

After seconds, maybe minutes, she felt Cole relax. She let out a deep breath and raised her head, swallowing hard past the lump in her throat. Her eyes blurred and she blinked to focus them. A quick glance showed the alley was empty except for her and Cole Wellington. Where was Cross?

She looked into the shadowed face of her protector, shivering as his black eyes honed in on her. He was dressed all in black, as she was, but his somber attire didn't represent godliness or even sedateness. Instead, it lured, tempted, threatened . . .

Up close, she could see the dark shadow of beard stubble and laugh creases on either side of his mouth, though she'd never even seen him smile. All the dreams of wanting him that had haunted her since his kiss last summer crashed back and her insides melted in a sudden burst of desire.

A pulse hammered in his throat. His heat curled around her, burning chills across her body beneath the robe and her underclothes. They stared at each other, an awkward silence building around them.

His gaze flicked to her lips and her pulse sped up. Softly, he said, "I think he's gone."

"Yes." Belatedly, she remembered her hands on his

shoulders and jerked them away. She pressed against the wall to distance herself from him.

Cole stepped back. Thick brows snapped together in a frown, his gaze black steel in the darkness. "What the hell was that all about?"

Regina took one wary step then another along the wall away from him, moving into the alley. She had no intention of telling him. Already Elliot had discovered part of her secret, probably endangering him. "Thank you very much. I don't know what I would've done if you hadn't . . . been here."

It felt strange, thanking a man for holding her against the wall. The same man she'd fled from last year. She backed away from him toward Main Street. She had to get to the docks. She would be safe there until she could figure out where to go. Certainly not the orphanage.

Cole followed, his lithe movements making him appear to barely move. "You're somethin' else, Sister." The words snaked around her, leaving little doubt that he was not complimenting her.

"Thank you." Regina glanced toward the saloon and back. Where had Cross disappeared to?

Cole matched her backstep with a forward one of his own. "I don't know many nuns who go tearing through the night with a man on their heels."

"You helped me and I'm grateful, but I owe you no more than that." Again, the desire to confide in just one person swamped her. And, as she had for the last eighteen months, she pushed it away. It was too dangerous. "You're free to go about your business."

"So you can go about yours?" His gaze raked over

her, peeling the clothes from her body, the same hot
look he'd worn last year. "What exactly's goin' on under that veil?"

Her head snapped toward him. "*You* are rude.
Even when you're not drunk."

He grinned, exposing a flash of white teeth.

She stared at him, her gaze defiant, his penetrating.
She couldn't linger here another minute. No one else
could learn her secret, especially not when she was so
close to finally getting Wendell Cross. She took another step back, then another until she was at the front
edge of Doc Warren's house.

Cole didn't move, but his gaze pinned her as effectively as Cross's knife had in the lean-to only moments
before. "Everybody has 'em, you know?"

Her gaze swerved to his, her foot faltering at his
confident tone. "Has what?"

"Secrets. And they're bound to be found out."

Her heart sputtered as he named her fear. She drew
herself up and gave him the tone she reserved for little
boys caught looking up girls' dresses. "As much as I'd
like to stand here and pass the time, I really can't."

"You've got a fast mouth for a nun."

"I wouldn't expect you've known many nuns, Mr.
Wellington." She backed away, searching the street
over her shoulder.

He stayed where he was, draped in pitch-black
shadows, one half of his face lightened by the moon.
"Guess you know what you're doin'."

"Of course." She hoped her teeth didn't chatter on
the lie. In truth, she had no idea what she was doing,

but she had managed this long. She couldn't weaken and allow herself to trust anyone now, certainly not him. "Thank you again."

She stepped back and turned to the left.

In that instant, an arm clamped around her throat and a voice rasped in her ear. "Look here what I found."

James Cross! Regina's heart clenched. In the span of a heartbeat, his knife flashed into view. She tensed and he tightened his grip on her, raising the blade to her throat.

Behind her, she heard the click of a gun then Cole's voice, lethal and quiet. "Drop it."

Cross laughed, actually chuckled in her ear, and twisted around, dragging Regina's feet across the parched earth as he turned her with him. He faced Cole, his voice cracking like flint against rock. "Perhaps you didn't see my little friend."

Cole's gaze flickered to the knife and back to Cross. Regina battled rising panic and loss of breath. Before, she had managed to knee him in the privates and get away. But what about now? The flat side of the blade pressed to her throat. One fraction of a movement would turn the slicing edge into her skin.

Had she sacrificed her life for all these months only to die at the hands of Wendell Cross's brother and cause another man's death as well?

Her half-formed plans for escape disappeared as James Cross pressed the blade to her throat. She felt a hot sting and cried out.

Cole dropped his gun and in what must have been

the flicker of Cross's eye, dove for the man holding her. Cross pushed Regina in front of him like a shield, but Cole launched for the man's knees.

Cross buckled forward into Cole. Regina felt a sharp sting then a burn in her right shoulder as she hurled herself away from the man who had been holding her. She stumbled against the wall of the saloon, her ragged breath mocked by the loose clackety notes of the piano.

She pushed herself to her hands and knees, crying out as searing pain gouged her back. Reaching over her shoulder, she touched a warm stickiness. Nausea rolled through her and she fought it back.

Behind her, she heard the meaty thud of flesh on flesh and turned. Cole and James Cross circled. Silver moonlight glinted off the blade between them. The knife arced and twisted in the shadows, striking close to Cole's face. Regina's gaze darted around, searching for a rock or Cole's revolver.

"Get out, damn it!" Cole yelled at her. "Go!"

She wanted to run, but she couldn't do it, not when he was risking his life to help her, again. Trying to ignore the pain in her shoulder, she squinted into the darkness for the gun. She could see nothing except small wisps of dirt kicked up by the men's scuffling boots. Chills raced across her skin, burrowing even under the thickness of her robe and underclothes. Her teeth chattered; pain clawed through her with every breath.

Finally, she spotted the ivory-handled revolver. James Cross had kicked it down the alley to the edge of the saloon. Struggling to her feet and holding her shoulder, Regina made her way to the corner and bent to pick up the gun.

Noise from the saloon swelled in her ears. Sweat slicked her chest and neck and between her fingers. Her shoulder and arm burned. Goosebumps rose on her back and she shivered. She turned in time to see Cole Wellington go down on one knee, holding his forearm.

"Get the hell out of here, Sister!"

The searing pain in her shoulder gouged deeper, spreading tentacles of fire across her shoulder blades and down her spine and arms. Her fingers fumbled with the hammer. She knew how to handle a gun, yet her hands wouldn't obey her mind. A cry of frustration erupted from her. The gun wavered before her eyes then separated into two. She looked up to see Cross bearing down on her.

She shrank back against the wall, trying to thumb the hammer back. Her strength seemed to seep right out of her. The gun grew heavy, straining the muscles in her arms. A hand clamped onto the skirt of her robe. She tried to pull away, but had no energy. Cross's face distorted and swam before her.

Abruptly, the pressure on her robe eased and she stumbled against the wall. The gun flew from her fingers and thudded into shadow. Cole had James Cross on the ground, landing heavy blows to the small of his back.

As though she watched a distant memory in her mind, Regina saw the two men fighting, heard the grunts as fist met softer flesh. Her shoulder went numb. A peaceful void beckoned.

She struggled to keep her eyes open, knowing she had to take Cole's advice and leave. There might never be another chance. The pain bloomed again, crowding out reason, desperation, even the desire to flee. Darkness pulled at her, but she fought it. She couldn't let James Cross catch her.

Digging her left elbow into the rock-hard ground, she tried to scoot herself into the shadows where she couldn't be seen. A flare of reason surfaced and she knew she was going to pass out. Panic rose. The void and a feeling of helplessness lapped at her.

Suddenly she saw a dark figure leaning over her. The scream died in her throat as she recognized Cole Wellington. "Please, help me."

He knelt beside her, his voice coming in harsh gasps. "This is no time to faint, Sister."

Aware of the cold chill of her blood and the solid warmth of Cole's hand on her arm, a black haze clouded her vision and she lost consciousness.

Cole stared down at the nun lying on the ground. Damn it all, the worthless woman! The worst was over and she had fainted.

His shirtsleeve was ripped and his left forearm stung where the knife had split the skin. He ignored the pain and plucked up the pistol, sliding it into his holster. He shoved an arm under her back. A sticky warmth spread over his palm and his gaze jerked to her.

Blood.

Not his from the nick he'd sustained, but hers. She hadn't fainted from fright. She was injured. A quick spark of panic flared. He scooped her up in his arms then turned.

The man still lay in a huddled heap and Cole stepped over him, kicking at the knife within the man's reach. The blade skittered across the slab of ground and pinged against the wall of the saloon.

Blood seeped into Cole's palm. He stared down at the nun's face, pale and drawn against the blackness of his shirt.

He had to get her out of here before that bastard with the knife woke up and came after both of them. Who was he and why was he chasing a nun? Cole stared at the woman, helpless and totally dependent on him. In his arms, she looked fragile and still frightened. Sensation pulled deep in his gut, but he ignored it.

A grunt alerted him and he spun on his heel. The other man was moving, his hand searching the hard ground for his knife. Cole took off at a brisk walk, heading for Doc Warren's then realized the doctor's house was silent and empty. He stopped suddenly, his gaze swinging around to find his horse in front of the saloon.

The nun had been afraid for her life and Cole's presence had done little to discourage the man chasing her. She needed medical attention, but Cole couldn't wait for Doc Warren to return. Judging from that little scene in the alley, she wouldn't be safe anywhere in town. Nor would anyone around her.

Cole knew this country like his own name and wouldn't be caught unaware by the man again. If he had to worry only about him and the nun, he could trust his own skill against that knife-wielding bastard. Decision made, he wheeled and headed for Horse.

The mare stood placidly at the hitching post. With one hand, Cole unlooped the reins. He laid Sister Regina across the saddle, climbed up, and struggled in behind her.

A low grunt of pain alerted him. He glanced over his shoulder and saw the man coming from the alley. Shifting the nun so she sat cradled between his legs, Cole gripped the reins with his left hand and kneed the mare into motion. With his right hand, he pulled his revolver and fired a warning shot over the man's head.

The man ducked behind the corner of the saloon then stepped out. The knife whistled past Cole's head, tweaking the brim of his hat. Hell, was the guy that good with a knife or just lucky?

Cole squeezed off two more shots, planting both in the man's right thigh. He stumbled and fell.

Cole kneed Horse again and the mare laid into a flat-out run down Main Street. He hunkered down, plastered against the nun's back. She lay limp in front of him, her chin notched in the crook of his arm.

As they galloped away from Calcutta, he looked over his shoulder. Men streamed from the saloon, probably in response to the shots fired, but the bastard he'd shot was nowhere to be seen.

Cole gave the mare her head, putting distance between them and Calcutta. He entered streams when he could, rode rock on the other side. When he slowed the mare, he was amazed to find they weren't being followed. He stopped and tied his bandana over the nun's shoulder and under her arm to staunch the blood then shifted her so she lay against his chest. He stared down at her.

What was he supposed to do with her? He wanted to take her back to town, but couldn't make himself turn around. The stabbing had happened when Cole had dived for the man and he felt a reluctant responsibility. Besides, she wouldn't be safe at the orphanage or anywhere, for that matter.

What kind of man would try to kill a nun?

Why would a nun be involved with such a man? None of it was his concern, he told himself. Whatever mess she was in had nothing to do with him. But there was the injury to consider. He didn't know how deep or serious the wound was. Or how much blood she'd lost. He couldn't leave her to fend for herself.

He stared down at the body in his arms, anger building as he took in the translucent skin, the straight almost too-wide nose, the dark silky lashes covering eyes he knew were the rich green of wet leaves. The couple of times he'd seen her in town he'd noticed those eyes.

Such flawless beauty on a nun. What a waste. "Hell."

He'd wanted a warm, willing woman. Instead, he'd gotten a fight that wasn't his and an injured woman. Hell, not even a woman, but a nun.

He should've had the whiskey.

An hour after they left town, Cole stood at the foot of his bed in Gage's house. After Sarah and the baby had died, Cole had sold their house and stayed here with his brother whenever he was in Calcutta.

He stared at the woman in black. He had no doubt the man would have killed her. And he had tried to kill Cole. Which was why Cole had gotten the hell out of there as quickly as possible.

She lay with her hands folded across her stomach as though resting peacefully, but the creases in her face attested to the pain she felt even in sleep. He knew he needed to look at her wound. Trouble was, how did he take off that damn habit?

The bed, a big, fluffy, rarely used piece, took the center of the small, air-stilted room. The lantern, brought from downstairs, spread a blanket of light over the bed, the scratched oak bedside table and porcelain washbasin.

Shadows striped the nun's face and hands, making the streaks of blood on her fingers look like bruises. Cole palmed his hat off, frowned, then dropped it on the corner of the bed.

He jerked open the window, taking a deep breath of heavy air that was no cooler than that in the room, and turned. At the edge of the bed, he looked down at her and tried to decipher all the clothes she wore. Urgency scraped through him. He knew he had to hurry.

A tight white cloth rode low on her forehead and gripped the sides of her face. The starched material continued down her neck and to the swell of her breasts. He remembered the soft cushion of them against his chest and his gut jerked. Disgusted at his reaction, he turned his attention to helping her.

A black, elbow-length veil covered her head. The sleeves and the robe from her breasts down were flowing voluminous black. Tied at her waist was a long strand of wooden beads with a crucifix on the end. She wore dusty sandals. One strap was broken, which explained why she had tripped when hurrying past him in the alley.

Again, he wondered why she'd been running.

She moaned and stirred on the bed, but didn't open her eyes.

Resentment churned. To term him a reluctant nursemaid would have been kind. He flat didn't want to doctor her. But there was no question he would. *If* he could get that contraption off to look at her shoulder.

He took the needle, thread, and whiskey he'd brought upstairs and walked to the other side of the bed. Blood stained the sheet like the spreading ripple of a scarlet tide.

He drew a deep breath. The memory of Sarah, bleeding to death in his arms, sliced through his mind. For an instant, he stood there, numb, his palms clammy. Then he sat down on the edge of the bed and stared at the woman there. He turned her on her side away from him.

The style and color of her clothing screamed that he shouldn't think of her as a woman. She was a forbidden, close-to-sainthood, never-had-a-man's-hands-on-her nun. He supposed he wasn't allowed to touch her, much less take off her clothes.

To hell with it. No woman was going to die in his bed, unless it was from pleasure. He pushed aside the black folds of the outer veil and sighed in relief that there was only one hook at the neck of the robe. The entire garment seemed to be one large square of material made to go over the head. It looked as though the white thing fit over the robe.

He rolled her to her back and she moaned. An ache wedged in his chest. With a swift motion, he unknotted the belt of beads at her waist and dropped it to the floor. He leaned closer to study the white material shrouding her neck and chest. Her breath fanned his cheek and a muscle clenched in his jaw. A seam ran down the center front of the white piece, but he could find no fasteners.

She moved suddenly beneath his hands and pushed at him. "Stop," she cried hoarsely. "What do you want? Who are you?"

"Don't tell me you don't remember our little meeting in the alley, Sister. I know I won't forget it for some time." Her hands were weak against his chest and Cole noticed she struggled to focus on him. Her eyes glazed with pain.

"Wh-Where are we?"

The raw fear in her voice tore at him and Cole relented. "At my brother's house."

He peered down at her. Her gaze searched the room, her face haunted and drawn. His earlier irritation faded and he sought to reassure her with mention of her friend, his sister. "We're only a couple of miles from Leah's place, between Calcutta and Farrell."

She stared at him for a moment, a lucid light coming back into her eyes. Her hand spread over her chest in a protective gesture and she glanced there. "Wh-What are you doing?"

"I need to get a look at that wound. Think you can help me get these clothes off? I'm havin' a devil of a time. So to speak," he added as an afterthought.

He was prepared for a blushing protest or maidenly outrage, but neither came. Weakly, she nodded her head and licked her lips. "Is it bad?"

"Don't know yet." He stood and walked to the door. "I'll give you a few minutes. Might as well strip to the skin."

"Skin?" Her voice was tentative and breathless.

"No time for modesty. You're bleedin' all over the place." He noticed her eyes, cloudy green from pain, and stepped out into the hall. "Better hurry, Sister."

He left the door open, turning his back so she would feel she had some privacy. A soft grunt and the creak of the ropes holding the mattress told him she was moving. He stared down at his hand, stained with her blood and swallowed hard. Looking at blood and feeling it were two different things. He tilted his head back against the wall, pushing away the picture of blood.

A few minutes passed with no sound from the room.

"How're you comin'?"

No answer.

"Sister?"

Nothing.

Cole pivoted and strode back into the room. She lay on her side, as he'd left her, but unconscious. She had managed to remove only the white thing from her neck.

Knowing he shouldn't waste more time, he sat on the bed behind her and gathered the thick folds of the robe. He lifted, gently easing the material over the wound. The earlier blood had already dried, causing the robe to stick to the chemise and skin beneath. He peeled the material away from her skin, relieved when she didn't move.

He picked her up and, with some difficulty, maneuvered the robe over the bulk of her veil and head covering. Tossing the robe across the bed, he laid her gently on her stomach and turned his attention to her shoulder.

The wound was in the fleshy part of her shoulder blade. Fresh blood welled from the cut while the old had dried and plastered her chemise to her back.

He'd have to take off the damn thing. With no more hesitation than as if he undressed nuns every day, he slipped the loops on the buttons running down the front of the loose garment, pulled it up, and dragged it over her head. Gently, he removed first one arm from its sleeve, then with more difficulty, the other.

If the Virgin Mary herself had been standing there, Cole couldn't have helped himself. He had to look. He knew he'd never get another chance. His gaze skimmed up over long slender legs to a firm rounded butt, taut waist flaring up to delicate shoulders. The wound gaped scarlet against the pale cream of her skin. Easing her on her side to check for other wounds, he glimpsed the curve of a full breast, the dusky pink of a nipple.

In a rush, heat flooded him and with it, the memory of the kiss he had stolen last summer. Even drunk, he had known she had a beautiful face, but he'd never expected a nun to be so perfect all over. He stared at her pale skin, knowing it would feel like honey and cream sliding under his tongue. This was probably God's idea of a great joke; the most untouchable of women was the most beautiful.

It crossed his mind that he should probably feel guilty, but he didn't. He stared for another full minute, simply enjoying the pleasure of something beautiful, which he hadn't allowed himself to do in a long while. Then reason returned and with it brutal reality. She was a damn nun!

And she was lying on his bed, bleeding all over his sheets. He rolled her to her stomach, ignoring the flawless skin stretched over taut muscles, and turned his attention back to the wound. Blood streaked across her spine and down under her arm; it soaked into the sheet bunched beneath her.

He swallowed for control and grabbed the cloth from the bedside table, wetting it with whiskey. Gently, but briskly, he dabbed at the wound and the area around it. She moaned, but didn't move.

He raised her arm to wipe at the blood, ignoring the tantalizing curve of her breast only a finger's length away. Once the cut was clean, he examined it. It was jagged, about four inches long, but not even a half inch deep.

The bastard must've reacted on reflex. There would be no muscle damage, but it would hurt like hell for several days.

Cole considered the wound, then the needle. He was none too good at sewing. Once, he'd had to sew

Gage's finger when his brother had gotten overly ambitious with a saw, but that was the limit of his experience. He had no choice. There had been no time to wait for the doctor.

Taking the needle in hand, he threaded it with black silk and leaned over her. "Sister?" Cole said roughly, loudly, in case she was coming out of her pain-induced sleep.

"Hmmm."

Cole couldn't tell if she had answered him or simply moaned. "You awake?"

"I think so."

"Damn, that's too bad." He wondered if she would drink the whiskey. He was going to have an even more difficult time sewing her up if she was conscious. "I've got some whiskey. You need to drink it."

"No." The voice was weak, but the determination strong.

Cole bit back a curse. "I wish you'd take it. You're going to have to be dead-dog-still for me to sew you up. It'd sure make me feel a lot better if you took a sip or two."

"No, I'll be fine. Just go ahead." She burrowed her head into the pillow, presenting her shoulder to him. Chill bumps rose on her clammy skin. The wound stretched wider, spilling blood to roll down her back to her taut waist. He gripped the needle and leaned over her. "You can yell if you want. Or curse. I won't hold it against you."

"Thanks." Her voice was thready. "I-I'd like it if you could do it quickly."

"Here goes." His voice softened as he positioned

the needle at the base of the cut. He felt compelled to apologize, in advance, for hurting her. "Sorry." Before he could think about it further, he pushed the needle through velvet-soft flesh.

She flinched, drawing her shoulder slightly away from him in reflex. Cole grimaced, aware of the sweat stinging his eyes, beading on his upper lip. His hand shook. He took a deep breath and came back through with another stitch.

His estimation of her rose by bounds in that moment. She made not a sound, just gripped the quilt on the bed until he thought her knuckles would pop through the skin. Her shoulder tensed, creating resistance to the movement of the needle through flesh. He knew the tautness of her muscle magnified the long drawing sting of pain left by each stitch.

On the third one, he felt her body go limp. He huffed out a breath, grateful she had passed out. Peering over her shoulder, he saw a lone tear seep from her eye and trail down her cheek.

He wasted no more time, concentrating on small even stitches and hoping like hell she didn't wake until he'd finished.

When she woke, he intended to find out how she'd gotten into this mess.

CHAPTER FOUR

Pain woke her. Persistent, searing, gouging through her shoulder. Her arm and hand ached, numb with sharp pinpricks of feeling. Regina fought to open her eyes. The air was thin and hot; a white sheet stuck to her bare skin. Downy pillows cushioned her head and she smelled whiskey.

Her breath rasped in the room and she struggled to think, to remember. The deep drone of frogs and crickets seeped through an open window. A lantern beside the bed cast wedges of light into the otherwise dark room. She blinked at the shadows writhing on the ceiling. Slowly she became aware of another presence and turned her head.

Cole Wellington sat in a chair in the corner, black hat pulled over his eyes. Long powerful legs stretched out in front of him. His hands were loosely clasped and resting low on his belly. She was dreaming, she realized. How many times had she dreamed of him in the same room with her? Except in her dreams he was in the bed with her. A warmth bloomed inside her, but the pain still persisted.

She came more fully awake and memory jolted her. Her eyes widened. It was no dream! The knife, the alley, James Cross. She remembered it all now. And she knew where she was. Gage Wellington's house. Cole had saved her from James Cross and brought her here. He'd looked at her wound and—

Regina's gaze dropped to her chest as she fully comprehended the rub of sheet linen against her bare skin. He had taken off her clothes! Every last stitch.

She pressed the sheet to her breasts then, with a sudden startling thought, raised a hand to her head. No, he hadn't removed everything. Thank goodness, he had left the headpiece. A relieved sigh escaped. If he'd seen her hair, he would have surely known she was no nun. Though she'd cut it close to her head last year—as payment for the habit she'd taken from the Sisters of Charity—she hadn't been able to make herself crop it again.

Admittedly, her hair was her pride. It was her best feature. Even her father had thought so. Straight, thick, and as black as a moonless night, he used to say it was the one feature she'd inherited from him. The joke had been a common one in their family because Worth Harrison had been bald. She felt the familiar mix of joy and resentment when she thought of her father. If only he hadn't become a detective and thrust them into a life of secrets and endless moves.

The pain in her shoulder burned hotter and she lowered her arm, breathing heavily with the effort. She wore her coif and veil, but nothing else. An embarrassed heat suffused her body and climbed to her cheeks. Before passing out, she had removed the guimpe at Cole's request. The thick white material that usually shrouded her throat down to her breastbone lay at stiff attention next to the bed.

Her chemise, stained with blood, was tossed across the end of the bed; her robe dangled onto the floor. She couldn't see her sandals or her rosary belt. She clutched at the sheet draped loosely over her, wincing as pain burst in her shoulder.

Judging from the thick stiffness there, Cole had also stitched her up. Yes, she remembered that now. Probing gently, she touched the bulk of bandage on her shoulder and her initial horror at her nakedness died.

The last man in the world she would have trusted had saved her life.

Equal parts resentment and gratitude flashed through her. She resented everything about Cole Wellington from his arrogant stance to the cocksure masculine promise that glimmered in his eyes. He exuded earthy sensuality like an elixir, dangling it in front of her own spartan, pure existence like gold to a covetous man.

Of all things, she resented this most about him. With one look he could make her feel like both a desirable woman and one who was completely naïve of the ways between men and women.

She wasn't ignorant, not completely. After all, Tab McClain had actually courted her for a time in Palmyra, before her family had moved yet again.

But she couldn't remember Tab making her feel this aware of her own body, this alive. Cole had made her feel tingly, shivery, *ignorant*, and all when he was drunk. Just looking at him now, legs splayed in rest, his latent power at ease, made her breasts tingle and grow heavy.

If things were different, if she weren't running, hiding, living a lie, she would've welcomed the feelings Cole Wellington stirred.

It wasn't that she *wanted* to resist him; she *had* to. Not only because she was posing as a nun, but also because, before now, she hadn't known when the charade would end. She wasn't free to pursue any other life until she knew Wendell Cross was behind bars, paying for what he had done to her father.

She shook her head at the ridiculous thoughts. As if Cole Wellington wanted her. Regardless of the kiss he'd branded on her lips, he, like everyone else, thought she was a nun. That kiss last summer had been the result of too much drink and some deep-scarring pain. She had seen it in his eyes.

Regina stared at the man slouched down in the chair, his black shirtsleeves rolled back to reveal thick wrists and corded forearms covered with dark hair. Had he spent the entire night in the room with her? She thought he had, though she could only remember gentle hands on her when he'd cleaned and stitched her wound.

A chill rippled through her and she touched the hollow at the base of her throat. Her skin was clammy. Pain gnawed at her. Weakness stole through her, sucking at her strength, clouding her thoughts. She had worked enough with Doc Warren to know that, due to all the blood she'd lost, she would have to rest for a while.

Closing her eyes, she allowed herself to drift away from the pain. A distant rational part of her knew she needed to get away from this man who haunted her secret dreams and get back to the children.

The children! Her eyes flew open. How could she have forgotten them? What would they think? Were they all right? Who would stay with them? Oh, Sweet Virgin Mary, what if James Cross came back to the orphanage tonight?

Panic surged and she raised up on one elbow. The movement sent pain shunting through her, cutting off her breath. She stilled, trying to ease the sharp ache in her chest. Taking deep breaths, she waited until the pain dimmed then she moved again.

She clenched her teeth and pressed the sheet to her naked breasts, inching toward her chemise at the end of the bed. Her fingers caught at the thin material.

"Well, well."

Regina jerked at the deep, gruff voice behind her and nearly toppled. The room spun. Her shoulder burned and she winced. She bit her lip to keep from crying out.

Clutching the sheet tightly to her, she drew in her knees. "I-I need to get dressed."

"Like hell." Cole rose from the chair, his boots thundering across the wooden floor. "You can't go anywhere. You can barely sit up."

"I'm a little sore, but I can move." Already her energy was waning. Embarrassed at her nakedness, she couldn't bring herself to look at him.

The sheet covered her breasts and around to her backside, but barely. She could feel his black gaze boring into the exposed length of her back. Chills skittered up her spine and she wished she could reach her robe. "I'm sure I can manage. I really need to get back to town. The children will be wondering where I am when they wake up."

"I imagine your friend will be, too." He moved in front of her, his waist at her eye level.

She raised her gaze to his, unable to halt the crash of awareness she felt. Heat stung her body and traveled to her cheeks. His eyes were too sharp, too intent on her nakedness, too promising. She swallowed. "Oh."

For a moment, she watched the play of shadow and light caress his rough features. Her body ached from exhaustion and the knife wound, but she had to get back to town. Who would watch the children? And what of Elliot? Had he even returned? She had to know.

Using the last dregs of strength, she waved her hand in a dismissive gesture. "Surely that man will be gone by now. He won't expect me to come back tonight. I've got to check on the children."

"Who is that man? What does he want from you?"

The questions were fired hard and hot. Her hand tightened on the chemise, embedding the material into her palm. She had hoped for more of a reprieve. "That's really none of your businesss."

"It is now."

"You saved my life and I'm grateful, but please

don't ask me anything. I-I'm not—I can't tell you anything."

"Please don't ask you anything?" His voice grated like steel on rock. "That man sliced you up good, tried to do the same to me. You've made this my fight now, Sister. I damn well expect some answers."

"I don't owe you any explanations." Forgetting her shoulder for an instant, she stiffened then winced when the pain bit at her.

"I *shot* him." Cole braced one hand on either side of her and leaned down. Big hands rested close to her thighs, trapping her. His breath burned her cheek. "Get it? Bang."

Her heart sputtered and dizziness assailed her. "Is he—"

"No, he's not dead." Cole's nostrils flared. The heat of his hands seared her through the thin sheet. "We managed to get away, but if he's looking for you, he's going to find me. At least for a few days. So, I'd say you do owe me an explanation." His eyes, as dark as frozen midnight, burned. A muscle flexed in his jaw and a hard smile twisted his lips. "Think of it as confession, if you like, but you'll tell me."

His voice was blunt and harsh, the way it had been the few times she had dealt with him, but he was absolutely right. He did deserve to know, but revealing the information could put him on Wendell Cross's list, if he wasn't already. Not to mention endangering her own life and her trip to St. Louis. Once again her life of secrets put her in a compromising position.

Fatigued and sore, her head spun. Her breath came

in shallow pants. She tried to draw in more air, desperate to ease the dizziness. "I-I can't."

"Damn it!" He reached toward her then stopped, seeming to remember her injury. Murder flashed through his eyes and he clenched his fists at his sides.

Muscles flexed up his forearms and drew her attention. Regina peered closer at his left arm and spied a thin long streak of red. "You're hurt! He cut you." Guilt rode her and she wished she could tell him the truth. "I'm sorry."

"It's a scratch. Don't change the subject." Fury burned in his eyes. Latent power surged from him, making Regina more aware of her own weakness. And nudity.

She wanted to make him understand. Pain clawed at her, muddling her thoughts. "Please, I have no answers for you. You don't have to worry about me. I'm grateful for all you've done and if you'll help me, I'll leave."

"Hell, you can hardly sit up in that bed, much less walk out of here. Where do you think you're gonna go?"

"I'm going back to town. The children need me."

"You can't."

His simple words weren't refusal, but truth. Because she knew they were, frustration made her snap at him. "Just because you helped me, doesn't mean you can tell me what to do." She lifted her chin at him though he wobbled in front of her eyes. Her shoulder pounded with pain and her entire body felt heavy and weak, but she repeated, "I-I've got to go."

"Suit yourself." His eyes glittered with a challenge. He shrugged, crossing his arms over his chest.

Her eyes narrowed. She struggled to keep her mind from straying to thoughts of rest. Was he going to let her go, just like that? She couldn't waste any time wondering.

She plastered the sheet to her naked backside and scooted toward her chemise. The pain sliced through her, destroying the last remnant of strength. Gripping the chemise and grabbing hold of the mattress, she managed to stay upright.

Sweat prickled her skin, burned the wound. The pain drilled into her shoulder and the base of her neck. She swallowed a great gulp of air and moved more slowly. With one hand, she spread the chemise so she could find the bottom opening. Her hands shook and a chill swept over her. She gritted her teeth to stop their chattering. Cole stood in front of the bed, watching with the concentrated gaze of a starved wolf.

Did the man intend to watch her struggle into her clothes? "Do you mind?"

"No, go ahead." He didn't move.

Anger rose, but she didn't have the energy for it. She wondered if she had the energy to pull the chemise over her head. She had to. The children needed her.

"What if you put them in danger?"

She thought the words were hers, but Cole Wellington's voice reverberated in the hot room. He had echoed her concern and she closed her eyes in realization. He was right. Again. What if James Cross followed her there? Or worse yet, what if he was already there? What could she do?

She had to get back to the children, but doing so might tempt Cross to use one of them to get to her. She would never forgive herself. Images of Laura, Bitsy, Micah, Cuff, Timmy, and Elliot flashed through her mind. Her throat tightened.

Silence pounded in the room. The song of frogs and crickets swelled, growing louder and louder. Tension knotted her neck.

Cole stepped up to the bed and said in a low, husky voice, "I'll go."

She froze, speechless with surprise. What had made him stop asking questions and volunteer to check on the children? Perhaps he was concerned for them. Whatever the reason, the simple offer did what James Cross and his knife had not been able to—drew tears. She knew it was a combination of relief, fear, and weakness, and cleared her throat. "Thank you."

He nodded, his gaze meeting hers. For a moment, she glimpsed unguarded emotion in his eyes. She thought it was curiosity and concern. In a blink, it was gone. "How many are there?"

"Six. No, five." The numbers circled round in her head. Images of the children crowded her memory then faded. "Three boys, two girls. Timmy's been adopted by your sister now."

"I'll be back." He frowned, a flicker of concern in his eyes. His gaze moved behind her to the pillow. "You'd better rest."

"Yes, I'll try." She didn't know if she could until he returned with news.

He moved to the door.

"Wait." Regina didn't want to ask him for anything more, but he was already involved. . . . "Could you take a note to Reverend Holly? Someone will need to watch the children until I return from St. Lou—until I return." She held her breath, watching him, hoping he wouldn't question her slip.

He had noticed her hesitation. His gaze bored into her and she saw the questions in his eyes. He took a step toward the bed and stopped. His gaze stroked over her then returned to her face.

Suddenly she was aware of being alone with him in the room, completely naked and as weak as a new baby. She couldn't tear her gaze from his. Every nerve ending leaped to life as much from wary caution as from the instant desire he seemed to evoke.

Cole jerked his gaze away and thundered out of the room.

Regina sat stunned, her senses befuddled by fatigue and pain. Where was he going? Was he leaving without the note? Who would watch the children? His footsteps echoed back along the hall then grew louder. She gave an inward sigh of relief when he returned with paper, ink, and a quill.

He laid a book in her lap—*Moseman's Illustrated Catalog of Horse Furnishing Goods*—and placed the paper on top of it. "There you go."

"Thank you." Holding the sheet up with her left hand and keeping her right arm as still as possible, she scratched out a brief message to Reverend Holly and signed it. Pain throbbed in her shoulder and her elbow. Holding back a sigh, she handed the note to Cole.

He tucked it in the back pocket of his britches. "I'll be back. Don't go anywhere."

"Funny," Regina muttered. Bracing herself for the pain, she scooted backward. Unable to use both arms for leverage, she managed only inches.

With a vehement curse, Cole rounded and came to the bed. He clamped one hand on her waist, the other behind her uninjured shoulder and hauled her up to the pillows.

The sheet dipped precariously low on her breasts and she froze. Her gaze lifted to find his fixed keenly on the swell of her breasts. Then his gaze rose to her mouth and lingered. A fine heat suffused her body; her heart slammed against her ribs. For a moment, she thought he might kiss her as he had last summer.

Then he laughed. Laughed!

Startled, Regina snatched the sheet up higher and stared. What *did* he find so funny?

He straightened from the bed and stepped back, still grinning. "Never had a naked nun in my bed before. Can't make up my mind as to whether I should get on my knees and ask forgiveness or climb in there with you."

"Mr. Wellington! I hardly think—"

"Yeah, I know. Not exactly what you're used to hearing, is it? Funny, but I can't help wondering . . ."

Embarrassment burned her cheeks. He was the strangest man, angry and hard one minute, laughing the next.

The laughter faded from his eyes and they narrowed. A heavy quiet invaded the room. His voice rumbled out, low and lethal. "What were you before you were a nun?"

Her heart sputtered and she met his gaze, though she wished she hadn't. He stared back at her, hungry, curious . . . suspicious. In a smooth whiplike motion, he turned for the door. "I'll be back."

With that he was gone, leaving Regina staring after him with a frown. She felt all shivery and hot inside and at the same time, indignant. She remembered how the light had faded from his eyes and cold reason returned.

Cole Wellington had saved her life. In repayment, he would want answers. Answers she couldn't give. Answers she knew he would ruthlessly try to get. She hoped she was up to the test.

Lean hot desire, spare raw energy coursed through him. Cole did not want to attribute those things to the nun, though he couldn't ignore them. His body was too hard, his blood too hot. He couldn't deal with this irrational attraction to a woman he would never have. A woman *no* man would ever have.

Uneasy with his response to her, he forced his thoughts to town. He wanted answers and he intended to get them. If not from her, then from someone or somewhere else. For that reason, and solely that reason, he had volunteered to check on the children.

Dim moonlight fanned across the ground. He dug his heels into Horse's flanks and the two of them raced over hills, through groves of trees and scattered creeks toward Calcutta. Sounds echoed in his head—the easy clomp of the mare's hooves across brittle ground, her occasional snort, the distant call of an owl, the persistent chirp of crickets and night crawlers.

He'd read the note. She had told Reverend Holly she'd been called away unexpectedly and would probably be gone a month or so. Cole knew it wouldn't take a month for her shoulder to heal. If he was guessing, she wouldn't be spending that time with him, either. So what was she planning?

As much as he resented it, his thoughts strayed to her. He'd unwittingly, unwillingly, been drawn into her secret. Anger rose and fell by varying degrees.

He couldn't help but wonder what she had been like before becoming a nun or what had made her choose that life. And he could not begin to fathom what she was hiding. People were almost never as they appeared and she was no exception. Even someone so seemingly pure and beyond reproach had secrets.

He intended to find out what Sister Regina's secrets were.

Half an hour later, he pulled up outside of Calcutta. He entered from behind the town, due west, and decided to walk his horse along the back side of the buildings up to the orphanage at the north end of town. The man with the knife could still be looking for Sister Regina, and Cole wanted to take no chance of being seen.

A hundred yards from the orphanage, he dropped the reins and left Horse in a stand of trees. The small frame building was dark and quiet. Testing the back door, Cole found it unlocked and stepped inside. It made the barest creak of noise and he stood for a moment, allowing his eyes to adjust to the lesser light.

He was in the kitchen. His boots made a hollow thump as he moved to the doorway. A bigger room lay beyond. Several chairs were scattered around; a child's wooden desk sat in one corner. The fireplace was dark and empty.

He moved down the hall, careful to walk quietly. He opened the first door on his left and saw three beds, one of them empty. Moving inside, he peered at the closest child. Boy.

Backing out, he closed the door and opened the one across the hall. Four beds here. Two occupied. Long dark hair streamed across one pillow. In another bed, a dark braid dangled over the edge. Girls.

Sister Regina had said five children. He'd counted four. Who was missing? Once Cole finished here, he'd have to go over to Reverend Holly's and deliver the note. Maybe the preacher would check on the children.

His mind touched briefly on the nun's lie. At least she'd relieved him of lying to the reverend. He opened the last door in the hallway, knowing the room must belong to her.

A tiny window, shaded by a square piece of fabric, allowed a milky wedge of light into the room. A narrow bed bumped against the wall under the window. Pristine sheets, diamond bright in the darkness, were tucked under the mattress and pulled taut, making a crisp rectangular box.

Close to the door sat a small dresser and beside that,

a canvas bag. Cole eased open the dresser drawers one at a time. In the top drawer was a chemise and a pair of pantalets. Underneath was a ragged, faded photograph. He walked over by the window and pushed the scrap of curtain aside. Moonlight rippled across the creased picture.

A bald man, a beautiful raven-haired woman, and a chubby little girl no more than three or four years old stared back at him. He could see a resemblance in the woman to Sister Regina. Her mother?

He slid the photograph in his shirt pocket and opened the next drawer. An extra habit and a medal of St. Augustine. There was nothing in the third drawer or the canvas bag, nothing in the room to give a clue what a knife-wielding bastard would want with a nun. Frustration churned. There had to be something.

He scanned the room then froze, senses attuned to the noises of the night. The hair on the back of his neck prickled. A distant creak sounded, the opening of a door. Muffled footsteps moved down the hall.

Cole turned, searching the spartan room for a hiding place. Dropping on all fours, he rolled under the bed and pressed into the shadows just as the door opened. His shoulders strained against the rope strung to hold the mattress.

He was too wide in the shoulders to be sandwiched into the tiny space. The slightest move would rattle the bed. He took a small breath of hot dusty air and peered into the darkness. He could make out a pair of boots and the cuff of britches.

A hiss of frustration sounded in the room then the

person in the doorway stepped back, pulling the door closed. Cole caught a quick glimpse of a form and registered it was a man, but he saw no features. The build was too slight to be the man with the knife.

Cole shut his eyes, listening hard. A door closed and then silence. After long seconds, he made a sweeping search under the bed with his hand. He found only small grains of dust. He rolled out and stood, readjusting his hat. After scanning the room a second time, he stepped to the door.

He took extra care to close the door quietly then looked in again on the children. They didn't stir. Walking silently up the hall, he stopped between the kitchen and front room, studying. He noticed nothing new. Both rooms were empty. The entire place was sparse and not given to hidden corners.

After another glance at the kitchen, he let himself out. His gaze lit on the lean-to a few feet away. Even though he knew it was probably used as a storehouse, he headed there anyway.

The door made no sound as he pushed it open, not even a small whine. A strong rich odor hit him in the face.

He placed the sweet, almost bitter stench of blood immediately—thanks to his days in the Union Army—and moved inside. A door that quiet meant someone had gone to trouble to make it that way. Why?

A hoe and a shovel leaned against the wall to his right. A lumpy burlap sack sagged in the corner. As his eyes adjusted to the light streaming in behind him, he spotted a bulky blanket.

He checked the sack in the corner, reaching in and grabbing a firm, dirt-encrusted potato. Leaning down, he tugged at the blanket. It didn't move and he felt a heavy weight inside. Cole knelt, unwrapped the blanket, and froze.

A man with dark hair and a graying beard stared up at him with blank eyes. At the same moment Cole registered the man was dead, he saw a slit throat and was assaulted by the coppery smell of blood. He turned his head away, fighting for a clean breath of air. After a few shallow gulps, he looked back. Thoughts tangled in his head, but it was shock that kept him still.

What the hell was going on with that nun? First a killer chased her through town and now he'd found a dead man in her lean-to. Was she involved with this man, too? Did she know him?

Questions hammered at Cole. Questions he knew she wouldn't answer, at least not willingly. Leaning over, he began going through the man's shirt pockets. He found nothing and moved to the man's britches. The pockets were empty as well. Cole felt around the waistband for a weapon or a pocketbook, something to show who the man was or why he had been killed.

His fingers skimmed across a bump in the waistband. He dug his fingers deeper and folded the band out. A small pocket was sewn there with something inside.

Anticipation rushed through him. He dug and pulled until he removed a piece of paper folded into a thin rectangle. He unfolded it and rose, moving to the doorway and into the hazy light. As he smoothed the creased paper, a picture of a man became clear. It was a notice for one Wendell Cross, wanted for murder.

Cole had heard of Cross, a corrupt sheriff from St. Louis or thereabouts. He was suspected of using his position to rob trains. Allegedly, he had passed on information about gold shipments to his two brothers, who then held up the trains.

Cole didn't recognize the man in the picture and felt a stab of disappointment. Wendell Cross wasn't the man who had chased Sister Regina with the knife tonight, although there might be a resemblance in the eyes and jaw. It was too dark to tell.

He folded the paper in half, prepared to put it in his pocket, when he noticed the writing on the back. Turning it over, he read: "Abe Grand Detective Agency, St. Louis, Missouri. 3-5-1."

The missive on the back could have just been the source of the wanted poster, but Cole knew better. Stunned, he read it again and turned his head to look at the dead man.

The man who lay in a pool of blood in the nun's lean-to was an undercover detective.

Did Sister Regina know? Was she somehow involved with him or the Grand Agency? Could she be an agent herself? He knew agencies like Pinkerton's had female detectives.

Cole stared at the man without really seeing him. Number 3-5-1 was a field agent. For security reasons, field agents were referred to by number, not by name. Cole knew that much from his brief experience with Abe Grand's agency. A little more than two months ago, he had traced Sutter to the detective agency where he was employed, only to lose his trail again.

In a small black book in Abe Grand's desk, Cole had found a list of numbers just like these. No names, just numbers.

The night clerk had sworn, with Cole's Smith & Wesson drilled into his temple, that only Abe Grand knew the agents' numbers and real names. Cole knew Abe Grand would die before he would reveal those names. And Cole would be exactly where he was now—nowhere closer to Sutter.

So he had come home to regroup, remap another strategy. Sutter had turned up last time chasing the James and Younger gangs across the state after the Monegaw Springs hostage incident. He would turn up again and Cole would be right behind him.

Stuffing the wanted poster in his back pocket, he left the lean-to and strode toward the trees where Horse waited. He would have to do something about that body. It wouldn't be right for one of those kids to find it.

Leading Horse until they were out of earshot of the orphanage, he circled back around Calcutta and came in from the south, close to the church. The white clapboard building was dark, but he dismounted anyway.

He knocked, then knocked again when he heard no one coming. "Reverend Holly? You in there?"

Did the man live here? Cole didn't know. He'd seen him only at Leah and Cabot's wedding and wasn't sure he would recognize him.

Cole pounded on the door again, but no one answered. He considered leaving the note under the door, but didn't want to risk the reverend missing it. Leading Horse, he headed across the street to the marshal's office. At least he knew Ted Sanders, albeit casually. Once Cole gave the nun's note to Ted, the marshal would probably check on things at the orphanage.

A lantern burned brightly over the door and another sat in the barred window. Cole opened the door and walked in, surprised to find the office empty. He stood undecided for a moment then became aware of voices coming from the street behind him.

He turned and walked out onto the porch. Marshal Sanders and two men came toward him. The two unfamiliar men carried something slung low in a sack between them. One man was about six foot three, slender build, with dark curly hair. He thought that might be Reverend Holly. The other man was about six feet tall and Cole could see as they neared he was only a boy, maybe fifteen or sixteen.

Between them they carried . . . something in a blanket. Something that looked like a body.

"Wellington? That you?" Ted Sanders called from a few feet away.

Cole frowned and moved down the steps for a closer look. "Yeah. I've got something for Reverend Holly." He turned to the man wearing suspenders and a white Sunday shirt unbuttoned at the neck. "That's you, right?"

"Yes, it is. What can I do for you?"

"Nothin' for me. I'm just delivering a message." Cole let his gaze go to the blanket-wrapped bundle the men were taking inside the marshal's office. He'd bet big money that the body in that blanket was the undercover detective from Sister Regina's lean-to. He'd gotten out just in time. How had Ted found the man?

The marshal stood back beside Cole, allowing the reverend and the boy to go through the door. "Can you come in for a minute? You might know this one."

"You got a body in there?" Cole's voice was normal, but he felt like he'd been kicked in the stomach.

Marshal Sanders followed the other two men inside and nodded to Cole's question. Reverend Holly bent over the dead man, eyes closed, murmuring a prayer. Cole stood stiffly, seeing the dead man's face. At least he'd been found and Cole wouldn't have to worry about one of the kids finding him.

He turned to Sanders, speaking in a low voice, "Sorry, don't know him. Where was he?"

"Rather not say." Sanders walked around his desk to open the drawer and gestured to the boy. "Elliot here found him."

Cole's gaze slid to the young man, surprised to see a hint of anger there. He nodded and Elliot returned the gesture. Cole noticed the boy's face was pasty; sweat rolled from his temple down the side of his face. Probably the first dead body the boy had seen. Memory flickered. He and Luke had seen their first dead man when they were twelve.

Reverend Holly turned from the dead man and walked to Cole. "What's this about a message for me, Mr. Wellington?"

"Oh, yeah." Cole dug in his pocket for the nun's note.

The preacher took it, his kind eyes tempered with concern. "Thank you."

"Sure." Cole opened the door to leave. "See ya, Ted."

"It's from Sister Regina!" The words exploded from the preacher.

Elliot's head whipped around, first to Reverend Holly then to Cole. His gaze narrowed in suspicion. Cole stared at him, not blinking.

The boy held his gaze, his mouth tight and drawn. "Where is she?"

"I just delivered the note, boy." Cole wondered at the protective hostility in Elliot's tone.

"She's been called away for a while." Reverend Holly smiled and folded the note, placing it in his shirt pocket. "It's all right, Elliot. She's fine." His gaze moved to Cole. The reverend smiled, though it didn't cover the speculation in his eyes. "Thank you."

Cole nodded. Behind the preacher's warm words lurked suspicion and worry. Did Holly think Cole had harmed Sister Regina? Cole gave one last glance at the dead man and stepped outside.

"How did you come to have this note, Mr. Wellington?" The preacher, his voice friendly but firm, stepped up behind him.

"I passed her on her way out of town." Cole looked over his shoulder, searching for Holly's reaction.

The man nodded, a thoughtful look crossing his face. Then he turned to the boy and clapped him on the shoulder. "Let's get over to the orphanage, Elliot. Looks like you'll be in charge for a while."

Cole tipped his hat. "See ya, Ted. Reverend. Elliot."

"Yeah." Sanders was distracted, already going through the dead man's pockets searching for identification.

Cole swung into the saddle and nudged Horse into a canter, careful to make sure he wasn't followed. Several times he pulled off the road, assuring himself he was still alone.

So, Elliot had led Sanders to the body. When and how had the boy found the dead man? Cole's trip into town hadn't yielded any answers, but a host of questions.

There was no doubt in his mind that the man chasing Sister Regina had killed Detective Number 3-5-1. But did the nun know who the killer was and what he wanted? Was she connected to Wendell Cross, a known outlaw? Did she know of the dead man in her lean-to?

Too many strange things had happened to her tonight for them to be coincidence. She had to know something. But what? And how could Cole get her to tell him?

He stared into the hazy night, but in his mind he saw her pale naked body in his bed; the fear and guilt *and* desire in her eyes when he'd kissed her last summer.

He replayed the arcing tension between them when he had moved her up to the pillows. She had felt it, too. Her eyes had softened with passion and confusion; her breath had quickened just like his. At the memory, blood rushed to Cole's loins. He cursed his physical reaction then realized it was the reaction of a man to a woman, not a man to a nun.

And suddenly he knew how to get his answers.

CHAPTER FIVE

Regina slept through the day and into the next night. She woke, staring into darkness. Blessed cool air drifted through the open window and she turned her face toward it. A strip of light slanted from the room into the hallway. With a mixture of relief and disappointment, she realized she was alone. She remembered waking once, sun streaming through the windows, and Cole forcing her to sip some broth.

After he had left to check on the children, she had slept. She hadn't meant to, had thought the pain would prevent it, but she had. She wanted to see Cole, to ask about the children. And James Cross.

Where was Cross? Lying in wait for her? What about his brothers? Lance Spradling had seen them in Texas, but were they, too, on their way to Calcutta?

Regina knew they would go to any lengths to keep her from arriving in St. Louis and testifying against their brother. Fear twisted in her stomach and settled like lead. Before, she had chafed at her protective anonymity, the forced lies. Now she craved it. She wasn't fool enough to believe James Cross would leave her be; she would face that danger alone as she had for the last year and a half.

Except for last night, when Cole had been the one to save her. The idea left her feeling unsettled and shaken. Regina knew she should concentrate on the children and planning for the journey ahead.

But her thoughts didn't dwell on either of those things. They stayed on Cole Wellington. Her gaze rested on the four-drawer dresser standing guard next to the chair in the corner. The only items on the dresser were a tintype of his sister, Leah, and her second husband, another tintype of his mother and father, and a comb.

Warmth burst low in her belly at the thought of him and spread up to her heart. She had seen a part of him others hadn't, a gentle part others probably wouldn't believe. A shiver of excitement worked its way through her.

Underneath that blunt, earthy exterior, he possessed a sensitive nature. Why else would he have volunteered to check on the children?

She became aware of the music then. Haunting, lonesome, poignantly familiar. The sweet strains of "The Blue Danube Waltz" played on a mouth harp wafted through the window with a teasing night breeze. Sensation pulled deep in Regina's belly. It was one of her favorite songs, though played by Cole Wellington, it became not a celebration of life, but a call for one, a seeking, yearning piece that pierced her heart.

It was the same song she had heard from the orphanage window last summer and gone to investigate. Even drunk, he had played it with enough feeling to bring tears to her eyes. And then he'd kissed her . . .

She pushed away the thought and scooted to the edge of the bed. The room spun for a moment then settled back into focus. Except for the sharp throb in her shoulder, she felt strong enough to get up and face Cole. Regardless of the questions she knew he would ask.

She levered herself off the bed, wobbling at first on unsteady legs. The voluminous outer robe slipped over her head with a small amount of trouble. The wool, a lighter and tighter blend for summer months, scratched at her skin, but she could not stand to put on the bloody chemise.

She stood for a moment, allowing the sharp sting in her shoulder to ebb to an ache. On legs that felt hollow from her two-day stay in bed, she made her way to the door. The lantern at the top of the uncarpeted stairs illuminated the way.

The music drew her, filling her with a sense of loneliness and knowledge that she had been right about Cole. He was more vulnerable than people realized, even his sister, Leah. Perhaps his frequent absences, the noncommunication with his family were the result of necessity rather than choice. Regina felt a prick of pain that had nothing to do with her injury.

Halfway down the stairs, she faltered. Cole was sure to ask questions, but she couldn't give him answers. After months of putting her life on hold, she could allow nothing to jeopardize the justice so close to being served on Wendell Cross. The excitement of finally being able to testify and exact vengeance for her father's murder thrummed in her blood.

Standing on the stairs with the slow, breathy sounds of "The Blue Danube Waltz" floating around her, she struggled. She would have to face Cole sometime. Perhaps he had changed his mind about learning anything from her. He had, after all, saved her life, stitched her wound, and taken care of the children. All without knowing a blessed thing about her.

Due to that, she told herself, there was an unusual bond between them. Both knew the other had secrets. They would respect that about each other.

Regina padded down the stairs, the smooth wood warm beneath her bare feet. The music swelled to a pause, then picked up as the last note faded into the night, causing her heart to squeeze. What had happened to make such a lively song so different for Cole?

The front door stood open. He sat on the porch, one brawny shoulder angled against a supporting post. She stepped into the open doorway, hoping he wouldn't hear her and stop. He kept playing. The music filled the night, plucking strings in Regina's memory. Her father had first taught her to waltz back when he was still the headmaster at a school in Chicago.

Her first ten years had been happy, loving ones. And then Worth Harrison had become an undercover detective. The family had begun to move, never staying in one place longer than it took for her father to finish an assignment. They moved to Missouri when Regina was fourteen.

As the years passed, her father spent more time in the field. His assignments became more dangerous, his homecomings shorter and farther between. Regina and her mother came to depend solely on each other. She knew her father loved them both, but she wanted him home and building a life with them.

She wanted to live in one place, establish relationships with people who could tease her about something she'd done years before, put down roots and make a difference somewhere. In an ironic twist of fate, she had found that at Calcutta. And it was all a lie.

She closed her eyes and lifted her face to the gentle breeze scented with wildflowers and loamy earth. Nights were her favorite. She needed those sacred moments after the children went to bed, when she could stand outside, remove her headpiece, and merge with the darkness that judged no man or motivation.

With her hair loose and flowing around her shoulders, she could pretend she was Regina Suzanne Harrison, a young woman who wanted nothing more than land and a place of her own. A woman who wanted to experience the touch of a man, the thrill of dressing for a dance, of sharing whispers with other women just like her.

But until Wendell Cross was brought to justice, she was Sister Regina, a *nun* who must control her every urge, guard every word and action, and forget she was half in love with the man who had ministered so gently to her last night.

"So, you're up and about." The words were quiet, etched with a predatory tone.

Her eyes flew open and she gripped the door frame

for support. Cole had moved silently in front of her. Potent power emanated from his rangy body. His ruthless black gaze scoured her face, tracked down her robe. A grin tugged at his mouth as if he knew she was naked beneath.

Her legs trembled, whether from fatigue or reaction she couldn't tell. She clutched her good arm around her waist and smiled. "Yes. I'm feeling much better."

"How's the shoulder?" He slid the mouth harp into his back pocket and leaned over to pluck up the neckline of her robe and peek at her bandages.

Stunned at his boldness, she pressed the scratchy robe to her breasts. Moist hot breath kissed the slope of her neck and a shiver ran up her spine. She was flooded with a sudden desire to lean into him and beg him to kiss her again. She imagined the shock on his face and bit back a smile. He thought she was a nun. It was better that way.

Remembering why she had come down, she pulled away slightly. "How are the children? Did you see them?"

"They're fine. I delivered your note." His eyes slitted as he considered her. "Seems you have a champion."

"Reverend Holly?" Puzzled, she tilted her head. Her legs still wobbled and she tightened her grip on the door.

Cole leaned against the opposite door jamb, his gaze scraping over her. "No, the boy. Elliot."

"You saw him? Thank goodness."

Cole's gaze sharpened on her. "He's with Holly."

She bit her lip, wondering if she should ask about James Cross.

"Didn't see your friend with the knife." Cole's voice was lazy, his gaze intense.

She tried a different tack. "Thank you for . . . saving my life and checking on the children."

"Uh huh." Tension scored his words, making her doubt the softness she'd seen earlier in him.

She raised one eyebrow though the movement seemed to take a lot of energy. "It's customary to say you're welcome."

"I want to know how grateful you are."

"I'm no fool." Her words came slowly as she prepared herself for what she knew was coming. "I know that man almost killed me and could've killed you."

"I'm glad you see it that way, Sister." His midnight dark voice caressed the words, reminding her again of his hot breath against her skin, his lips on hers. "I figure you won't mind telling me now about that bastard with the knife."

He wasted no time. Disappointment and anger flashed, but Regina reined in her temper, reminding herself that she had seen a softer side of him. He would listen to reason. "Cole, please understand. I have no answers for you."

"You mean you won't tell me. You're hidin' somethin' and I want to know what."

"I *can't* tell you. Can't you just leave it at that?"

"Like I should've left you to that bastard in town?"

"No." His words stung and again she fought back an angry reply, striving to appeal to the man she had glimpsed earlier. "I do thank you for helping me."

He edged closer, pushing her back from the door until his heat merged with hers and she could feel the brush of powerful thighs through her robe. "I want to know who that guy is and why he tried to kill you— us."

"I'm not asking why you sneak in and out of your family's life like a hunted man. Why can't you give me the same regard?"

" 'Cause what I do didn't nearly get you killed." He leaned full into her then, trapping her against the wall with his body. The dusky odor of warmed skin and a trace of lye soap floated to her.

Above her head, he braced one arm. He raised his other hand to her face and stroked her cheek. His gaze dropped to her lips; slowly he ran his tongue over his own. "You are incredibly beautiful. Do you know that about yourself, Sister?"

"I-I am a nun," she choked out. Panic fluttered in her chest as his heat shimmered against her face. The dark odor of the man assaulted her. Rather than push him away, she kept her arms locked at her sides, hands curled into fists. If she touched him, she wouldn't want to stop. "Don't you have any respect? If not for me, then for the Church?"

"All I care about is the way you melted into me last summer. I haven't forgotten that and I don't think you have either." His finger traced lightly over her cheek, around to her ear. He leaned closer, until she breathed from him. "I think you want me as much as I want you."

"Stop it!" Finally, she allowed the dam on her anger to break. Fear of her reaction to him merged with the fury. Desperate, she used the only means she knew as she stood her ground, staring him down. "I am a woman of the cloth, not some saloon girl you can handle and paw every time you get around. You may not respect my religion, but at least respect the fact that I am not like other women."

"Oh, don't I know that?" Instead of moving as she had hoped, or even getting angry, he stared into her eyes. A hungry, relentless smile spread across his face.

That smile traveled down Regina's body, unraveling in her stomach, and pooling in a flame at the center of her thighs. Her body's reaction spooked her as his words hadn't.

Trying to throw him off, she bucked against his chest. Pain shot through her shoulder, but she drew herself up to run. Cole's powerful body blocked her way, never moving. Instead, his left arm closed around her waist and his right hand cupped her head.

Even through the headpiece his heat seared her scalp. Just as he lowered his head, he whispered against her lips. "Come on, Sister. Give me what I want." The words were low and hypnotic, deliberately seductive.

Warm lips slanted across hers, molding, caressing, tempting. Regina pressed her lips together, squeezed her eyes shut, and allowed her anger to swallow every benevolent thought she'd had about him.

There was no softness in him, no vulnerability, no hidden gentleness. She felt like a fool for believing so earlier and allowed that anger to come, too.

He nibbled at her lips, sending shivers across her shoulders. She focused on the rage and let it heat her body, control her mind. Her lips stayed clamped tight and she felt small satisfaction in it. Instead a finger of sadness worked into her heart.

His tongue traced the seam of her lips, dipped into the corner. The wet silky play of his flesh against hers shot tingles under her skin. Her legs grew as weak as sun-warmed honey. Fighting for more than dignity, she focused her flagging energy on keeping her lips sealed against his coaxing invasion. Angry and wild with panic, she railed inside. A tear seeped out of her eye.

Dropping his hands from her, Cole pulled away. The abrupt loss of support caused her to take a balancing step back. She opened her eyes to find him staring at her, dark eyes glowing with anger and reluctant admiration. His nostrils flared; his chest rose and fell in rapid succession.

Her breath tore out in lung-stretching gulps. Exhaustion and the aftermath of anger set in, stripping her stamina and composure. The uncontrollable reaction to him beat against her will like hail on tin, punching holes in carefully erected armor. Regina didn't know if she could find the strength to walk, but she couldn't stay down here with him any longer.

She turned and stumbled for the stairs, only to be stopped by his voice. Raw, labored words hissed out. "I thought that would work for sure, but since it didn't, maybe this will."

She froze. He had planned to seduce answers out of her? Where was the man who had offered to check on the children, the man who had tenderly stitched her wound? She tried to ignore the pain that ripped through her, the inexplicable sense of betrayal. "Cole, I can't be any clearer. I have nothing to tell you."

"I think you do." His boots scraped the floor then he held something around in front of her.

Turning so the light from the stairway fell on his hand, she looked closer. A photograph wavered in front of her. A photograph of her family.

Shock and pure rage exploded in her veins. Tears burned her eyes. That photograph was the only thing left to her of them, their old life. She snatched it out of his hand and whirled, ignoring the arrow of pain through her shoulder.

"How dare you! You went through my things!"

"Damn straight." Tension coiled in his body. His arms and shoulders bulged tight against his black shirt; buttons strained with his heaving breath.

Her earlier image of him crumbled like charred wood. "That's the only reason you went there," she choked out, struggling against the tears burning her eyes. "The only reason you volunteered to check on the children. Did you even do that?"

"Of course," he said flatly. "I just took the time to look around when I finished."

"Took the time?" Her voice rose until she was yelling at full tilt. "Of course you would present it as a favor. Here I thought you were decent, caring, misunderstood. You're ruthless, a sneaking, conniving, lying son of a—"

"Uh uh." He moved with the deadly speed and grace of a springing mountain cat, pressing in on her and thumping the picture in her hand. "Tell me about this."

She wanted to tell him to go to hell, but she had spent too many months biting her tongue. She launched for the stairs. "I will not."

Undiluted rage poured through her, fueling her steps. How could she ever have thought he might care about anyone but himself?

Cole followed, his boots crashing against the wooden steps behind her. "Perhaps you'd like to know what else I found?"

"I'm not interested."

"I think you will be, although nuns don't have much, do they?"

At the silky smugness in his voice, she curled her fingers into her palm, squeezing until her knuckles ached. The anger was taking its toll on her weak body. Her shoulder throbbed. Each step came slower, burning the muscles in her thighs, along her calves.

"There were a pair of pantalets."

"Of course you would find those," she muttered darkly.

He kept step behind her. "The photograph, of course. An extra habit."

"Perhaps that will remind you of who and what I am." She reached the landing and started for the bedroom.

He followed close on her heels, too close, and his breath brushed her ear when he spoke again. "A medal of St. Augustine. Do all nuns carry those?"

"If they're of the order of St. Augustine," she snapped, walking into the room. How could she get rid of him? Would he hound her until she fell asleep from exhaustion? She stopped at the foot of the bed, wondering for the first time if she should tell him the name of James Cross so he would leave her alone.

Cole plastered himself against her, his chest cradling her back, his thighs hard and hot against hers. A whiskered cheek scraped her neck and his breath tickled her ear. "I also found a dead man in your lean-to."

His words were as gentle as a spring rain and jolted her heart to a painful stop.

Sweet Mary, Mother of God! He'd found Lance. Why, oh why hadn't she guessed when he thrust that photograph at her? Of course he would find Lance. Cole Wellington had gone there for the sole purpose of finding *something*.

Fear, anger, sadness, and welcome fury raced through her. The urge swelled in her to lash out at him, hurt him as much as he had hurt her.

She knew she was in over her head with him. She knew she should be careful. She knew she should control her anger.

Gaining a burst of strength from her fury, she turned and sidestepped him, looking for her sandals.

"What the hell are you doing?"

"I'm leaving."

"Not until I get answers. Why is there a dead man in your lean-to?"

"If I tell you anything, it will only jeopardize my life. I'm sure you don't care about that, but I do."

"Why will it put you in danger? What have you got on the man who tried to kill you last night?"

"Get out of my way." He blocked her as she tried to look under the bed. She straightened, the room spinning around her, and glared at him.

He glared back, his eyes hard, unforgiving. She swallowed, not sure how to handle any of this, and stepped around him to where her guimpe lay on the floor beside the bed. "I can't give you any answers. Surely you, of all people, can respect that."

"Can't give me any because you don't know, because you're protecting someone, or because you're one of them?"

Regina froze in her search of the room, her stomach dropping. Dread hammered at her, but she couldn't stop the words. "One of who?"

He crowded against her back and grated, "That dead man is a field agent for Abe Grand."

How had Cole Wellington learned that about Lance? And what else had he learned? The confusion in her voice wasn't faked. "A field agent?"

"An undercover detective," he stated baldly. "Is that what you are?"

"No! No, I'm not. Lance wasn't—"

"He was wearing identification."

"You . . . went through his clothes?" First, he'd ransacked her room, then a *dead* man? She whirled, her fingers curling into a fist to strike his jaw.

He halted her easily, smoothly reaching out to grip her wrist. "Now, now. Is that any way for a nun to act? What about 'turn the other cheek'? What would the Church think?"

"In this case, the Church would grant dispensation." The hot words blistered the air between them, but the pause served to right Regina's reeling temper.

Cole's amused taunt reminded her of who she was supposed to be, but the core of anger burned deep, tempting her to release emotions she shouldn't. Her fingers flexed, her wrist still captured by his bruising hold.

"Sheathe those pious claws, Sister, and tell me what I want to know."

She was tempted, so tempted to confide in just one person. Curse his arrogant hide! It was almost as if he knew the truth about her and dared her to tell him all of it. But no, he couldn't know she wasn't truly a nun.

They stood toe to toe, his brute power pressing in on her, her chest heaving with anger and exertion.

Green eyes speared deep black ones. Every handsome line in his face was tight, drawn into carved stone. The laugh lines around his hard mouth were creased with anger and impatience. His lean rangy body was as taut as a drawn bow. He wouldn't rest until he had answers.

"W-What did you do with Lance?"

"Me? Nothing. Marshal Sanders has him now."

"Marshal Sanders?" Her eyes widened; her heart skipped to a triple beat. Cole had turned in the body to the marshal. Had he also told him where he found the body and what had happened to Regina last night? She stood staring at him, not wanting to give him the satisfaction of seeing he had rattled her, but needing to know if she should expect a visit from Ted Sanders.

"Don't worry. I didn't turn in the body. I believe the boy, Elliot, led Ted to the lean-to."

"So you didn't . . ."

"Tell him about you? Not yet. Which doesn't mean I won't. And I wouldn't expect Ted to be as patient as I've been."

He had been as patient as a vulture swooping down on a fresh carcass, but Regina didn't feel now was the time to point that out. How much could she risk? With frustrating certainty, she knew she had to tell him something. Part of the truth, but not all. It was better to give Cole some information than risk drawing in yet another uninvolved party and possibly threatening her safety.

Meeting his flinty gaze, she relaxed her rigid arm and opened her fist, palm up, showing him she would withdraw.

Long seconds ticked between them as he contemplated her face. Seemingly satisfied, he released her and she rubbed her aching wrist. She backed toward the bed and sat down, as much from fatigue as to hide her shaking. The ache in her shoulder had flamed to fire again, burning with icy heat.

"I-I knew Lance, Lance Spradling, was an undercover detective. He was a friend of mine."

"How did you know him?"

She sorted through the truth, searching for answers to satisfy him until she left—she'd already decided. "I met him in St. Louis a couple of years ago."

"Was he a detective then?" Cole stepped up to the bed until his knee brushed the mattress. Heat surged from his body to hers. Anger still ribbed his voice; he sounded harsh and winded.

Regina stared at the tip of his black boots, lost in

the memory of the night she had met Lance at Abe's house. The night of her father's murder. The memories took her mind briefly from the pain in her shoulder. She answered with a sad smile, speaking of Lance but thinking of her father. "He's always been a detective."

"What was he doing in your lean-to?"

She had no intention of telling him the lean-to was a safe place for the detectives, but could she satisfy him with sketchy details? "He came to give me some information."

"What?"

"I won't tell you that. I will say—"

"Damn it!" He shifted, his anger swallowing the space in the room.

"I must get to St. Louis by the first part of September." Her gaze sparred with his. Had she meant to tell him that? Her body hurt; her mind felt downy and thick, but she had told him nothing that would endanger her business with Cross.

Cole shifted closer, threatening in a more subtle way than he had before, but threatening just the same. She thrust out her chin.

His chest and shoulders swelled and she knew he was struggling to control his anger. He cocked an eyebrow at her. "And if you don't get there?"

She glanced at her shoulder. "Haven't you figured that out?"

"What part does he play?" They both knew he referred to the man with the knife.

Regina hesitated, unsure about how much she should reveal. Cole stood unyielding and dangerous in front of her, barely leashed power coiled in his body, capable of exploding at any moment. Her shoulder throbbed; fatigue seeped through her bones, sucking her energy, draining her will. What could it matter to tell him now? He would not know how James Cross was related to her business in St. Louis.

She unconsciously placed a hand on her injured shoulder, trying to soothe the fresh flare of pain. Her bandage felt sticky, matted against her skin. Was she bleeding again? "His name is James Cross."

"Cross!"

The word exploded from Cole's lips with such force and familiarity that Regina immediately regretted naming the man. "You know him?"

"I've heard of him. Who hasn't?" Cole pivoted on one heel and paced the length of the bed. "He and his brothers are about as well known as Jesse and Frank."

"You're on a first-name basis with the James brothers?" Dread hooked into her, pulling tight in her stomach. She shouldn't have told him.

He ignored her question and strode over to stand in front of her. "How do you know him?"

"I don't really."

He shot her an impatient look. "Try again, Sister. I assume you do know he's a murderer."

"Well, I'd guessed that," she said dryly.

"How in the hell did you come to be involved with someone like that?"

She pressed her lips together and stared up at him, trying to keep her gaze locked with his. Fatigue swirled through her, dissolving the small strength she had.

Her lids felt heavy, as if she were drugged. He would get nothing further from her.

"Oh, we're back to that, are we?"

"I'll leave tomorrow."

"And go where?" He looked angry and amused at the same time.

"St. Louis, I guess."

"You goin' by horseback, stage, what?"

"I-I hadn't thought about it. Yet."

"Probably should. I don't think you've seen the last of James Cross."

"I could wait at the orphanage." She had no intention of doing so. She had only spoken to hide her panic.

"Endanger the children." The words were calm, matter-of-fact. He eased down in the ladder-backed chair and shucked off his boots. "And you're too weak to even put on your clothes."

She glared at him, torn between anger and shock at his obvious intent to stay in the room with her. Before, she had been unconscious and it hadn't seemed important. But now . . .

She hated his logic, hated his smugness, most of all hated that she had to stay here at least one more night. There was no mistaking the wet heat spreading on her shoulder.

He was right, of course, even if he didn't know she was bleeding again. Her strength had ebbed right out of her, like yolk from a broken egg. She wouldn't make it far.

He stretched out in the chair and pulled his hat low

over his eyes. "Holy hell, James Cross. What do they teach you at those convents?"

She blew out the lamp and eased down on the bed, aching for the day she could send Wendell Cross to prison and tell Cole Wellington to go to hell.

The wool of the robe suffocated her, made it hard to breathe. Huddled under the sheet, she peeled off the robe and dropped it on the floor. After considerable groping, she came up with her chemise and managed to pull it on. The effort left her breathless with fatigue, her shoulder throbbing. She pulled the sheet up to her chin, shielding herself from Cole.

As her eyes adjusted to the darkness, she could just make out Cole's hat still covering his face. Better for him than Marshal Sanders to know about James Cross, but Regina still chafed that she had been forced to tell. She couldn't risk disclosing any more information. Tomorrow she would have to leave.

Sadness washed over her and she pushed it aside, closing her eyes. She was better off on her own. She *was*.

CHAPTER SIX

The nun was his ticket to Luke Sutter and he was going to use her.

Endless months of tortured dreams, hate, and loss were riding on her connection to Sutter and Cole couldn't turn away from this chance to kill the demons inside him. Guilt at the idea of trying to seduce a nun battered him, but it wasn't as strong as the hate, the marrow-deep need for revenge.

The next morning, just as the sun pinkened the horizon, Cole swung down from Horse, wrapped the reins loosely around the hitching post, and stepped up to the door of Calcutta's telegraph office.

For the first time in his eighteen-month chase of Sutter, Cole wavered. It had little to do with the memories of his one-time friend that sometimes sprang upon him unaware, like their first fight over who had caught the biggest fish or the time Luke had lied and confessed that he, not Cole, had broken Corrie Wellington's favorite porcelain figurine.

Cole's hesitation came instead from an injured nun in his bed.

Want, need, anger, and frustration coursed through him. How could he feel so much for a woman who wasn't really a woman? There was the trouble. Cole shouldn't think of her as a woman, but he did. And always had.

He'd scant been around nuns in his lifetime, except that brief stint in St. Louis two months ago. He'd never reacted to them except to acknowledge the respect they garnered and absentmindedly afford it to them.

There was nothing absentminded in his reaction to Sister Regina. He wanted her. Bad. And if he'd believed in her religion, then he would have believed he'd burn in eternal hell for wanting her. But he didn't believe. His reaction to her disgusted him, but even more it clouded his mind, blurring the goal that even his family hadn't been able to sway him from.

Since he'd found the dead agent, Cole hadn't been able to escape the idea now hammering at his conscience. At first it had sneaked through his mind, flickering to life then dying of guilt. But he couldn't ignore it any longer.

Sister Regina was, albeit indirectly, his link to Sutter. Perhaps his last link. Twin pictures flashed through his mind—one of her, one of Luke and Sarah.

He felt again the brush of the nun's lips against his, the near-surrender he had sensed last night.

Crowding that memory came the one of Cole walking into Luke's barn, finding him and Sarah wrapped in each other's arms like skin turned inside out.

Cole gripped the knob of the telegraph office door. He couldn't, wouldn't allow the futile feelings he had for the nun to interfere with a search he'd lived, breathed, and slept for nearly two years of his life. He had ruthlessly set aside everything in his way. His home, his farm—hell, even his family. He would set aside the nun and his guilt, too.

He pushed open the door, anger overwhelming his hesitation about Sister Regina, refueling the determination to get Sutter. He wouldn't be the only one to benefit from this plan. Whether she wanted it or not, she needed someone on the trail with her.

Hershel Waldrup, a man with thinning silver-white hair, pushed his wiry frame out of the chair behind the waist-high desk and tipped his worn conductor's hat at Cole. "G'morning, Cole. What can I do for you?"

"Need to send a wire to St. Louis."

"Yessir." The man stepped over to the metal apparatus, placed two fingers on it, and looked expectantly at Cole.

Cole pushed his hat back further on his head. "I'd rather write it down."

"Certainly." The man reached into one of a dozen pockets in the desk and laid a piece of paper and a pencil in front of Cole.

He considered the shortest way without giving away his identity to inform Abe Grand that he was bringing Sister Regina to St. Louis and began to write. The door behind him opened and he paused, not eager for company. He shifted as a man stepped up beside him.

"Morning, Hershel. Wellington." Marshal Sanders stood at Cole's elbow and raised a hand in greeting.

"Marshal." Cole's shoulders tightened and he stalled over the brief message, unwilling to reveal anything to the lawman beside him. Cole knew Lance Spradling was a detective for Abe Grand; did Ted Sanders know?

Sanders took off his hat and placed it on the desk. "It's gonna be a hot one today. You got any messages for me, Hershel?"

"Not yet. I'll sure let you know when I do. I know you're anxious."

"I'd appreciate it. How's Delilah holding up?"

"Fine. The heat gets to her sometimes, but her cough is better in the summer."

"Tell her I said hello." Sanders turned for the door, slapping Cole on the back. "Nice to see you again, Wellington."

"Thanks." Cole looked up then, his gaze sliding from Hershel to Sanders. "Any word on that find you made last night?"

"Not yet. That's what I'm waiting on."

"Good luck." The pressure on Cole's lungs eased. The longer it took Sanders to find out anything about Lance Spradling, the better for him and Sister Regina.

The marshal left, but Cole couldn't relax. He kept his sights on the door.

Hershel read the message, "Grand Stop. Will bring your *sister* Stop. Will release to Sutter only Stop. St. Louis September 5 Stop. Reply urgent Stop."

"That's right," Cole affirmed.

The older man grinned as he moved to the side of the desk. "Going to St. Louis, are you?"

Cole leveled a gaze at him.

Hershel's smile faded a bit. He licked the tip of the quill and wrote on the paper. "I'll just sign your name—"

Cole grabbed the old man's wrist. "No name."

"But how will he know who it's from?"

He released Hershel, ignoring the question. "I'll wait for a reply. It won't be long."

"All right." The other man sounded disappointed, but began tip-tapping on the machine.

Cole faced the door, watching the street, keeping an eye out for James Cross, though he doubted the man was fool enough to go traipsing around town. The telegraph office was quiet, but outside, the town hummed with life.

Two towheaded boys raced past the window, their bare feet thumping on the planked walk. Next door, keys rattled as Stern's Mercantile opened for business. From the docks, a steamboat trilled. Horses clopped down the street; wagon wheels squeaked and seats creaked.

Inside the office, an oily dirt smell trickled into Cole's awareness along with the waxy odor of the ink he'd used. The clickety-clack behind him came to an abrupt stop.

"There you go." Hershel wadded up the written message and threw it into a bin. "Should be a while."

"Thanks." Rather than sit, Cole stood where he was. Tension played at his shoulders and neck as he tried to reassure himself about the nun. He might be using her to help himself, but his presence would help her, too. He ignored the fact that she hadn't asked for his help.

It was a trade—her connection for his protection. And Abe Grand wouldn't be stupid enough to turn him down. Before long, Grand would hear about Detective Spradling's death, if he hadn't already. And he would realize the threat posed by James Cross.

If she was telling the truth.

The thought came to him suddenly and just as swiftly he dismissed it. She had to be telling the truth. He was counting on it.

This might be his only chance of getting Sutter and her only chance of getting to St. Louis alive. Cole tried not to think of the betrayal on her face when he had pulled the photograph of her family from his pocket.

He told himself this plan was mutually beneficial, but that didn't halt the pull of muscles across his chest and shoulders. Nor the feelings of guilt and manipulation he felt, though the determination was stronger.

He resented his reluctance and questioned everything she had told him. Had she told the truth? Grand's answer would be the proof.

He didn't have to wait long. Within an hour, the black machine on the desk began clicking. Cole pivoted. Hershel hurried over to scratch something on a piece of paper. The machine went silent as abruptly as it had started. The old man glanced at the paper, frowned, and pushed the message across to Cole.

One word glared at him. *Agreed.*

No questions, no negotiations, no games. Cole stared at the word lettered in bold black on a faded piece of newspaper, then crumpled the message in his fist.

Anticipation, relief, and excitement all coursed through his body. His hands shook and his breath rattled in his chest. He was closer to Sutter than he'd been in eighteen months.

The sense of triumph faded as he began to imagine what it would be like to finally gain revenge. Sadness and confusion sifted through him. He tried to ignore the heaviness pulling at his heart, the pain that spread in a pulsing sting through his body.

Thanking Hershel, he walked out the door and into the blinding sun, hating himself more in that instant than he ever had. He knew it would only get worse. He still had to tell the nun he was taking her to St. Louis. And he didn't know how to do that without lying.

Across the street, at the back corner of the warehouse marked Wellington and Montgomery, James Cross stood in a slight wedge of shadow. He watched as the man he'd fought in the alley mounted a dun mare and rode out of town. He rode easily, with coiled power, his rangy muscles poised for action, and scanned every alley, every inch of the street. Looking for him, James knew.

The dense heat prickled his skin. Sweat trickled down his temples, between his shoulder blades, even pooled to burn the wound beneath the bloody bandage on his right thigh. He rubbed his throbbing leg and, despite the pain, a slow smile stretched across his face.

James had sweltered and bled in this stinking hole for two days, waiting. For this.

The man in black had ridden off with Regina Harrison. He might know where she was; he might not. Either way, he was the only lead James had. Since James had last seen the woman, he'd spent one day unconscious, one day digging in his leg for the two bullets put there by the man in black. James figured he owed them both.

He pushed away from the weathered building, checked the empty street, and walked to the telegraph office.

At the door, he paused, glanced over his shoulder, then pulled his gray hat lower to shield his face. A dusty faded blue kerchief came up to cover his nose and jaw. From a slender sheath belted at his waist and easily hidden by his arm, he pulled his knife. Sunlight bounced off oiled metal.

He wrapped his fingers around the carved ivory handle as gently as if he were holding a woman's hand. The muscles of his palm absorbed the sinew of the weapon; it became an extension of him. He went inside and the door clicked silently shut.

A few minutes later, he stepped outside. Without using the knife, he'd gotten what he wanted—a name.

Cole reined Horse to a stop as he topped the knoll facing Gage's house. Through the feathery tops of pines and silver maples, he could see the barn and paddock and to the east, the two-story white clapboard. Plain except for the porch that squared the entire place, the house stood proud and gilded in the first glow of day. His gaze went to the window on the second floor and his eyes narrowed as he thought of the woman inside.

She would be furious, no doubt. A grin flashed and he started down the rise. He'd hidden her robe, taken it, in fact, in his saddlebags to town. After her half-hearted attempt to leave last night, he couldn't take the risk that she might try again.

He still wasn't certain why she had abruptly given up the fight though she had looked tired and pale. Conscience twinged at the way he had pushed her for answers, but he shrugged it off. By being drawn into her fight, he deserved to know everything about James Cross.

As Horse ambled down the slight rise and weaved between the trees, Cole shifted in the saddle. The day was still young, retaining the freshness of morning before being burned to sultry heat as the sun rose higher.

He thought he had come to terms with his decision about using her to reach Sutter, but the whole idea still nagged like a sore throat. He had to do it. She was his last chance.

He watched the window for some sign, expecting to see or hear her. Instead, the house was quiet, eerily still. Cole glanced around the front yard, taking in the grass withered from green to gray-brown, the black earth cracked and shriveled in the August heat. Not even a pulse of wind whispered in the air.

The silence pricked at his nerves. He slid off Horse

and dropped the reins. Not bothering to take her to the barn, he slapped the mare's rump and took the wide steps to the porch two at a time. The door swung open easily; inside, he stopped and listened.

Not a sound. Not the creak of a bed nor the impatient slap of bare feet on the wood floor. Surely she hadn't left without her clothes. For all her courage and bravado, he couldn't imagine it.

Silence reigned—heavy, ill-fitting. Cole stared up the stairs, laying a hand on the smooth-shaved banister. "Sister?"

Nothing.

He tried again, his voice louder this time, anger edging in. "Sister Regina?"

Again, no sound.

She'd left, by God! Panic had him bounding up the stairs. How would he get to Sutter? Triple emotions surged through him—anger, disbelief, concern for her safety. His heart thundered in his chest as he rushed to his bedroom. He came to a complete stop in the doorway. His heart lurched then resumed a heavy beat.

She lay in the bed, as still as a marble statue, just as she had when he'd left over two hours ago. No muscle moved. He couldn't detect the rise and fall of her chest. Her eyes were closed, the dark lashes making the hollows deeper there. She was pale, unnaturally so, the color of paste.

Dread hammered at him, stepped up his heartbeat again. He frowned and walked to the foot of the bed, staring at her. The sheet slanted across her chest, tucked under her arms, revealing the modest neckline of her chemise. Her skin was pasty, as motley gray as that of her face.

After a moment, he saw that her pulse fluttered in the hollow of her throat, but his relief was guarded. She had lost a lot of blood. Asleep she looked helpless, frail.

Sister Regina might have her secrets, but he'd had no right to treat her as he had; to push, prod, threaten, *seduce*. Self-loathing cut a swath through him and left him with an uneasy emotion—regret.

For nearly two years, he'd done whatever he'd had to, pushing aside everyone and everything to get the man he blamed for his wife's and baby's deaths.

And what about Sutter? Cole's mind taunted. Will you give up your ill-gotten edge from the nun? Take her to Abe Grand without demanding Sutter in return?

He pushed the questions aside. He would have a few days to think about it while she took a much-needed rest and healed up.

Four nights later, Regina sat on the porch listening to the soul-soothing sounds of "Amazing Grace" on Cole's mouth harp. The trills and vibratos brought a texture to the song, a wailing quality that pleased and provoked thought at the same time.

He had brought her downstairs tonight, at her request. He'd seemed reluctant, almost determined not to bring her, but he finally had. Tension pulsed from him. There was a wariness in his eyes as he looked out into the night, in the way his shoulders braced tight. Though he played the mouth harp with an easy rhythm, he was alert, sharp-edged.

She sat in a ladder-backed chair, her robe now washed and stitched, by Cole no less. There was something different in their relationship, though she couldn't quite say what. It wasn't the things he had done for her; the sewing, cooking, helping her to the bath and water closet. It was the way he had done them.

He had been . . . kind, and she didn't trust it.

She closed her eyes, humming the tune to "Amazing Grace," and allowed her thoughts to settle on Cole. Earlier, he'd brought her rich venison stew, hot fresh corn, and biscuits with honey. She saved the biscuits for last, savoring the hot bread and the sweet tastes of butter and honey.

From the doorway of the bedroom, he'd said, "I suppose you'll be wantin' more of those." His tone was polite, almost teasing.

She nodded. "I'm sure I won't get food like this in St. Louis." She clamped her mouth shut, wishing she hadn't referred to the trip. Shoulders tight, chin lifted, she had waited for him to demand further answers about Cross or how she had come to be involved.

He hadn't asked any questions. He had simply nodded and gone about the business of taking her tray downstairs.

She didn't understand it, wasn't sure she believed it, and sure didn't trust it. Cole Wellington as a dark, impatient man intrigued and even intimidated her upon occasion. As a caring man, he scared her to death.

His blatant attempt to seduce answers out of her several nights ago still blazed fresh across her memory. And her heart. He'd been in her room every night since. Though he hadn't tried anything else, she didn't trust this new side of him.

Yet, here on the porch with him, touched by the light from inside the house, listening as he began to play "The Streets of Laredo," she felt a peace she hadn't felt since the death of her mother.

The last rich note drifted into the night. "You asleep over there?"

"No." She smiled, opening her eyes. The soft evening enveloped her. The air was heavy with the scent of bruised grass, thirsting earth, even the smell of horses on Cole's clothes. "That was beautiful. How did you learn?"

"I taught myself during the war." He tapped the instrument against his palm and looked at her. "We spent a lot of time waiting for orders."

"I've always wished I could play an instrument."

"Didn't they teach you at the convent?"

Perhaps real nuns did learn, but Regina didn't know. She answered with a smile in her voice. "No."

She could feel his gaze on her, as tangible as a hand. His voice rumbled out like the slow announcement of a summer thunderstorm. "I could teach you. It's not hard."

Regina glanced over her shoulder, met his shadowed eyes. She wanted to. Oh, how she did. Some secret part of her strained toward Cole every time she was around him. It wasn't wise to fan the things she felt for him, but she was leaving tomorrow. "I'd like that."

He moved closer, scooting his chair so that he sat partially behind her, his shoulder touching hers. He held the instrument out to her. The thin bar was light and wooden with a silver plate on top that read "M. Hohner." It looked small in his hand; in hers it stretched the length of her palm.

"Now, you hold it so." He reached around with one hand to guide her own. Long fingers hot on her skin, he took her left hand and pressed the mouth harp between her thumb and forefinger so that they paralleled the top and bottom of the instrument. "There. Low notes to the left. Where your thumb and first finger join."

"Like this?" She gripped the instrument, her skin tingling at the smooth feel of metal still warm from his hands.

He adjusted her finger and thumb further toward the back edge. "You want enough room for your lips to get a good seal."

"Okay."

"Use your right hand to form a chamber with the left hand around it." He drew her right hand up and cupped it under the mouth harp so her fingers edged over the top of the instrument and met her left hand. "Adjust your hands until you're comfortable with the grip."

His heat curled around her; leather and the dark richness of his own scent played havoc with her senses. Her hands trembled and she forced herself to concentrate on his voice, his instructions. She moved her hands until she felt what she thought was a natural hold.

"The notes are numbered left to right. There are ten holes, thus." He drew a finger along the side facing her. His finger brushed her thumb and sensation tickled her skin. He pointed at the hole on the left end and his voice lowered, stroking over her. "Feel each hole with your tongue."

Startled at his words as much as at the intimacy of his voice, she jerked her gaze to him. Was he joking?

One corner of his lip tugged up in a half-grin. He stared at her, waiting.

Tentatively, she touched her tongue to the bar, the sensitive skin tingling when she felt the moist warmth he'd left behind. She found the first hole on the left and counted spaces.

"You only have to remember to ten, okay?"

"Okay." Her voice was soft, breathless with anticipation, and she berated herself. He was giving her a mouth harp lesson, nothing more.

"Good. Now to get a single note, you either lip it or block it with your tongue."

Her gaze sliced to him. Was he really teaching her to play the instrument or was he up to something else entirely? He simply stared at her, eyes unreadable. Her lips felt parched; her throat ached. "I don't know about this."

"You can do it. Wrap your lips around it so only the inner part makes contact."

She stared at him, caught in a swirl of emotions—

uncertainty, anticipation, a sense of forbidden excitement.

He continued, his gaze trained on her lips. "The moist part of your mouth. Otherwise you'll lose air out the sides. Don't wanna do that."

"No." She could barely control her breathing and desire tugged deep in her belly. The instructions whirled in her head. What had he said? She frowned, looking back to the instrument.

He leaned closer, his breath burning her cheek. "Imagine you're kissing someone." He gave a short laugh. "A lover, not the Pope's hand."

Was he laughing at her? Her gaze jerked to him and she stared blankly. An intense desire to kiss *him* knifed through her.

"You weren't always a nun, were you?" His voice was whisper soft, deep and provocative. "Think back."

All she could remember was kissing him outside the orphanage. She blinked. This was not a good idea. Her skin tingled; sensation fluttered in her stomach. He seemed to be enjoying it. Too much. She couldn't let him see how he affected her. She raised the mouth harp to her lips and tried to do as he'd told her.

"The trick is in the breathing. You blow out or draw in. Gotta learn to close your nose."

"How do I do that?" He was near enough that she could feel his breath on her cheek, see the shadowed whiskers beginning on the lower part of his jaw. A shiver jumped across her shoulders.

He grinned. "Blow out your mouth, breathe in your nose. While you're playing."

She gave him a dubious look. "All right. I'll try."

With trembling hands, she lifted the instrument to her mouth again. His scent, dark and mysterious, lingered and her lips tingled. For an instant, she froze in shock. Warmth curled in her belly. She breathed in and a whining note twisted out of the mouth harp. She puffed out another breath, grimacing as a flat *waaaa* yawned out.

Behind her, Cole chuckled. Without warning, his fingers brushed the side of her cheek and barely touched her lips. "Don't let any air escape the sides of your mouth. It takes a little practice, but you'll get it."

He pressed the mouth harp back to her lips. She tried to concentrate over the heat shifting through her body. She blew a tentative breath through the small holes, imagining that his lips were there, too. A thin high note whistled out.

"Wait." He reached over and pressed his fingers below her breasts, in the hollow where her ribs met. "Breathe from here, rather than your mouth or throat. Relax. Breathe evenly."

His hand stayed at her chest, searing through the cloth of her robe. How could she concentrate, let alone breathe, when he touched her so familiarly? Danger danced along her nerves. She stared down at his hand, large and possessive against her body, then lifted her gaze to his.

Tension tripped between them. The silent song of the night swelled in her ears. She thought she could hear Cole's heart pounding. Or was it hers?

He swallowed and removed his hand. "Breathe in pauses. It's easier. Watch me."

He lifted her hands in his. Curling his large calloused hands around hers, he put the harp to his mouth and blew out, drew in.

She could feel no air, but the heat from his lips and cheek scorched her hand. His palm was hot and rough against her hands. A shiver rippled down her spine. Her attention fixed on his lips sliding over the bar and her mouth dried up.

He played a series of notes, then pushed the instrument toward her without releasing her hands. "You try it."

His hand seared hers as he guided the bar gently over her mouth. His moist breath still lingered on the instrument, stroking her lips every time she blew. She could almost taste him, rich and dark and salty. Sensations tumbled through her, sharp enough to bring pain.

He spoke in her ear, something about blowing on holes one and four, but a wave of desire sliced through her. So pure, so intense, she caught her breath. Her hands shook. Light seemed to pulse through her body, sending channels of warmth to all her nerve endings.

"Ready to try a song?"

She blinked up at him, her heart pounding, as if she had just finished first in the horse race at the county fair. "Yes."

He showed her a sequence of notes and under his careful tutelage, she stuttered through "Mary Had a Little Lamb." On her own, she tried twice more. The last time she made it through smoothly, with perfect notes, until Cole's breath tickled her ear.

A sour note lanced the night and she stopped. "Oh, bother."

"You almost had it."

"I love it." She turned to him, their shoulders brushing. His lips were close and warm breath stroked her cheek and nose. She looked into his eyes. "Teach me something else."

"I'd like to." The words, seductive and low, weighted the air between them.

Regina didn't think he meant to answer that way because he grew suddenly still. The mood shifted from mouth harp lessons to something else entirely.

Even with her limited experience, she knew that and couldn't ignore it. Helpless to run from him, not wanting to, she watched him. His gaze lowered to her lips; she felt them burn, anticipating his.

He leaned closer, giving her the choice. His breath mingled with hers and stirred a warmth inside her.

Desire axed straight down her middle. She swallowed, her heart slamming her ribs, her lungs so constricted she could barely breathe. She wanted to taste him and lifted her chin so that her lips feathered his.

She felt his indrawn breath. His gaze burned into hers, naked hunger and sharp frustration. She felt it, too, in a tight knot low in her belly.

Abruptly, he shoved back his chair and rose. "I almost did it again, didn't I?"

"Wh-what?" The sudden loss of him left her cold and bereft.

"It's sometimes hard to remember you're not . . . like other women."

Regina stared up at him, heart rushing, palms sweating. She wanted to say something, anything, but words tangled in her throat.

"What made you do it? Don't you want someone to share your life, give you children?"

"I . . ." She shook her head, helpless to answer, still reeling from the fact that she had invited his kiss.

He stood in the shadows and drew in a deep breath. His voice was low and rusty. "Best be getting in. It's late and you're probably getting tired."

She closed her eyes briefly, thankful and yet frustrated that he hadn't kissed her again. She was glad darkness shadowed her flaming cheeks.

For a few moments, they had enjoyed a new ease in their relationship, a closeness she'd experienced far too little in the last months. Now he was pulling away from her. Though it ripped at her heart, she knew it was best.

He waited until she was inside before he followed to walk silently up the stairs beside her. She had wanted him to kiss her, craved it. And he hadn't. It seemed he had finally accepted what she was and she hated the thought.

She was next to the bed before she realized he hadn't followed her into the bedroom. Turning, she searched his face. "Are you going out?"

Indecision then fleeting hunger flashed across his features. "No. I'm sleeping in Gage's room tonight."

"Oh. Of course." She didn't argue. How could she? To him, she was a nun—forbidden, sacred. He had no business in here now that she was practically recovered.

The thought saddened her, made her want to rail at the injustice of it all, curse the quest for vengeance that took every chance from her.

"Good night then." She hoped her voice sounded normal, not hurt.

"Good night." He closed the door and she could hear his footsteps cross the hall. Another door closed—Gage's bedroom.

Regina eased her outer robe over her head and clasped it to her breasts as she sank down on the bed. The chair in the corner sat empty. His gun was gone from the dresser as was his mouth harp. No sign of him lingered; only the faint odor of whiskey and the dark scent that was Cole's.

Loneliness swelled through her. She stayed awake well into the night.

CHAPTER SEVEN

Regina walked quickly toward the barn, glancing over her shoulder and up to the window. The sun bathed the yard, barn, and corral in a pink glow of early morning light. She needed some time to think, some time away from Cole.

Especially after last night. He surrounded her, his dark musky scent, his devil-knowing eyes. She could still feel his heat pressing in on her, the ache in her lips that could be assuaged only by his. Even now, her breasts tingled and grew heavy with a need she didn't fully understand.

Last night she had wanted to give herself up to his cool ways, hot hands. Tell him the one secret that she should use to protect herself from him—that she wasn't a nun. But it seemed that finally he had decided to respect what he thought she was. So she hadn't told him. In the brutal light of day, she could be glad of that. But not in the night.

Cole made her want what she couldn't have, at least not until Wendell Cross was in prison. She should be anxious about getting to St. Louis, ready to put her father's murderer behind bars. And part of her wanted to go.

But another part of her felt trepidation and fright. She couldn't forget James Cross and knew he hadn't forgotten her. That frightened, uncertain side wanted to stay here, forget about time and her commitments, her vows, and pretend she had a chance at a life with Cole.

After last night, she knew she either had to tell him the truth about herself—which would jeopardize everything she'd held sacred for all these months—or leave. The choice was simple, but far from easy.

She approached the paddock, smiling as a brown mare with a white streak down her nose trotted over. The mare stuck her nose through the rough-cut slats of the fence and Regina rubbed the plush muzzle.

The paddock was large and roomy enough to work the unbroken horses. A smaller area, connected to the west end with a gate, was used for refining the horses' skills once they learned the basic rein and voice commands. During the day, several horses used this area and were allowed to roam the hills directly behind the house.

Last night, Cole had put the animals in the barn. Regina walked inside, feeling easier away from his too-sharp gaze. While the man intrigued her, he also made her defensive and very possessive of her secrets. She knew she had to tell him she was leaving. She didn't dread the telling; she dreaded the going.

A moment of quiet was all she needed to shore up her guard and she had slipped out here, assuming he still slept. There had been no sound of movement from his room as she passed.

The barn was hollow, drafty almost in its largeness. Two wide doors opened it and Regina left them ajar to let in the morning light. Straw and oats marked the hard-packed earth floor; the dusty smell of hay and the pungent odor of manure sifted through the building.

Two rows of stalls ran the length of the barn, back to another set of double doors. Except for one, the stalls were filled.

As Regina approached, the horses nickered in acknowledgment and snorted. With the exception of Cole's dun mare and a paint gelding, all the horses were for breeding. There were eight in all, different colors and sizes, but all with classic blood lines evident in their streamlined strength, the clean dense bones, intelligent eyes. Though beautiful, all were sturdy working horses.

Even as little as Regina knew of horses, she could tell these were all handpicked by a man who knew the animals. Had Cole had anything to do with this or did they all belong to Gage?

She opened the stall doors, allowing the horses to wander out to the paddock. One mare, a kidney-red bay with black mane and tail, passed and Regina stroked the mare's nose, smiling as warm breath moistened her palm.

Cole's mare whinnied in recognition as Regina passed. She stopped at the next stall to stare at the horse there. A black and white paint with expressive onyx eyes regarded her with alert wariness and open curiosity. Regina reached out a hand and waited. The horse's nostrils twitched. The gelding moved closer, sniffing her outstretched hand and up her arm. When Regina stroked a hand down his thick neck, he stood still. She smiled.

"Goin' somewhere?"

Her heart jerked in her chest and she whirled. Cole stood in the doorway, hands clenched into fists at his sides. His denim britches melded over lean hips and thighs. The top button was unfastened as though he'd pulled on the britches in a hurry. He wore no shirt and beads of water shimmered on his collarbone. Dark hair dusted his chest.

Her gaze followed the cleft of muscle and bone down a ridged abdomen to the line of hair below his navel. Her throat ached. Warmth fingered through her stomach.

The sun made a halo behind his head, streaking his black hair with prisms of blue, gold, and red. Though her heart sank at his aggressive posture, she soaked in the picture of him for later.

He stepped into the barn and rested his hand on a delapidated wagon frame to his right. A muscle flexed across his chest. "Well? Are you leaving?"

She swallowed. "It's time."

His steps were slow and measured. He stalked toward her, gauging the distance between them as though he would only allow himself to get so close. His black gaze pierced her, held her rooted to the spot. "I suppose you have a better plan than you did a few days ago?"

"Yes. I'll be taking the stage to St. Louis."

"You'll be takin' a horse. And travelin' at night."

The arrogant assumption that she would do as he said made her back stiffen and her eyes narrow. "Perhaps you haven't noticed, but I don't have a horse."

"You can borrow one of these."

"Of course I can't. Your brother isn't here for me to ask." She took a step toward him, anger unfurling in her belly with the same annoying speed as her awareness of him.

Cole walked past her, toward the stall that housed his dun mare. "You'll be with me. You don't need to ask."

Shock held her speechless for an instant. "I . . . haven't asked you to go."

"Well, that's just the kind of man I am. Lucky you." He reached over and stroked the mare. His hands glided softly over the mare's nose and he caressed the velvety underside of her jaw. Regina could swear the mare's eyelids fluttered shut in pleasure.

She felt a pang watching him, remembering last night when those hands had been so gentle on hers. Pulling her gaze away, she allowed her earlier anger to wash out the desire. "I can't afford to pay you. I don't need you."

"I don't want your money. And, yes, you do need me."

"Why?" Suspicion sharpened her voice. She narrowed her eyes.

"A nun, alone? Easy prey."

"I've done very well taking care of myself, thank you. I'm sure I'll continue to do so."

"Yeah, you did a great job back there in town."

She flushed with anger. "There's no need to remind me. That's the only time and you just happened to be there. If not you, it would've been someone else."

"Maybe. But chances are you won't make it to St. Louis on your own, not with Cross on your tail."

"Now, see here—"

"You couldn't even make it out of Calcutta without getting carved up." He continued as if she hadn't spoken, as if she weren't standing there itching to throw something heavy at his head. "You seem to have an unusual knack for getting into trouble. You'd think with that habit you wear, it would be easier to avoid."

"Are you quite finished? Because I'm not going with you. I mean, you're not going with me." For heaven's sake, the man had her so rattled she couldn't even speak properly.

"I doubt you'd even make it to Cape Girardeau, much less St. Louis."

"Your concern is touching, quite unbelievable in fact, but unnecessary."

"You need someone who can handle a gun."

"I can handle one very well, thank you," she returned hotly, then wished she hadn't. She doubted most nuns handled guns, a fact that wouldn't escape the man in front of her.

As she'd feared, suspicion narrowed his eyes. But after a long moment, he asked only, "Do you have a gun?"

She didn't, but his high-handed manner chafed. Though she would welcome Cole's company, she didn't trust his off-hand offer to go with her, nor his persistent argument that he should. "Guns don't solve everything."

He gave her a look that said she might as well have claimed a man didn't need air to breathe. "They solve most things. I'm going, so you can just quit jawin' about it."

"I am not 'jawin'," she gritted out, struggling to keep from losing her temper. Why was he offering to go? Simply because she was a nun?

"I don't want it ridin' on my head if you run into trouble. Leah would make my life miserable."

"Well, aren't you charming? You can take your concern and—"

A gunshot split the air and a bullet drilled into the door behind her.

Cole lunged, pushing her toward the floor and into the empty stall where the white stallion had been moments before. Another shot rang out; a bullet whizzed past.

"It's Cross, isn't it?" Regina scooted and slid her way into the corner, her shoulder twinging. Cole's chest and knees bumped her back and buttocks as he crowded behind her.

"We're damn lucky he's not as good with a gun as he is with a knife," Cole whispered roughly. "Can you see him?"

Regina craned her neck and shifted lower, trying to get a good look. She could make out light and the foreleg of a horse about a hundred yards from the door. "I see someone. I think it's him."

"Damn." Cole's hot breath steamed her neck. "Let

me over there. How did he find us?" He bit out the words, his voice still low, and suddenly froze as though he'd realized exactly how Cross had found them.

Regina bit her lip. "Do you think he followed us from town? That he's been waiting all this time?"

"No." The word was slow and rich with thought, but certain.

She sent him a sharp look over her shoulder, almost able to hear Cole's mind clicking as he tried to figure it out. Stale air thickened the barn; Cole's breathing, harsh and quick, tangled with hers. Sweat slicked her palms.

"Send out the woman, Wellington." Cross's voice shattered the hushed stillness of the barn. "She's the one I want."

Regina's heart twisted in her chest. Outside, she could hear the nicker and shuffle of the horses. Behind her, Cole's mare bumped against the stall. The paint let out a low neigh, his feet thumping the hard earth floor. Regina glanced back at Cole.

He pressed closer to her, his bare chest hot through her clothes. The heady smells of dirt and horseflesh meshed with the darker scent of Cole in the cool dimness of the stall. He turned his head, his jaw brushing her head as he scanned the small box.

Staring once again through the slats, he hollered to Cross, "You want her, come in here and get her."

Regina elbowed him in the ribs, glaring.

Cross's voice boomed into the barn, bouncing back through the building. "Come on out, lady. You don't want to be responsible for another death, do you?"

"Go to hell." Cole twisted around to search the floor.

Regina wanted to yell the same thing, but instead she edged closer to Cole. "Why don't you shoot? He's already used two bullets."

He turned a look on her so cold, so utterly furious, that she shrank back. "Well, now, why didn't I think of that?"

Apprehension bloomed. Her gaze slid over the muscled chest dusted with black silky hair and down the bare nut-brown skin that sheathed taut muscles. Bowstring tight waist. Lean hips encased in tight black denim. Devoid of a holster or a gun. She froze, shock and terror grinding in her stomach. "You don't have your gun?"

"I came out here in a little bit of a hurry. I thought you were takin' off."

"I thought people like you went everywhere with their guns." She huffed out a breath and turned around to crawl on her hands, searching for a shovel, a broom, anything. "Well, there's nothing in here. Now what?"

Cole was silent for a moment, his body rigid. His eyes glazed as if focused inwardly on the problem. He gave a jerk of his head. "Come here."

She scooted over, trying to catch a glimpse of Cross through the slats, but he had moved and she couldn't find him.

"I'm going out back and try to sneak up on him."

"You can't fight him! You don't have a weapon."

"We don't have a lot of choice here. You'll have to

go for the gun. I don't like it, but I think I can buy you enough time to get to the house."

"But—"

"It's beside the bed." He peered through the slats then turned to her. "When you get a clear shot, take it."

"Kill him?" She shuddered, not doubting her aim but her ability to kill another person.

"I can't figure you, Sister. First you want me to shoot, now you don't want to." Cole gripped her arm. "Look, it's you or him. This guy's going to haunt you till he's dead."

She stared at him, dread knotting her stomach. Keeping her eyes on his, she nodded. "All right. Tell me when."

"Follow me to the doors then wait for my signal."

She nodded.

Cole pushed himself to his feet and helped her up. His hand was hot and steady in hers. She squeezed, taking strength from him. He dropped her hand and turned, edging along to the stall door. She pressed close against him, not touching but close enough that she could feel his heat, the reassurance of his muscled back brushing her robe.

Her breathing was rapid and jerky; her hands clammy. For all the words she'd thrown at Cole moments ago about taking care of herself, she was glad he was here. They edged along the outer edges of the stalls toward the back doors.

Cole guided her into another stall and Regina slipped into the shadows, watching his face for the sign to run.

"Cross, you coming in or what?" Cole yelled, cocking his head in wait for the answer.

The answer exploded in a whine of gunfire. Regina let out a yelp of surprised alarm. Bullets dug ground, spitting dirt and wood as they drilled the barn.

Cole's jaw tightened and his gaze sliced to her. "Okay, now we know where he is."

"Now, Wellington, you can come out and bring the lady. Or I can come in and pick up what's left."

Regina thought Cross's voice sounded closer and stepped out to peek around Cole to the door. On the far side of the paddock, she saw a blur of horse and man. She pointed, whispering, "Is he moving?"

"Yeah." He pressed her back with his arm across her middle.

Another round of gunfire, slow and measured, cracked the air. Bullets drew a line of holes across the wall opposite them. Sunlight dribbled through new holes and speckled the barn floor.

"Hell, how many guns does he have?" Cole turned and gripped her shoulders. "I'm going to open the back doors then we're ready."

She nodded, fighting down a wave of hysteria and sickness.

"Don't go soft on me or start spouting religion. Just get the damn thing and save my hide."

"All right." She stared at him, wanting to say thank you, be careful, don't go. The words tangled in her throat. They were words she shouldn't say, words he probably didn't want to hear.

He nodded sharply and tore his gaze from hers. "I'll be countin' on you."

She pressed close behind him as they inched their way down the row of stalls.

"Come on, lady. Get it over with. You'll have to send your regrets to St. Louis."

James Cross's voice flicked at her uncertainty, but she kept her gaze trained on the supple muscles of Cole's back, now drawn tight in tension. A bullet whizzed by, nicking a stall door and ricocheting off into the murky light. Regina winced and commanded her legs to keep moving.

Her entire body trembled and she clenched her fists, striving for control, fighting off the panic that edged her mind. Another bullet then another spattered the air, popping into a wooden beam in one of the stalls.

They reached the door. Her palms were sticky with cold sweat; moisture trickled between her breasts. Cole slid the lever and opened the wide double doors. Sunlight streamed inside, blinding as it swallowed up the dusky interior.

"Be careful." She reached out and squeezed his arm.

He stared into her eyes and for an instant she thought he might kiss her. "Aim straight."

He slipped out the door and plastered himself against the building, easing his way to the left. Regina waited until he reached the corner. He looked back, his face tight and fierce and gave her a nod. She took a deep breath and bolted for the house.

A volley of gunfire erupted and she buried her head in her arms. Bullets whizzed and whistled through the air, exploding like steel on stone. Her feet flew over the hard ground, one ankle twinging as her foot rolled outward. She caught herself short of stumbling and leaped the steps to the porch, hurtling inside the open door. Without a pause, she veered for the stairs.

The noise of gunfire grew louder, swelling shot for shot, until it seemed there was a rhythm. A macabre crashing dance that reverberated through the trees. Regina rushed into the bedroom and straight for the dresser.

Plucking up the gun, she ducked to crawl around the bed and edged to the window. She peered over the windowsill, the gun heavy in her shaking hands, her legs watery.

Cole was nowhere in sight. Neither was Cross. Bullets still sang through the summer day, sending birds and rocks and pieces of tree bark scattering. She scrambled for the stairs.

Once down, she inched to the front door and gripped the gun tight with trembling hands. She managed to get the hammer back, fighting the nausea building in her stomach. Her lungs burned as she tried to draw a steady breath.

Peeking around the door frame, she searched for some sign of life. All clear. Wiping her hands on her skirt and getting a better grip on the gun, she vaulted outside. In a spinning leap, she cleared the porch and ran for the barn. Through the open barn doors, she could hear the pop of gunfire.

She reached the back side of the building, wondering how long their ammunition would hold out. She realized then that the gunfire was no longer directed at the barn. James Cross was shooting elsewhere and someone was shooting back.

But who? Cole didn't have a gun. Fear scraped at her, raising ugly images. Was someone with Cross? More than one? The shots never ceased. She pressed her fingers to her temple, straining to identify the pattern she could only hear. For every single shot, two echoed in rapid succession. There were at least three guns.

Where was Cole?

The shots faltered for an instant then a single shot sounded in the distance. Two shots answered, directed away from the barn. Regina frowned, unable to tell what was happening.

She stepped closer to the door, moving her head only fractionally to peek inside the barn. Who was shooting? Was Cross leaving?

Frustration and uncertainty pounded at her. Abruptly, Cole appeared in the opposite doorway. More shots rang out, definitely dimming now, farther away.

"Cole!" Regina's heart lurched and she rushed toward him. She skidded to a stop, stopping just short of throwing herself at him. There was no blood, she noted with relief.

His gaze skipped over her, the hard edge softened by concern. "You okay?"

"Yes. Are you?"

"Fine."

Her gaze shifted over his shoulder. "Who's out there?"

"My brothers." He dragged an arm across his fore-head, drawing her gaze to the flex of muscle. He held out his hand for the gun.

She relinquished the weapon gladly. In the distance, she heard another shot then a holler. Only then did his words penetrate her fog of relief. "Your brothers! What are we going to tell them?"

He slipped the gun into the waistband of his pants at the back and cocked an eyebrow. "Tell them?"

"About me?" she said. "And Cross."

She stared at him, trying to curb her frustration and the residual of fear. A pause tightened the air between them.

"Nothing. It's your business."

She studied him, searching those black eyes. He held her gaze and relief shifted through her. "Thank you. Again. It seems I owe you another one."

"One of these days I'm gonna collect." His voice dropped, slipping over her like warm midnight that shimmered with the promise of secret pleasures. His tone brought back memories of the night before.

Her face flushed; her body heated and tingled. Distantly she was aware of horses drawing near, the low hum of voices outside the barn, but she couldn't concentrate on them. As she stared into Cole's black eyes, smoldering with banked fires she was coming to know firsthand, she realized suddenly the real reason she hadn't wanted him to go to St. Louis.

He reached for her and on reflex, she stepped away. Anger, then realization lit his eyes. A sharp pain pierced her heart. For all the lying and deceit, the habit was her only protection. She couldn't let him find out the truth, until she was ready to confess.

"Well, I see you're up to your usual." A voice abraded the silence. Gage Wellington rode up to the doorway of the barn and swung down from his horse. Emmett, the oldest brother, dismounted behind him.

Gage walked inside the barn, jerking his thumb toward the rise where Cross had been hiding. "What the hell was all that—ma'am?"

He caught sight of her next to Cole and stopped, staring. He blinked then frowned. "Sister?"

"Hello, Gage." With his auburn hair and stubborn chin, the youngest Wellington resembled her friend, Leah. Regina peered around to offer a smile to the oldest brother, whose dark hair and features looked more like Cole. "Emmett."

"Nice to see you again, Sister." Emmett took off his gray felt hat and nodded. His gaze slid from her to his middle brother and a speculative gleam fired his gray eyes.

Gage stared at Cole, who let the obvious question about why Regina was here remain unasked. And unanswered.

Silence settled in the barn like the first thin ice of winter. Gage shuffled, threw another glance at Regina then looked at Cole. "What's going on here?"

"Unfinished business," Cole answered easily. "You got here just in time."

Gage opened his mouth then closed it, exchanging a look with Emmett.

Regina took the cue. "Excuse me. I'm sure you three would like to talk." She stepped past Cole, giving him a look she hoped he understood. *Please don't tell them anything about me.*

He gave her a flat stare, no promises.

Emmett smiled and moved aside so she could walk through the doors. Gage stared, belatedly jerking off his hat as she passed. An embarrassed self-conscious smile flashed across his face.

She walked outside, uneasy about leaving Cole to fend for her, not at all sure that he would. She squinted against the glaring sun and rounded the corner of the barn.

"What in the holy name of sanity is she doing here?" The words exploded from Gage.

Regina flattened herself against the building, feeling no compunction about eavesdropping.

Cole watched Sister Regina walk out, allowing himself finally to feel the relief at finding her all right. Even though he'd known Cross was lurking about, Cole had been surprised anyway. Which just went to show how far his mind had strayed.

He thought way too much about that nun and the way her lips had brushed his last night, the instant desire that had burned along his nerves and down his belly.

"Why is she here, Cole?" Gage turned on him.

"It's a long story."

"Make it short."

Cole glanced at Emmett, who waited patiently. "She needed a place to stay for a few days. She's leaving tonight."

"And you?"

"Well, you're here now, so . . ." Cole shrugged, trying not to feel the pull of home and the woman he'd cared for the past few days.

"Of course you're going after Sutter."

"How was the trip?" Cole was glad to change the subject, though not necessarily to Sutter. "The two of you are back early, aren't you?"

Gage snorted, walking to the corner and yanking his gloves from his hands.

Emmett grinned, eyeing their youngest brother. "He didn't get exactly what he wanted at the sale."

"How's that?"

Gage took a deep breath and scowled. "There was a perfect pair of the most gorgeous black Percherons you've ever seen. A stallion and a mare. I got the stallion."

"And the mare?"

Emmett laughed. "That would belong to Miss Quinn Spencer. A spunky woman and a cunning horse buyer to boot."

"Hah!" Gage spewed out, slapping his gloves on his thighs. "She's a damn man masquerading as a woman. Sneaky wench."

"Shrewd," Emmett corrected.

Cole grinned. "I think I'm beginning to get the picture. You tried to, uh, charm her out of offering for the mare and she turned you down flat."

"It was the funniest thing I've ever seen." Emmett settled his hat back on his dark hair. "The day of the sale, there they were, outbidding each other to spite themselves. Gage wasn't about to give up the stallion and Miss Spencer wasn't about to give up the mare."

"Well, where is this mateless specimen of perfection?" Cole walked to the barn door and looked out.

Emmett followed to lean against one side of the door and thumbed his hat back on his head. "Coming in on a boat sometime tonight. He is beautiful. Black as the tarhills, with silver markings. Both of them. At first you think they're charcoal, not quite black, but it's like there's silver powder sprinkled all over 'em. The mane and tail go from black to silver as though dipped in moonlight. I've never seen anything like it."

"I bet that mare was something else."

Emmett raised his eyebrows and grinned. "So was Miss Spencer."

"It's a damn good thing I came back today, to accommodate your schedule and all." Gage returned to the original subject, his voice heated.

"I wouldn't have left the horses."

"That's reassuring."

"Listen, you're back now. What difference does it make?" Cole's shoulders tightened as he felt his younger brother walk up beside him.

Gage leaned against the door frame on the other side of Cole, mirroring Emmett's stance, except for the anger coiled tight through his body. "Why can't you give it up, Cole?"

It sometimes seemed as if this search for Sutter had lasted his whole life, but Cole didn't say so. "I'm close now. I'll find him and when I do—"

"You'll kill him," Emmett finished, his voice tired and sad.

It was easier to take Gage's blustering temper than Emmett's quiet recriminations. Unease pulled at

Cole's gut. His business with Sutter had assumed complicated proportions in the last few days. All because of that damn nun. "Yes, I'm gonna kill him."

"He was your best friend, Cole." Gage glared at him. "That man was just like a brother to you. Doesn't that matter to you at all?"

"Any generous feelings I had for him, brotherly or otherwise, ended when I found him with Sarah. He took what was mine," he reminded them through clenched teeth. "Doesn't that matter to you two at all?"

"Of course it does." Emmett took off his hat and ran a finger along the brim. "We just wish you could get on with your life."

"I am."

"You call this livin'?" Gage's voice cracked with anger. "You're mired in the past. There's no livin' in that."

Cole met Gage's eyes, his voice raw with pain and remembrance. "They betrayed me. A man I would've died for and a woman I did die for."

Gage closed his eyes, regret and frustration pinching his features.

Emmett's voice came low. "Gage is right, Cole. Hell, you're letting your life ride right past you and all in the shape of a bullet. It's time you made peace, quit roaming. Stay here and help Gage with the horses. I've never seen anybody work horses like you two."

"I can't stop until I get him." Not for the first time, Cole wished he could forgive as easily as Emmett. "If you can't understand, can't you at least leave me in peace?"

"All I understand," Gage snapped, "is you used to be a hell of a lot more forgiving and certainly more alive. I hate to think what would happen if Emmett or I 'sinned' against you."

Gage's choice of words scraped across Cole's nerves. He didn't need any reminders of the nun or that he was using her to get to Sutter. "It was betrayal, pure and simple."

"I don't think either Luke or Sarah meant for anything to happen," Emmett put in. "Maybe Sarah just never got over him."

"Well, that would be the logical answer, wouldn't it? Why else would she plan to run off with him while carrying my child?" Again, ugly doubts about the baby scraped at Cole. *Had* that baby been his? Or had she been sired by Sutter?

Emmett shook his head, his voice heavy. "That doesn't sound like Sutter to me."

"You weren't there, Emmett. You didn't see them together. And those years he was gone, those years we thought he was dead, he changed."

"Like you have? Like we all have?" Emmett reminded quietly. His gray eyes darkened with anger, a rare thing. "I'll tell you what I do know. This has soured you until you're not the brother I knew. I'm not sure I want to know you now."

Cole's eyes narrowed at the fierceness in Emmett's voice. Cole didn't betray it, but the words shook him to his soul.

His older brother's anger made Cole feel as if he'd given an accounting of himself and fallen short. "Damn, I'm tired of explaining myself to you two. I'll be leaving tonight."

Emmett stilled, sadness dulling the steel fire of his eyes. "I'm glad you're always gone so Lee and Selinda can't see what their uncle has become."

Cole's gut twisted. He kept his face carefully blank, but the pain gnawed at him. "I'm sorry you feel that way, Em, but this is something I have to do. Sutter cost me my wife and my child and I'll see him pay for every last bit."

"Luke may have wronged you, Cole, but you've taken those things from yourself." Emmett jammed his hat on his head and walked outside.

A knot of pain clogged Cole's throat. He turned to Gage, a bitter smile twisting his lips. "I trust you to put it in less philosophical terms."

"This time I agree." Gage walked out the door, grabbed his paint's reins, and vaulted into the saddle.

Cole stared until his brothers disappeared over the knoll, headed toward the town of Farrell, Emmett's home. Recriminations echoed in his head; fire burned his gut. He agreed with every damn thing they'd said. Yet he couldn't stop hunting for Sutter.

He'd come too far, sacrificed too much. What kind of man would give up when he was so close? A fool, that's what.

He'd worked, sweated, bled over Sutter for too long. He couldn't live with himself if he quit. It was like paddling toward a waterfall; you knew the threatening drop loomed ahead, but you were helpless to turn around.

He couldn't quit. Not until Sutter got a share of the pain that Cole had lived with for the last eighteen months.

CHAPTER EIGHT

Regina thought about leaving, but only as long as it took her to walk to the house. Cross had nearly killed them both and she couldn't bring herself to strike out on her own just yet. Her heart finally settled to a calm beat though a fine trembling still seized her arms and legs. The danger was past for the moment, allowing other thoughts to capture her attention. Her emotions seesawed.

Relief tangled with suspicion; gratitude with curiosity. She stood at the window of Cole's bedroom and watched as Gage and Emmett rode away.

Cole hadn't told his brothers anything about her. She had stayed outside the barn long enough to learn that. But she had also learned more about Cole Wellington. He was tracking someone named Luke Sutter and his brothers didn't like it.

The sun pulsed through the glass to heat her face, each ray seeming to throb and echo the beat of her heart. Cole had spent eighteen months tracking the man he believed responsible for the death of his wife and child.

Regina had learned from Leah of Cole's loss, but she had never connected the deaths of his wife and child to his frequent absences. Nor had she imagined the tensions caused in his family by his vigilantism. Were Gage and Emmett upset only because Sutter had once been Cole's best friend or was there more?

In a flash of irony, she realized what she shared with Cole, and how differently they handled it. Where she worked for revenge against Cross through justice, Cole sought revenge through retaliation. Compassion swelled, making her heart feel too large for her chest. Yet even as she hurt for him, some part of the conversation she'd overheard needled.

It was the way he'd spoken of his wife, Sarah. Regina had expected to hear love in Cole's voice, but it had sounded more like possession. As though the issue were that his friend had taken something Cole owned rather than someone he loved. Perhaps Cole hadn't loved Sarah.

Surely he had, Regina told herself. Perhaps her suspicions about his wanting to go to St. Louis were coloring her judgment. Why was he so determined to go?

He had steered the conversation with his brothers away from her, for which she was grateful. He had let them draw the conclusion that he was continuing after Sutter when she knew, even though she hadn't agreed, that he was planning to go with her to St. Louis. The whole picture seemed off-kilter.

Looking back on it now, she wondered if this Sutter person could have anything to do with Cole's decision to accompany her. Perhaps Sutter was in St. Louis. Cole was not a man given to easy conversation or confidences and Regina didn't hold out any hope that he would tell her.

Cole crossed the yard toward the house, glancing up at her in the window. His eyes were masked by the glare of the sun, but she could tell he was staring at her. Even from here, she could see the corded strength of his bare shoulders, the strong square hands gripping his revolver. Her heart turned over in her chest.

Did he have business in St. Louis? Or was he indeed going along for protection because she was a nun? She didn't want to believe that.

She had come too close to trusting him once, to believing she'd seen a secret gentle side of him. A part of her still believed that, or yearned to. But she couldn't afford it, certainly not now when she was so close to Wendell Cross.

Cole's boots clattered over the front porch, thundered across the floor in long strides to the stairs, and thumped heavily as he came up. Regina turned as he walked into the room. Every nerve immediately tingled at his nearness.

"Agree with me now about needing a gun?" Dark brows arched up and satisfaction glinted in his black eyes.

Irritation burned. "Yes."

"Cross is gone. For now," he added flatly, his gaze boring right through her. "I'd say you can look forward to more surprises on our way to St. Louis."

She considered telling him she didn't want him along, but knew it would be a waste of breath. He would come whether she wanted him to or not. "All right, you can go."

There was no thanks, no surprise in the dark eyes, just a matter-of-fact acceptance that told her he hadn't been waiting for her permission. She fought off a quick burst of annoyance.

He walked over to the dresser and dropped his gun. The ivory handle thudded heavily against the wood, causing Regina to start. Cole slid a hand over his hair and turned toward her. "We'll leave at dark."

She nodded, trying to figure out what he was up to, feeling compassion for the loss of his wife and daughter and ambivalence about his quest for a man he once considered his best friend.

"You're mighty agreeable." His midnight eyes squinted at her. His skin glowed bronze from the hot sun; perspiration trickled down his right temple and he thumbed it away.

Her throat tightened. She wanted to offer sympathy about his wife and knew he wouldn't welcome it. Was he still in love with Sarah? Her mind rejected the notion—he didn't act like a man who pined for lost love.

His heat surrounded her, beckoned her, and yet suspicion still lurked. Maybe not suspicion, but a frustrating knowledge that everything wasn't as it appeared.

He planted his hands on his hips, fingers splayed. His gaze scraped over her, igniting sparks of feeling along her legs, belly, breasts. "You'll need to get rid of the habit."

"No." Even she was surprised at the panic that

edged her voice. She gripped the skirt and buried her fingers in the woolen folds.

He raised one eyebrow.

She turned away from him. Was her reluctance only because of the familiarity of her habit? "I have nothing else to wear."

"We can fix that. We'll stop at Stern's on the way out of town."

"I can't go there. People will see me."

"I'll get what you need."

"No! I-I can't." As much as she had wanted to wear "regular" clothes, she could hardly imagine herself in them. Somehow the thought made her feel vulnerable to Cole. And he would know immediately upon seeing her long hair that she was no nun. "We'll be traveling at night. You said so. No one will see us."

He stepped up until his chest crowded hers. "Don't be a fool."

"I'm not." She fought rising panic. "I simply think you're creating a problem where there is none."

"Me?" His eyes snapped with impatience. He dragged a hand through his hair and an ebony lock fell carelessly onto his forehead. "Be smart. Cross will be looking for a nun, not a real, er, normal woman."

She licked her lips, unable to deny his logic, yet wanting to. If she told him she was not a nun, would he forgo the trip? The thought panicked her. Though she would never admit it to him, she wanted his protection. Uncertain and apprehensive, she raised a hand to her veil and stepped away.

He grasped her upper arms. "Cross made it out of

here today. He'll be waitin' for us, but he won't be lookin' for you if you're dressed differently."

"Well, he will be looking for you," she reminded with an edge to her voice. She pulled away from him, again moving to a safe distance. Her arms burned from the heat of his hands. "It won't take him long to figure out who I am."

"That's why we're goin' at night. And if he asks, nobody will have seen a nun."

He said it so simply that fresh resentment flooded her. She knew he was right. She stared at him, studying him, weighing his words.

He reached for her then, a quick movement that startled her. Purely by instinct, she drew back.

Anger flared in his eyes, wild, uncontrolled. His jaw tightened. "What is it? Afraid some man might pay you a little attention? Don't worry, I'll be there to discourage that."

His deliberate sarcasm left no doubt that he didn't consider that a possibility. She ignored the flick of pain at his words and lifted her chin. "Maybe I'm not worried about *other* men."

His eyes narrowed and he advanced on her. "Still haven't forgiven me for that kiss, huh? Or is it yourself you haven't forgiven?" His voice dropped, silk and midnight. "For likin' it."

Anger flashed red before her eyes. "You're full of yourself."

"Don't worry, Sister. I like a woman who knows what to do with a man, not one who hides behind a veil."

His words cut her like a sharp stone on tender flesh.

At that moment, in spite of the pain, she realized that her protests had only made him contemptuous of her. Whether she wore the habit or not, he would consider her a nun from now on.

She glanced down at the floor, away from his pointed stare. She didn't believe he was taking her to St. Louis for her own protection. He'd had an ulterior motive for checking on the children and probably had one for accompanying her on the trip. But the fact was she needed help and wanted him to go.

Swallowing her trepidation, she nodded in agreement. "All right. I'll wear something else."

"We'll leave as soon as it's dark." He stepped around her and walked out the door, leaving her feeling bereft and alone and as though she were teetering on a broken branch high above rushing water.

As soon as the first silver light of dusk edged the trees, Cole made a sweep of Gage's house and the surrounding area, looking for James Cross. He harbored no illusions that the bastard had given up. Cross was merely biding his time.

Satisfied the outlaw was not within a mile's radius of the house, Cole hastened Sister Regina to the barn and onto one of the gray mares. He offered her a hand up, but she hurriedly stepped into the stirrup and away from him.

He tried not to feel anger at her obvious distance. He should be glad of it. God knew, he hadn't been keeping any of his own. After last night, the heavy ache of desire had settled low in his belly and remained there.

He mounted and led the way out of the barn, mindful to stay close to her, but not touch. She rode carefully, as though getting her bearings. In the white light of the moon, her skin glowed like porcelain, smooth, unblemished. Her lashes cast dark shadows along the molded cheekbones and her lips were full.

Cole shifted in the saddle, easing the now familiar warmth that spread through his loins. Days ago, he had gotten over the startling irony of Sister Regina's beauty. He wanted this woman and she was forbidden to him. Not by his choice, perhaps not by hers, but forbidden just the same.

She was someone he'd never have, someone he should forget. But he couldn't forget the perfect rose and cream skin, the full breasts, the vivid green eyes that had smiled at him before she'd discovered how far he would go to get answers.

With a low grunt, he jammed his hat further down on his head and glanced over at her. She sat stiffly in the saddle, her hands wrapped with knuckle-white tightness around the horn and reins. She appeared alert, wary, just as Cole was. They both knew the importance of secrecy and tonight it was of the utmost.

He was intrigued by her almost desperate refusal to discard the habit. Even now, she seemed to wrap herself in it as though it were a shield. Perhaps it had been so long since she had worn regular clothes that she felt uncomfortable. Somehow he thought it was more than that.

More and more about her didn't add up. There had been a flare of panic in her eyes when he had accused her of being afraid of the advances of a man. She hadn't hesitated when he'd questioned her about her abilty with a gun. What kind of nun was she? *How much of a nun was she?*

The thoughts twisted and wound through Cole's mind, setting his insides aflame with impatience and resentment. Why should he care about this woman? Except for the fact that she was his ticket to Sutter, she should have no pull on him.

But she did. With a chill, he realized the draw was stronger than he had allowed himself to think.

He wanted Sutter, bad enough to taste revenge like copper in his mouth. But he wanted this nun, too. He would have one and never the other.

Knowing that didn't stop him from wanting both.

They rode through trees then forded a stream. Rocks climbed the bluff on the far side and Cole waved Sister Regina ahead as he checked behind them to assure they were still alone. They kept off the road, shadowy figures slipping between trees and staying in the next creek as long as they could.

Finally the road flattened out in front of them. In the moonlight, the gold of Calcutta's lights twinkled. Tension coiled tight across Cole's shoulders. Putting a finger to his lips, he stopped Horse and turned to the nun. "We'll walk the horses in and go around the back side of the livery."

She nodded, her face drawn and pinched with concern. Huge eyes stared back at him, pleading for reassurance. He couldn't give her any. The success of their trip depended on them getting out of town without being seen, especially her.

They dismounted and tiptoed in silence, their shad-

ows twining and separating as they stayed close to the
trees. Air hung hot and heavy. Cole could hear the
pounding of his heart, the deep-drawn breath of
Horse, the whisper of Sister Regina's robe against the
hard-packed earth. They approached the back side of
the livery and pulled themselves against the building,
hiding in the darkness.

He found a rock and used it to weight the reins to
the ground. Motioning for the nun to stay where she
was, he sidled up the alley between the livery and the
marshal's office. The moon burned high in the sky,
making the shadows scant and shallow, spreading un-
commonly bright light over the dark dirt of Main
Street.

From inside the stable, he heard a snort and the
heavy thump of hooves. He peered into the street, immediately alert at the quiet stillness. The hair on his
neck prickled.

Silence swallowed the town, except for a low hum
of voices coming from down the street. Lights glowed
from the marshal's office, Clemma's Restaurant and
Boardinghouse, and Stern's Mercantile at the far
north end of town. Other than that, there were no
signs of life. No boys scampered in and out of the
shadows, eluding their mother's calls to come in. No
voices echoed in high and low pitches from the Blue
China; the piano sat stoically silent.

A chill rippled across his neck. Where was everyone? Though it was late and most places were closed
for the evening, the saloon was always booming.

Easing his hand down to his holster, he thumbed
off the leather strap and slid the gun up. He backed

inside the open doors of the livery stable. Satisfied the place was empty, he went outside for Sister Regina.

"It's awfully quiet," she whispered. She pressed close against him. His body throbbed at her nearness, but he told himself it was from caution and apprehension and kept moving.

He eased around the corner and headed for the doors before he realized she was no longer behind him. Alarmed, he jerked around and sighed in relief and exasperation as he spied her at the corner of the livery looking toward the orphanage.

The pain and longing on her face pulled at him and for an instant he let her stand there. She took a step toward the street—he didn't think she even realized it—and his hand shot out.

"No, Sister." He pulled her to him, steeling himself against the glimmer in her eyes. "You can't."

Her eyes searched his, pleading, struggling. "I know. I just wish—"

"Come on." He tugged at her. When she wouldn't move, he tried again, softer. "Come on."

He placed himself at her outside shoulder and herded her into the livery. The lantern, turned down low for late night visitors, cast a soft glow through the small musty interior. Moonlight slanted a small triangle inside the door and they moved into deeper shadows toward the back stall in the corner. Hay and dust saturated the air and tickled Cole's nostrils. Behind him, the nun sneezed.

The shuffle of a horse answered her. They both froze, their tension heightened by the awkward and unusual silence which draped the town like sagging

Spanish moss. Cole felt as if he·were swimming a channel in the dark—anxious to escape, blind for a sense of direction.

"What are we doing?" Sister Regina whispered, stifling another sneeze.

He motioned her over into the corner, judging her whereabouts by the glow of the white coif. "I'm going to get you some clothes. Something's goin' on in town, so we might be able to get away without being seen."

"If we leave now, we'll have a good head start on Cross."

"Maybe, maybe not. But you're not wearing that habit. We were lucky this morning. Let's not give him any more help."

"It wasn't my fault he found your brother's house."

"I didn't say it was." He paused and his voice was low as he stared into the darkness. "I'd sure like to know how he did that." Cole had thought he wasn't followed on his way back from the telegraph office. How had James Cross found them? What else had Cross learned and where was the bastard?

It could've been the heavy pall of silence over the town or just not knowing exactly where Cross was, but Cole felt trouble coming. He wanted to be well out of here before it hit.

"I'll be back." He turned to walk out of the stall then stopped, glancing over his shoulder. "Stay put."

"I don't see what it would hurt if I went over there for a quick minute." Her voice was thick and he knew she was fighting tears. "I haven't seen them in over a week. It's not right to leave like this."

"You don't have a choice. Don't do it." Cole reached for her and she stepped back against the sagging wood of the stall.

Her eyes met his then. Even in the darkness he could see the flare of irritation. "All right. I'll stay here."

He paused, ready to take her word for it and wondered if he should. "Shouldn't take me long."

"Hurry."

He gave a quick bob of his head and left. Want and need and the urge to reassure her plagued him. A tight smile curled his lip. How was he supposed to reassure a nun? Especially when just the sight of those green eyes trained on him set his skin aflame. As much as he couldn't abide his reaction to her, he also couldn't seem to stem it.

Outside, he turned his attention to the sounds of the night and the stillness of the town. Instinct from his months of stalking Sutter, often hidden like this, took over. He kept to the shadows, gliding from the marshal's office past the bank and edging around the saloon.

Three voices from inside the saloon trickled to him. A bottle cracked glass and slid across the wooden counter. No sound from the piano. He heard a low masculine laugh then the shuffle of cards. Upstairs, two lights glowed from windows facing the street. One of those was Shell's room and he wondered who she was entertaining.

He had never explained to her about the night he'd gotten back to town. He felt a little bad for that, but he'd been occupied with the nun. Strange, he no longer felt resentment for his unwilling assistance. The realization unsettled him, but he shrugged it off.

The quietness of the saloon, and the town, puzzled him. He couldn't figure it. Even at Christmas, the Blue China boomed. Like Clemma's Restaurant was now.

He didn't stop on his way to Stern's Mercantile, but he noticed the commotion at Clemma's. The entire place glowed with gaslight. Voices were indistinct murmurs, but rising and falling in a tangled lull. People crowded the doorway, the doors propped open to accommodate the crowd and let in what little air there was this late in August. A window on the top floor was open. Lantern light flickered from there; shadows undulated on the ceiling.

What was going on? He didn't have the time nor the inclination to find out. Whatever it was, was a godsend. Was "Someone" watching out for the nun? He would get the clothes and within minutes they would be gone. No one would ever know.

Except the person from whom he bought the clothes. And if anyone cared to speculate as to why Cole was buying women's clothes, he would be long gone with Sister Regina by then.

He walked inside the store and looked around. A lantern hung on the wall by the door, casting the room in shadows and half-light. Cinnamon and spices scented the air as well as the rich deepness of new leather and the dark-sweet smell of molasses. Barrels lined the walls, filled with shiny nails, pickles, apples, cakes of soap, cornmeal, and flour. On the shelves across the store, he saw shoes, bridles, and belts.

At the opposite end of the store, next to a window, sat a rack of ready-made clothes. He strode between the tables of fabric bolts, shovels, hoes, and picks to peer at the hanging dresses illuminated only by the burning light of the moon streaming through the window.

"Perhaps this will help you find what you're looking for." A silky voice sounded at his elbow and the lantern appeared at his shoulder.

Light spilled over the rack and glared back from the window. Cole glanced around to find a blonde with slanted tawny eyes staring at him. "I just need a few things."

"I'm Chloe Stern. I'll be glad to help you any way I can."

Any other time, Cole might have found her caressing voice amusing, but not right now. He didn't answer as he shoved his way through the rack, holding up one dress then another. Guessing at the nun's size, he slung two dresses over his arm then walked down the aisle toward the shoes.

The blonde followed, quiet now, but staring with open interest as though trying to decipher a puzzle. Cole didn't think he knew her.

"I'll need a gun, like this." He slid out his Smith & Wesson and showed it to her. "And some underthings. A chemise and petticoat, some stockings."

She looked startled, but hurried off to get the items. Cole held on to the shoes, one dress, and the revolver. Minutes later, Chloe had wrapped everything else in brown paper.

He slid the gun into the back waistband of his britches and nestled it in the small of his back. With his back to the wall, he kept one eye on the street, one eye on her. "Sure is quiet tonight."

"There's a town meeting. At Clemma's," she offered in a subdued voice.

Perfect. Cole laid a twenty-dollar gold piece on the table, took the package and his change, and strode out the door. "Thanks. You've been very helpful."

The shadows swallowed him as he slipped along the street toward the livery. Once inside, he blinked to adjust his eyes to the soft glow of light. "Sister?"

She stepped out from the stall and waited for him to approach. He thrust the shoes and dress—a red, green, and blue calico—at her and moved closer as a mutinuous look crossed her face. "There's no time to waste. There's a town meeting goin' on and if we hurry, we'll be gone before it lets out."

She stared at the clothes, her lips tight. For a moment, he thought she would renew her protests. Then with a sigh, she went behind the stall. Cole turned his back and tried to concentrate on planning their journey. They would first cut west to Sikeston then head northeast, sticking to the bluffs around Cape Girardeau.

His mind played with possibilities, but his ears honed in on the sounds behind him. Cloth whispering against skin, the steady sound of her breathing at her exertion, a low sound of despair.

"I can't get the dress fastened." She stepped up behind him, impatience and irritation scoring her voice.

Cole turned to see her back presented to him. She still wore the veil. He moved it aside so he could help her. His hands shook as he lifted them to the tiny glass buttons and a curse hissed out.

Her chemise showed only the pale skin at the base of her neck and the shadow of the bandage on her shoulder. He was in a sorry state indeed if such a small sight affected him. But he knew it was more than that.

Only hours ago, she'd sat inches from him, warm and eager lips brushing his. The memory of the mouth harp lesson brought visions of alabaster breasts and swollen nipples and he remembered with aching clarity every inch of denied flesh.

He finished, his hands hovering at her back. The dress was big, but not distractingly so. His gaze tracked the narrow shoulders to the nip of her waist and the flare of her hips.

Gone was the vague shape that had been hidden beneath the black robes. In front of him stood a woman, curved, angled, flared as though a sculptor had brought fantasy to life. He stepped away from her, his hands curling into fists. "Done."

She turned slowly, one hand pushing the veil over her shoulder, the other smoothing down the front of her skirts. Pleasure and confusion mixed on her face as she stared down at herself.

Cole let his gaze flow over her, taking in the soft defined curves, the proud thrust of her breasts beneath the bodice. A hard rush of blood shot through his body. Pulling his gaze to her face, he gestured to the veil. "Don't forget that."

She bit her lip and with slow movements removed

the headpiece. The slim column of her neck was revealed, creamy in the dim light. Without the dark shroud, she looked slight, vulnerable. Cole waited, his breath jammed in his chest.

Her gaze flashed to his and he read doubt and trepidation there. "I feel indecent somehow."

"I reckon these clothes will take some gettin' used to." And not just for her. He shifted, his gaze glued to her hands as they fumbled with the coif wrapped turban-like around her head.

The white material slipped off in her hand. At first, Cole thought her dark hair cropped close to her head. Then she pulled pins from the back and scrubbed her fingers through it. A cloud of black settled around her to hang just below her shoulders. She closed her eyes and tilted her head back, her face creasing in intense pleasure.

Twin emotions of desire and surprise warred within him. Her hair was thick, silky strands of it curling onto the puffed sleeve of her dress. Though he didn't know what he'd expected, this somehow wasn't it. He had thought she was beautiful wearing the habit. With her hair down, she was striking, bewitching actually. Cole blinked to reassure himself she wasn't a figment of his imagination.

She was the same woman, yet nothing about this woman warned men away. Nothing about this woman cautioned of the forbidden.

Rather, there was a ripeness, an untested sensuality in her features, the exposed length of her neck, the now visible swell of her breasts.

Her own joy in escaping the confines of the veil released something inside him, something hard and fast and utterly primal. Desire bit deep in Cole's gut. Before he realized what he was about, he reached out and lifted a soft strand of hair. It curled around his finger, lightly teasing.

She opened her eyes then, spearing him with a direct look.

He froze, his gaze locked on hers. Her green eyes, usually shooting fire at him or banked with wariness, were unreadable. Cole untangled his finger and pushed past her. "Ready?"

She didn't answer. He could hear her moving around behind him, gathering her clothes. He stared out the livery door, impatience and frustration gnawing at his gut. He had wanted to thrust his hands into her hair and his body into hers.

He clenched his teeth. He had known the trip would be difficult for him in terms of keeping his mind on pure thoughts where she was concerned. Any chance of that had just been blown to hell. He had never expected her to look so tempting, so . . . worldly. She *wasn't* worldly and he needed constant reminding.

He clamped down on his rioting thoughts, forcing himself to concentrate on the world outside the stable. The meeting was still in progress.

"I'm ready." She appeared beside him, slightly breathless, her hair gliding around her shoulders. In her arms, she carried the habit.

He reached out to take her elbow then stopped himself as he saw her lips press primly together. If he hadn't known better, he would've thought she was laughing. He moved outside and motioned her to follow.

Voices carried clearly down the street, some raised in anger, others murmuring underneath. Cole reached the corner of the livery and turned, ready to motion her in front of him, but she had disappeared.

Shock and panic sheared through him. He bolted for the stable. "Sister?"

"I forgot my shoes." She met him at the door, carrying the pair in her hand.

Relief was a sharp pain in his chest and he growled, "Come on."

He pushed her ahead of him this time and followed behind, scanning the street. The ground vibrated and Cole heard horse's hooves then the rattle of a buggy. They had reached the corner of the building when a familiar voice called out.

"Cole? Is that you?"

Leah! Cole glanced around, pushing at the nun and trying to get her around the corner. She stopped dead and turned into him.

Their noses bumped and Cole swore at the fire that curled in his belly. "Go."

"That's your sister."

"I'll talk to her." He pushed the nun toward the alley. "You go on."

"I thought that was you. Where have you been? Emmett said you were watching Gage's place, but I haven't seen hide nor hair of you these last few days." Leah pulled the buggy to a stop in front of the livery doors, threw the brake, and jumped lightly down.

"Are you leaving again? Oh, I'm sorry." She stopped, staring at Cole in embarrassment. "I didn't realize you were with someone."

"It's me, Leah." Regina stepped around Cole and into the light.

"Sister Regina?" Leah gasped. Her gaze darted from the nun to her brother.

Cole scowled and glared at the nun.

"It can't hurt for me to say good-bye."

"Good-bye?" Leah stepped up to them. "What do you mean? Didn't you just return?" Her gaze shifted from Regina to Cole and back again. "Are you . . . together?"

Cole glanced over at Regina and found her gaze on his. "Look, sis, we've got to get out of here."

"But, Sister Regina, I thought you were gone. Reverend Holly said—"

"I know," Regina broke in. Cole put his hand on her arm. She stopped and flashed him a defiant look, stepping toward Leah. "I have to leave. I can't explain right now. It's very complicated."

Cole could imagine Sister Regina's urge to confide in Leah, but there was no time for that. A sudden swell of noise drew his attention and he glanced across to the restaurant. A clot of people filled the doorway then spilled out into the street like water overflowing a pitcher.

They hadn't seen him and the nun yet. He grabbed her arm and backed into the alley. "Let's go, dammit."

"Cole Wellington, she is a nun! You unhand her this minute." Leah's voice rang out, loud and startling, cutting through the murmur of voices.

An abrupt silence descended and all eyes swung to Cole and the nun.

After a stunned pause, an unidentified masculine voice boomed. "Look, it's her! We know she's no nun. She's been lyin' to this town for months! Let's go!"

Shock jolted Cole's brain.

Beside him, Regina choked out, "Oh no!"

The crowd moved forward and in a flash of panic, Cole saw his connection to Sutter disappear. He tightened his grip on her arm, dragging her down the alley with him. Angry voices followed them.

"Not a nun?"

"Is it true?" Leah's voice, hurt and disbelieving, penetrated the confusion. "Sister Regina?"

"Come on! We deserve the truth!"

The crowd surged forward, a sudden rush of stampeding feet as they swarmed into the alley, jostling and jockeying for position, teeming like ants on a hill.

Cole and Regina were at the back corner of the livery stable now. Only a few more feet to the horses.

She struggled against his hold and strained toward the people behind them, her voice breaking. "Let me go. Let me explain."

He clamped an arm around her waist and threw her into his saddle, vaulted up behind, and rode as if running for his life instead of hers.

CHAPTER NINE

Not a nun, not a nun. The words pounded through Cole's head with each strike of Horse's hooves against the hard-packed earth.

He didn't even wonder if it was true. He'd seen the look of shock, absolute horror on her face. Damn! All this time. He should've known. She'd been hiding too much. Her easiness about guns, her reaction to him.

Surprise was too mild for what he'd felt when he'd heard it. There was shock, some denial, even a bit of righteous anger until he reminded himself that he had his own secrets.

Regina had fought him even as they galloped headlong out of town, trying to hurl herself out of the saddle and pleading in a hoarse voice, "Please, let me explain."

Now she was slung across in front of him, her legs pinned under his left thigh, her breasts pressed into his chest. His arm curled around her waist, hard and tight. Relentlessly, he pushed Horse, trying to gain as much ground as he could. The mare responded with every bit of strength she had, but it was a struggle carrying two people.

Fleetingly, the lie brushed his mind. She'd fooled even him, who had learned not to take anything at face value. Anger surged through him. In response he pulled her closer, insinuating his thighs even more intimately against her hip. His arm around her waist tightened and he shifted her body. "Spread your legs and ride straddle."

He took perverse pleasure in the dismay and embarrassment that crossed her face, but she did as he said. She swung her right leg easily over the saddle horn and leaned into the wind. The action brought her butt slamming into his groin with revengelike accuracy. His body responded, hot and swift, but he had more to concentrate on than the desire that shimmered just below the surface.

Someone was following them.

A quick glance over his shoulder confirmed the silhouette of a lone figure on horseback, steadily following. Cole wondered, with a knot in his belly, if it was James Cross, but he couldn't see to prove it.

The nun's—no, not a nun—*her* new position gave them more mobility, but Horse was still carrying two. Instead of heading west toward Sikeston as he had planned, Cole shot straight north, for the only place that might be able to help them.

He veered west when the trees began to clump in stands then thicken into a forest. They tore through pines and sugar maples, the night air hot and thick in his chest, the moon polished silver in a clear sky and reflecting light like a mirror. Cole cursed, knowing whoever followed would have no trouble tracking them.

Branches tore and clawed at them, scraping and slapping their faces. He pushed *her* down in front and pressed his chest to her back.

He used only his knees to command the mare. Horse was so well trained she didn't need the reins. He held them loosely in his hands, clamped around in front of the woman and keeping them both in the saddle.

They gained miles and the terrain changed in a blur. Flat ground swelled into hills. Trees thinned, giving way to bushes and boulders. Horse's dark gold coat gleamed with lather in the moonlight and her sides heaved with labored breaths. Beneath his thighs, Cole felt hard pumping power and despite it, the animal's thick, slowing movements. Another glance over his shoulder showed the other rider in hot pursuit, gaining ground.

He couldn't push Horse any harder. She was working her heart out already. With a quick flash of satisfaction, he spied the ledge of rock in front of them. The mare scrambled up, finding footholds in the shadows and pulling herself to a flat landing before stretching out again. They hit the ground with a jarring thud and he heard a soft *oomph* from the woman under him.

Suddenly the bluff loomed before them and Cole checked his relief, knowing they weren't safe yet.

Abruptly *she* jerked back against him, jarring his

chin with her head, burying his face for an instant in the thick cloud of hair. "Stop!" she yelled. "There's rock straight ahead."

"Shut up," he growled, pushing at her hair and trying to see over her head. Silky strands of black clung to his hand and he shook them free with annoyance. He never slowed down, but headed straight for the face of a steel-gray bluff and the almost invisible path that cleaved the rock.

He felt her sharp intake of breath, heard a cry of horror. Flinching from the expected collision, she curled into his body. He braced himself against the impact and pulled back on the reins.

The mare skidded to a stop, shoed hooves skidding sharply on slick rock. Immediate blackness swallowed them. Frigid air stripped Cole's breath for an instant and stung his nostrils. The cave sheltered them, but only complete silence would save them.

He hoped like hell Cross didn't know about this cave. Cole and Luke had discovered it quite by accident the summer of '64, just before Luke had headed east to work undercover for the Union and Cole had left with the 15th Missouri. Chased by guerrillas, they'd backed into the shelter and been able to fight their way out by superior strength of ammunition. He smiled at the memory before he could stop himself.

"Where are we?" In the dead-weight silence, her whispered words bounced off the walls, almost booming in Cole's ears.

He clamped a hand over her mouth and slammed his body into hers, threatening, trying to communicate the urgency. She stiffened, but seemed to understand and didn't struggle.

Seconds limped into minutes. Cole had no idea how long they sat there, his sweat chilling in the cold temperature and sticking to his skin. At first he could hear nothing except his racing heart. The silence itself pounded in his ears.

From inside the cave came the drip, drip, drip of water into a pool, Horse's labored breathing, the heavy thunder of Cole's heart. From outside, he heard the harsh scream of an agitated owl, the raucous curse of a bluejay and then what he waited for—the crackling sound of breaking twigs, the creak of a branch being pushed aside.

He listened hard for the sound of metal striking stone, the horse climbing the rock toward them. Cold sweat trickled between his shoulder blades and his temples itched. *She* drew in a strangled breath behind his hand and he relaxed enough to allow her to breathe.

The cave smelled of mold and dirty water and the fetid odor of something rotten underneath. His heart slowed down; his hands steadied as he focused on shutting out every noise except the sounds beyond the cave. He stilled and allowed his mind to sharpen and narrow. He could hear the scrape of one leaf against another, the patter of little feet as a critter scurried across the hard earth, the *whrrr* of a wing as a bird settled on a branch.

He heard the deep labored breath of an animal, the creak of a saddle. A twig broke. A rock skittered and knocked others loose. Then silence.

Cole sat motionless, his body curved into hers, hot in front, cold behind. He removed his hand from her mouth and squeezed her arm in silent command. She nodded and he eased his butt over the lip of the saddle onto Horse's steamy rump.

He twisted at the waist to stare out the mouth of the cave. The moon glowed, flooding the rocks and landing with light as strong and constant as the gas used in big cities now. Slowly his eyes focused, picking out shadows and translating them into a broken branch, the beak and head tuft of a partially hidden owl, the rough surface of a boulder.

Then he saw Cross. There was no mistaking the man now, not with the moonlight painting his face in severe clarity. He was limping, but surely and slowly leading his horse up the rocky incline they had scrambled up only moments before.

Silently Cole slid from Horse's rump to the ground, careful to step lightly. He put a hand on Regina's thigh to warn her. Even so, she started at his touch.

She—he didn't know what the hell to call her— turned toward him. He felt it, but the blackness was so complete he could not even see his hand on her thigh. Through the chilled fabric of her dress, he could feel the surge of heat and firm muscle of leg underneath. He could also feel fear and anger radiating from her.

In the barest whisper, she spoke, "Are we safe?"

In answer, his hands closed over her taut waist. She stiffened, but he hauled her down from Horse and against his chest, breathing in her ear, "Cross is out there. We've got to get to the back of the cave."

She nodded, bracing her hands on his shoulders. He eased her to the floor, holding her tight to muffle the movement. His hands slid up her trim back, soaking in her warmth for a moment before he grabbed her hand and started into the darkness.

It was as though someone had stitched his eyes shut and covered his head with heavy black velvet. Even with the cool of the cave, the darkness was suffocating. He felt his way along rough walls slimed with water and moss and God-knew-what-else. The fetid smell of gritty sand and decayed animal remains hung in the chill air and the ancient rock that walled them in.

He felt each step with one careful foot in front of him. His boots slipped on an occasional slickness and sometimes a small saucer of water. Her hand, cold and small, gripped his tightly.

The walls were closing in. He couldn't see a damn thing and had no way of knowing where they were. He fought down rising frustration and reassured himself by knowing if Cross came in here after them, he wouldn't be able to see any better than Cole could.

He stumbled, his foot dipping into a hole as big around as his thigh. Behind him, she gasped. Chills skittered up his spine, not just from the cold air. He had seen holes big enough for a man to stand upright. Cole caught himself and hugged the wall. She pressed tightly against him, her heart thumping in magnified tat-tats against his arm.

He drew in a gut-deep breath of relief that he'd caught himself in time. The silence clanged all around them, laced with hidden disasters, secluding and menacing at the same time.

His hand curled around hers, seeking the warmth they shared. From his mind, he stripped away the feel of her soft body next to him, the exotic scent of her, the thud of his own blood pounding in his heart, and focused.

Gurgling sounds. Drips echoing off the rocky walls. A squeak from an animal. Bat, most likely. Cole's breath curled out, warming his cold lips and nose. It was a few seconds before he realized he also felt a warm draft at his backside. He shifted, searching for the pocket. Definite warmth. Another way out?

It had to be. He gripped Regina's hand, relaxing when she tugged at the pressure. Taking another tentative step forward, they inched along the wall toward the possible second exit.

They turned a corner, zigzagging around a sharp curve. Rock scratched his cheek. They moved slowly, methodically, Cole feeling their way with his hands and feet, relying totally on his senses of touch, smell, and hearing. They stuck to the narrowest of paths by putting one foot in front of the other. She followed silently, her hand clasping his with knuckle-aching tightness.

Then suddenly a point of light flashed. Cole blinked, wondering if he had imagined it. He took another step and halted, then drew in his breath. Up ahead was a small dot of light. It mushroomed as they walked closer, shedding enough light for Cole to see they stood at the back of a tunnel.

There was another opening! Triumph hummed through him though tempered with reason. Cross was out there somewhere and Horse was still in the cave where Cole had left her.

Cole squeezed Regina's hand and let his eyes adjust, able now to pick out craters in the floor. They moved between thick shoulders of rock and soon stood several feet from the opening. Moonlight glimmered off wet walls, picking up lines of red and blue-black in the rock formations.

He halted, every sense prickling, unease tightening his shoulders. He thrust the extra gun he'd bought at her, along with a handful of bullets. "Just in case."

He edged up to the mouth of the cave, trying to focus all his attention on James Cross and not on the woman behind him. Tension coiled tightly through his shoulders, trimming his breath to shallow draws of air. He reached the opening, startled anew at the brightness of the moon, the wide patches of landscape now revealed.

The leaves of a young oak, a black-green in the hazy light, drooped listlessly in the humid air. The moonlight streamed across the grassy area in front of the cave, picking out pebbles, twigs, even tiny yellow flowers poking through the ground.

A thud was his only warning.

A horse darted across the mouth of the cave. In that split second, Cole pushed Regina back against an outcrop of rock and flopped to his belly.

He drew his own gun and eased the hammer back as he scooted behind a small jag of rock. Bullets exploded into the cave, whining against the rock and shattering stone. Chips of granite rained down on

Cole. He fired back, but crouched as he was behind the rock, he couldn't get a clear shot.

He flipped the cylinder and shoved more bullets into his gun as he crawled across the cave and toward Regina. The sound of gunfire roared and swelled, crashing and blasting inside the cave as though their weapons were cannon instead of revolvers.

Cole risked a glance at Regina and found her on her knees behind a nature-made battlement of granite and limestone. Darkness masked her face, hollowing her cheeks, shrouding her eyes into deep-set glittering stones. She returned fire, squeezing off careful shots in answer to every one of Cross's.

Cole dove behind her and rolled to his knees. "Cover me."

"Where are you going?" She didn't stop firing or even turn around, but he could hear the panic in her voice.

"You're doin' fine. I'm goin' out."

"Cole, please!"

There was a desperation in her voice that tugged at his heart, made him wonder if he felt it because now he knew she wasn't a nun. He felt warmth and something else, something he couldn't think about right now. He ignored the tug and crawled past her to the mouth of the cave.

He stuck his head out just at the bottom edge of a broken-off piece of rock. His gaze scanned over earth now plowed from bullets, a grayish-blue flower, the glimmer of wetness on the rock in front of him. No Cross.

Then from the corner of his eye he saw a blur of movement.

He rolled, slamming into rock and squeezing off a shot at the same time. A bullet whistled by his head, close enough to burn across his right temple. He fired in that direction. No return fire. Cole squeezed off two more shots.

He heard a groan then a heavy thud. Rocks clattered loose, spinning and tumbling in a spray of gravel.

Cole lay on his back, gun aimed to the spot. Had he gotten Cross? A plume of smoke curled from his gun; gunpowder scorched the air, heavy in the cold dankness. Cole moved slightly, gauging, waiting for another shot.

A horse whinnied and he bolted upright. Cross was getting away! Hell and damnation! He lunged to his feet, wincing as pain burst in his head.

Hooves pounded into the night, crashing through brush and bushes. Cole leaped out, gun leveled. The thunder of hooves faded into the night.

Glancing around, he took in the bullet-battered ground, the tall trees that stood quietly, the rocky ledge that led to the cave. He walked to the ledge, peering over a drop of more than ten feet, but he could tell nothing in the thick underbrush.

A dark spot on the ground caught his attention and he knelt, touching it. It was wet and clotting the dry earth. He raised his finger, rubbing at the dark smear there. Blood? Had he hit Cross?

Cole straightened and stared out over the moon-spattered trees, then looked north. Moonlight showered over the rolling hills, glittered off the face of another bluff miles away, but there was no sign of Cross.

Regina came up behind him. "Is he gone?"

"For now." Cole glanced around at her, taking in the milky paleness of her face, the remnants of fear in the big eyes. "He's hit, but I don't know how bad."

She stared up at him, then alarm widened her eyes. "So are you." She reached up a hand to touch him, but he drew away.

He ran a finger over his temple, touching the burn. "He just grazed me."

"You should at least clean it."

"Later." Cole turned back to stare down the ledge and over the valley that stretched north.

Beside him, Regina moved closer. She didn't speak, but stood near enough to touch his arm with hers as though she needed the contact of another person. He knew the feeling. After every bloody battle of the war and some he'd fought since, he'd needed the same comfort, the reassurance of hearing another person's voice, the shaking relief that he was somehow still alive.

His conscience urged him to put an arm around her or take her hand, but there were too many things she had yet to tell him.

He didn't move to touch her, but neither did he move away.

James sucked air through his teeth and felt it bubble out his nose. He'd lost blood, too much this time.

Damn Wellington! The bastard had blown a hole the size of a twenty-dollar gold piece in James's gun hand and lodged another bullet in his bad leg. Same one that was infected, but the back of the thigh this time rather than the front. The shot had knocked him down the incline, giving him an escape, and he had taken it.

His time was running out and he knew it.

James lay flat over the saddle, his hands tied to the pommel with the reins. He bobbed and slid with each step; pain ripped through his body in burning arrows, but he urged on the stallion. The smell of his own blood soured in his nostrils. Heat crawled on his skin; mosquitoes buzzed around his head.

They rode through the night, James dozing at intervals and waking to steer the horse north. He was dying. He knew it. But first he had to leave a message for his brothers. Somehow Wendell or Pat would make it to the cave.

At dawn, James woke. The stallion stood in front of a wizened hickory tree with a split trunk. His body felt light, numb of pain. Noises exploded all around him. Vultures circled overhead screaming in mockery. The stallion shifted, his shoed hooves striking like cymbals in James's head. A twig snapped with the resounding crack of a whip.

Through the cloud of poison and pain in his mind, he saw the cave. He prodded the stallion over to the entrance and untangled his hands from the reins. Cuts and leather burns crossed his palms, but he could feel nothing. He tumbled from the saddle, grunting when his infected leg hit hard rock.

His breathing came slower, heavier. Pat's and Wendell's faces swam before him. He called to them in his mind.

Up on the damp shadowed ceiling of the cave, he thought he saw an angel wink. It was time, he knew. As soon as he did this one last thing.

Heady relief, fear, anger. Too many feelings crowded in on her. Regina felt disoriented and strangely let down. Chills slid under her skin and her breath rattled in her chest. On the edge of hysteria, she took inventory of herself and her surroundings.

The moon crackled like a white hot flame in the pewter sky. Her right sleeve was torn and a scratch stung her upper arm. Her jaw and hip ached from the harsh, buffeting ride from Calcutta. Her shoulder, still tender, burned.

Her secret had been revealed. James Cross had found them. And nearly killed them.

She stood next to Cole for a few minutes, trying to rein in her rioting senses. A kind of frightening exhilaration flooded her body, releasing the guilt. All the lies, the threats posed to her friends and the children, were gone now.

She was operating on shock. She knew it, but couldn't stop the panicked laughter bubbling up from her throat.

Her body shook until she could swear her ribs rattled. Through a dazed fog, she saw Cole turn toward her and frown. Her knees buckled and she grabbed for his arm.

"Hey, you okay?" His voice was low and concerned. He gripped her arm, steadying her.

Regina swallowed, soaking in the musky scent of him, the steady strength he exuded. She felt out of control, spinning, whirling, and struggled to regain mental footing. "I'm sorry. You seem to be handling this better than I am."

"Had more practice," he said warily.

His dry words gave her a vestige of control, though she was still breathless. She pulled away from him. Her legs were as liquid as new cream and fear still clawed her stomach. Her will crumbled and she thought she might simply fall apart. But she struggled to hold together the ragged edges of her control.

"I think we'll stay here for the night." He walked over to the mouth of the cave, peered inside, then turned to survey the rocky ledge where they stood.

Regina eagerly turned her attention to that, taking deep breaths to calm her shaking nerves. "What would you like me to do?"

"Wait here while I get Horse." He disappeared around the bulbous nose of the rock and reappeared in a few minutes with the mare. He moved around picking up twigs and breaking off overhanging branches. "I'll build a fire. You see what you can find to eat in the saddlebags."

"All right." She swallowed, rubbing her hands together, wondering how they could sweat and also ache with cold. She moved next to the mare and pulled the saddlebags down. "Biscuits and cheese. Some ham wrapped in paper." Her words came slowly, her body shaking so hard her teeth chattered.

"How about some coffee?"

She dug into the other bag and pulled out a coffeepot with a leather pouch inside. Gripping the pouch tightly as though it could help her hold on to her sanity, she opened it and inhaled the bitterroot odor of coffee beans. "Yes. Here it is."

He already had a fire going and she carried the bread and meat she'd found over to him. She turned away for the coffeepot and reached for the canteen hanging on Cole's saddle. Her hands shook. Where was Cross? Was he even now watching them?

She tried to carry on as Cole was and managed to pour water into the pot, splashing only a little on her dress. She carried the pot over to him and he placed it on a rock at the edge of the small fire.

A sudden *whrrr* sounded in her ears and something furry brushed her cheek. She swatted at the air, stifling a squeal. Her control slipped another notch and she wrapped her arms around her waist, holding tight.

"It's only a bat. Don't worry."

"A . . . bat." Her voice was calm, but her control splintered. Her legs gave and she sank down on the ground. "Oh, Lord. I can't believe this." Her teeth chattered as though with the cold, running her words together. "Where is he? Aren't you worried about him? How can you be so calm?"

"Because if he comes back up this way, we'll hear him," Cole answered matter-of-factly. It should've soothed her nerves. Instead they stung with raw energy. The townspeople's parting words pealed through her head—*been lyin' to this town for all these months*.

"I didn't tell the children good-bye. What if I never see them again? Or Leah? Or Elliot?"

"Hey." He stepped over and knelt in front of her. "You're fine. Just a little shaken up. It's normal."

"Normal? My life hasn't been normal in a long time." She choked back a sob, willing herself not to cry, not to give in to the emotions shearing through her. She rocked back and forth, trying to warm herself, stem the fear that grew colder in her blood. She was hardly aware of his hands gripping her arms. "I can't do this. I can't do this."

"You did just fine a while ago. Held your own like a veteran." Cocking an eyebrow, he added, "Saved my butt."

She stared up at him, focusing on his steady black eyes, the reassurance of his hands on her. "I did?"

"Sure."

Her breath rattled out and she tried to clear her head. She shifted so that Cole's arms draped her shoulders. She strained toward the warmth of his body, the security of his chest. Somehow she knew she would feel safe there, even if James Cross was standing a foot away.

Cole stiffened, his features closing against her, his muscles taut as he released her and moved away. "Let me get you a blanket. Stay put."

Her gaze followed him as he stood and walked over to the mare, taking down a blanket rolled behind the saddle. She wanted to ask him to sit beside her or hold her hand, but the words locked in her throat. She hugged herself and huddled further into the rock at her back, scanning the area for any sign of Cross.

Cole bent and settled a rough wool blanket around her, creating an instant web of warmth. "Better?"

His tone was civil, his action polite, but Regina felt the tension, the impatience pulsing from him. She could guess why.

Her heart had stopped when the truth about her had been exposed. Cole had heard it, too. "Cole, I need to tell you—"

"I think I know." The words were clipped, terse.

She lifted her head, hope sparking inside her. Had he figured out the information she carried to St. Louis was related to Cross and tied to her lies? "You do?"

" 'Fess up." A bitter smile twisted his lips, the lips she had wanted on her own just moments ago. "You're really a 'Pink,' aren't you?"

"Wh-what?"

"No more games." He towered over her, his spine as stiff as a rifle barrel. Anger smoldered in his eyes and his voice was low and grainy, edged with steel. "You work for Allan Pinkerton."

CHAPTER TEN

A "Pink"? The term often used to describe Pinkerton's men shocked her into silence. Cole thought she was a detective, an operative!

Some of her fear dissolved into confusion. Barely able to string together more than two words, Regina sat staring at him. The ringing in her ears was replaced with the sudden thud of her heart. "I—I've never worked for Allan Pinkerton."

"All right then, Abe Grand. An agent's an agent."

"It's not like that."

Powerful shoulders shifted. Shadows and white light played over his large body, menacing in its whipcord strength and sudden tension. "You expect me to believe you're disguised as a nun for all this time, runnin' with detectives and criminals, but it's 'not like that'?"

"Yes." Having something else to focus on other than James Cross pumped some strength into her. She rubbed her pounding temples. "If you had let me explain in town, you'd understand."

"If I'd let you explain in town, we'd be dead and probably some others along with us. Confession may be good for the soul, sister, but timin' is everythin'."

She recognized the blurred endings of his words, a sure sign of anger. Sensation trickled back into her arms and legs. The chill faded from her hands, but she still felt ragged, out of control. She strove for steady mental ground, but she still reeled from her forced exit from Calcutta and the shock of having Cross so close behind them. "You had no right to take me out of town like that."

"You're welcome." He knelt in front of her, pressing her into the rock, trapping her with an arm on either side of her head. "Let's hear it. How long have you been an agent?"

"I'm not an agent!" Her voice was shrill and she took a deep breath trying to keep her teeth from crashing together.

"Bull! You know too damn much about how they operate. The dead man in your lean-to was an agent and you're goin' to St. Louis to meet one of the most well-known operatives in the States." He was practically yelling in her face, his features rough and frighteningly harsh in the moonlight. "Don't expect me to believe you're not involved up to your pretty green eyes."

She had wanted to tell someone the truth for so long, just share the burden of her lies, but not like this. All the guilt hurtled back. She took a deep breath and met his gaze, forceful, commanding. "It's true."

His black eyes snapped with fury; a muscle flexed in his jaw. "I knew it."

"Not that," she added hastily. "What they said in town." Only Elliot had learned the truth. Had he been the one to tell the others? If so, why? "I'm not a nun, but I'm not a detective either."

"Then what?" He waited, anger drawing deep lines around his mouth and jaw.

She swallowed, unsure now that she was faced with telling the whole story. The pain of her parents' deaths had been safely locked away for over a year. But she knew this time Cole wouldn't settle for anything less than the entire truth. Tears choked her and she stared down at the tips of the shoes he had bought her, struggling for control. "My name is . . . Regina. Harrison."

"Bravo." He was unimpressed, his mouth hardened to steel, eyes blazing. Long swollen seconds dragged by.

She licked parched lips, wanting to tear her gaze from his and unable to. "I'm involved with Abe Grand because I have some information for him. That's the truth."

"And your connection to Detective Spradling? James Cross?"

"I told you how I met Lance. And James's brother, Wendell, is the real reason I'm here."

Still kneeling, he shifted. Power rippled through his thick thighs and his gaze impaled her. "Go on."

She swallowed, dropping her gaze. Suddenly she was back in the nightmare of that frigid February night eighteen months ago. Rough ugly voices. Her father's gurgling cry for her to run. The knife blade glinting in the moonlight, streaked with Worth Harrison's blood.

She flinched at the memories, still sharp, still inflicting that ache of guilt. If only she had waited for her father at the farmhouse as he'd instructed her. But instead, dazed with panic over the death of her mother, she had sought him out at the detective agency. She raised her gaze to Cole. "I saw Wendell Cross murder a man. I'm not a detective, but a witness."

He didn't speak for a moment, his eyes boring into her, tension creasing his face. "Isn't it the criminal who's supposed to hide out, lie, take advantage of people?"

"I never took advantage of anyone!"

"No? What do you call your relationship with my sister? The good reverend? Those kids, damn it!"

"They're my friends, all of them. I couldn't tell them. At first I was too afraid then I saw that it could endanger them."

"So why didn't you leave?"

Cole's black eyes skewered her soul and she glanced away. She'd asked herself the same question hundreds of times over the last months. "I couldn't. By then, I was operating a safe house for the detectives."

"Holy hell!" He surged off the ground, power rippling through his body. "With those kids right there?"

"Until James Cross showed up, no one but the detectives was ever there."

The scowl on his face grew deeper, carving new lines. "You were waiting there all this time, pretendin' to be somethin' you're not, just for them to catch Cross?"

"Yes, and they finally did. That's why Lance came

to me. And why he was killed." She still felt some responsibility for that even though Lance had known the risks of his job.

"Killed by James Cross?"

"Yes. Abe and Lance and several other detectives caught Wendell Cross going over into Mexico and now they're bringing him back for the trial."

"So you're goin' to St. Louis to testify?" He paced to the mouth of the cave and back.

"Yes." She fought to control the anger that stoked a latent fire inside her. Cole deserved answers, but he was interrogating her just as he had that first night.

"Why would you sacrifice so much?" His voice turned cold, scraping across her raw nerves. There was a subtle hint of some deeper emotion she couldn't define. "Was that man your brother? Husband? Betrothed?"

Her stomach cramped with the memories still thumping their way into her mind; the relief at finally finding her father to tell him of her mother's death then the shock and gut-twisting fear when Worth Harrison had been murdered in front of her. She fought the sting of tears. "That man was my father."

Cole's gaze shot to her, weighing, studying. Compassion flickered then it was gone. "Why were you there?"

"My mother had just died, a lung condition." The words were dull and flat. How long had it been since she'd allowed herself to think of this? Pain drove through her. "I had to tell him. I couldn't wait—" The resentment, controlled and fed for eighteen months, burst inside her. "I couldn't wait for him to come home, to be in between assignments to find the time for *us*."

"He was a detective? For Abe Grand?"

"Yes, one of the best." Her voice was bitter, but she didn't care. It was one of the things she both loved and loathed about her father.

"I knew you were no nun," he spat. "You're too easy about guns and killin', too damn beautiful."

The contempt in his voice caused her to spring up and glare at him. "I've done nothing wrong—" ·

"Cross saw you that night."

The calm observation startled her and served to crack her defenses. "Yes," she answered quietly.

Cole stepped up to her, his boot stubbing her shoe, his thigh brushing the fullness of her skirt. "So that's why the disguise. Why a nun?"

His question was asked with the same intensity, the same drive that fingerprinted everything he did. Just like her father, she realized dully. A shiver of warning tripped down her spine. He wouldn't rest until he had all the answers. "I never meant for it to be anything other than a way to escape Cross."

Rage flooded her then, vindicating, reassuring the decisions she'd made. She stared into the night, the trees and rock and moonlit ground blurring into a vision of painful memory. "He chased me with my father's blood dripping from his hands, staining his clothes.

"I found Abe that night. The next morning he took me to a convent near the docks and left me with one of his men." She took a shaky breath, explaining how Detective Poindexter had gone out to make sure the area was safe for her, but had never returned. "And Wendell Cross showed up across the street, waiting for me. I was afraid Mr. Poindexter was dead, which he was. So I took a habit and left my hair as payment."

"Your hair . . . then why isn't it cropped?"

"I couldn't do it again. I was careful to always wear my headpiece."

He was silent for a moment, his gaze tracking over her with solid purpose. In a quiet voice, "How'd you get to Calcutta?"

"I arranged passage on a steamer, bound for New Orleans. But we never made it."

"The boiler explosion," he said flatly. Everyone within a hundred-mile radius knew about the boiler explosion in Calcutta's harbor.

Cole's gaze sliced to her, still hard. "So you set up housekeepin' with the orphans."

"I didn't plan to," she snapped and instantly regretted it. Hadn't she questioned the morality, the wisdom of that herself?

"Elliot was on the boat. That's how we met. His brother, Joel, died during the trip. After the explosion, Reverend Holly asked if I would stay awhile, for Elliot. I agreed." She stared down at the ground. "Then I couldn't leave."

"Because they hadn't found Cross?"

"No," she whispered past the knot in her throat. "Because of the children. I wouldn't have made it through the year without them." She realized a tear was streaking down her cheek and scraped it away with the heel of her hand. "After a while, the reason I was there didn't seem to matter."

"Yeah." His voice was tired and crusty, sifting through the night like old ashes. There was a wealth of understanding in that single word, but he didn't offer it.

She stared over at him, standing against the rock face of the cave, half-invisible in the shadows of a large oak tree. His gaze met hers.

In that instant, some part of their relationship shifted from distrust to respect. Both had done, at times, what they had to do.

Cole's gaze flickered over her face, lingered a moment on her lips. They tingled as though he'd touched them. For the first time, Regina understood the breadth of what she'd revealed tonight. She couldn't comprehend the possibilities in their entirety, but she did know they had to do with Cole. Would he treat her as a woman, as she longed for him to, or with the same second-thought respect he had when he'd thought she was a nun?

Standing on the ledge with him, warm air stroking over her body, she felt heat uncurl in her belly. His gaze meshed with hers.

The kinship in his eyes died and was replaced by fleeting pain before being shuttered against her.

She wondered if he was thinking of Luke Sutter or Sarah. Slowly the realization trickled in—her secret was out. The guilt at her lies still lingered, but there was relief. At last she'd told someone. The knowledge sucked the strength right out of her. Her legs folded and she sank to the ground.

"Well," she said. "Well."

Suddenly she felt as if she were skimming over the

trees, high above the world. Energy surged through her and disbelief and giddiness. The ground in front of her blurred and the flames of the fire melted into an orange mass. Distantly, she heard Cole's voice.

"Aw, damn." The words came through gritted teeth. "Damn."

She realized she was crying, but couldn't contain the sheer joy that bubbled out of her. She tried to reassure him. "I'm fine, but I can't help it. It feels so strange to be rid of the disguise."

She sniffled and plucked at the multicolored calico, the flowers flowing into red and blue with no discernible pattern. Tears streamed down her face, cleansing, rebuilding some part of her that had died when she was unaware. She felt a refreshing sense of renewal and anticipation. Laughter mixed with the tears.

A hand settled on her shoulder and she turned to find Cole kneeling beside her, frowning as if he feared she had come unhinged. "Are you laughin'?"

"It just feels," she hiccuped, "so good to tell someone, get it out in the open." She swept her hands down her bodice and raised her gaze to his. "Thanks for the dress. It's the first one I've had in—" She frowned, blinking, trying to remember. ". . . years."

"About two," he supplied.

"Yes." She giggled, still dizzy with the shock of telling Cole. Her breath was spare and her chest ached as though she had strained her lungs by running some great distance. Somehow the dress represented the comfort and security she had missed the last few years. She glanced down at the ripped sleeve and sobered. "I've already torn it, I'm afraid."

"Don't worry. There's another one in the saddle-bag."

"For me?" She stared, openmouthed, blinking against the threat of new tears. "You bought me two dresses?"

"Oh, hell, if I'd known it would make you cry, I wouldn't have told you."

"I think anything would make me cry right now." She dabbed at her eyes, floating on the joy and new sense of freedom she was experiencing. "Thank you."

She looked up at him and found his gaze riveted on her. Wonder, confusion, bafflement shifted through his eyes, but there was something else. A flicker of desire.

She caught her breath, her gaze dropping to his lips. At that moment, she wanted nothing more than to be held in his arms and kissed. Kissed the way a man was supposed to kiss a woman, with no secrets, no lies, no sense of the forbidden.

Cole's gaze sharpened on her, the rugged planes of his face heightened by shadows. His head lowered.

Time ground to a halt and her stomach dropped. She didn't even breathe, afraid to break the spell and send him running. Then his lips touched hers.

Softly at first, as though she might shatter. Heat skipped down her arms. She trembled, parting her lips under his, silently asking for more, reveling in the fact that she could. His mouth opened over hers, firm and bold, hot, wet. One brawny arm pulled her close and she curled her hand around his neck for support.

His tongue dipped inside her mouth, stroking the sleek heat. Her muscles jerked. Her breasts crushed into his chest and she strained closer, unable to silence the moan that worked out of her throat. He took her leisurely, as if it were his right, and tenderly, as if he wanted it to remain that way.

Her heart turned over in her chest. *I love you.* The words welled from the deepest corner of her soul, but were silenced by Cole's lips on hers.

The secret part of her heart unfolded and drew him in. His scent sang in her blood, beat in her heart as she knew it always would.

Abruptly, he pulled away. Pain and frustration chased across his features, a longing so fierce her throat knotted. He quickly masked it. His voice was hoarse and choppy. "I think you'd better get some sleep. I'll take the first watch."

Desire scraped through him, pooling in a fiery knot in his belly and rushing in a hot flood to harden him. Pleasure was edged with pain, caution battled with savage lust. All through the night, it plagued him. Yet despite the lust, he couldn't quite think of her as a normal woman.

Like everyone else, he had believed she was a nun. He had known she had secrets, known she had more information than she would reveal, but he had never, never imagined she wasn't truly a nun.

When he looked at her, he expected to see her as she'd been in the habit, beautiful, but pristine, forbidden. Instead he saw a slender raven-haired woman, striking and sensual, in a multicolored calico dress. The conflicting images wound the frustration tighter, pulling invisible cords of tension across his shoulders, up his belly. His head throbbed with the dual images so prevalent in his mind.

Even in the glare of early morning light, as he scoured a mile radius of the cave, torturous dreams of Regina's vivid eyes haunted him. First smoked with passion as they had been last night, then frigid when she learned of his deal with Abe Grand. And she *would* learn of it.

Cole clenched his teeth and grabbed for Horse's saddle, swinging up. Last night, he had not allowed himself to go back to her, not even to check and see if she slept. He didn't trust himself.

In the still cool shadows of the woods, he found old deer tracks, a thin and frail snakeskin, a bobcat den, dark stains of blood on the earth below the ledge, but no sign of James Cross. Where was the man? There were no human prints, no sign of horse hooves in the stubborn earth.

Cole stood still, waiting for the instincts that had served him so well in the past. They were silent, over-ridden by the guilt that fluttered at the edges of his mind. All through the morning, he tried to escape the fact that he was using Regina to get to Sutter.

The guilt sliced through him, shredding his confidence, mangling his judgment. The feeling had been spurred by the kiss. And it hadn't.

So open, so giving, seeking something from him. A secret part of him had opened up; he'd felt possessive tenderness and a desperate need to bury himself in her. He'd never felt that with a woman. Certainly not with Sarah.

Yet he couldn't go to Regina. Not with the plans

he'd made with Abe Grand. Not when involvement with her would risk catching Sutter. A gust of fear chilled him. His priorities, so carefully guarded, so selfishly implemented, were muddled. Sometime—when?—he'd come to care about this woman.

Last night, his first thoughts had been for her safety, her welfare. He could tell himself it was because she was his only link to Sutter, but it wasn't true. Increasingly, he'd had to remind himself of Sutter and why he was involved with Regina in the first place.

With no sign of James Cross, Cole didn't want to waste any time. After a quick breakfast, he and Regina mounted Horse and rode out. They veered slightly east behind the bluff to skirt a large patch of dense forest and headed north again.

They were a safe distance away from Rebel Cave, where Jesse James and his band had been spotted several months ago, and Cole wanted to keep it that way.

As they rode, confusion played at the edges of a mind once resolute with purpose and unyielding in decision. Just as strong was the urge to comfort, the urge to accept the same from her. Something deep inside him cried out for it, something he'd covered in the last months with hate and cunning and vengeance.

It was more than physical. There had been a recognition of common ground last night, though he hadn't verbalized it. A new respect for her had been born. She had been subjected to trauma and horror and defended herself the only way she knew. He couldn't condemn that. She had better reasons than he did for some of the things he'd done.

Even so, the double images of her sparred in his

mind. He tried to keep a mental distance from her as they rode. It was impossible to keep a physical one because she sat behind him on Horse. Her breasts burned into his back; her arms circled his waist. She trusted him.

Sweat trickled down his neck and soaked the collar of his shirt. It was becoming increasingly difficult to keep his mind centered on James Cross and extremely important to find her a separate mount.

What was he going to do about her? He'd felt her response to his kiss last night, as eager as his own. And also her hurt when he'd pulled away. The desire built to razor edge inside him, twisting the muscles of his gut, lashing his mind until he answered even her most casual questions in monosyllables or grunts.

He felt as if he were drowning, pushed down by some weight greater than his own. His conscience, effectively schooled for months, was rousing, giving orders, pulling at the pain inside him. He wanted more than one night with her and had since he'd found her bleeding on his bed. He knew he could've made love to her last night, but his conscience wouldn't allow it.

He needed to make a decision about her before he did something stupid. A sense of urgency uncoiled within him, a potent reminder of the raging fire as she started in his blood. He would have to forfeit either her or Sutter.

He tried to focus on Cross, searching for signs of disturbed ground, horse manure, broken twigs. No echo of sound followed them over the rolling hills. Despite his renewed effort at concentration, Regina was always there, as constant as the moon in the sky. Pulling at him, beckoning with unspoken promises.

Even when they purchased another mount, using money Cole had gotten from the sale last year of his and Sarah's house, he couldn't ignore Regina.

He soaked in the sight of her, aching to touch the cloud of her hair, as dark and silky as a mink pelt. He wanted to haul her up to his chest and plunder her soft mouth, delve beneath that bodice to the rose and cream breasts. The musings were so vivid he swelled against his britches and shifted uncomfortably.

He couldn't keep his gaze from her, even when she shyly met it with her own, full of questions and apprehension. He found himself waiting in anticipation for those emerald eyes to turn on him and smile. A smile that kicked him in the gut and tingled in the soles of his feet.

The trim straight back, the delicate hands carefully holding the reins, the ripe swell of her breasts, the long line of her creamy neck. His fingers itched to stroke her skin, thumb her nipple to rousing awareness, scrape over the velvety softness of her belly and lower. . . .

He cursed. This was supposed to have been a job, a means to an end, calculating, shrewd, business only. He told himself he wasn't in love with her. Not so soon. But even the bond of simply caring was strong enough to skewer his plans.

A long-denied part of him yearned toward her, softening his heart, but his mind stayed hard and brutally focused on Sutter.

He knew he had to choose, but couldn't make himself let go of the hate that had driven him since Sarah's and the baby's deaths. Not even to take the promise of something pure and bright.

He was going to leave her. Dump her somewhere and continue on without her.

It might have been foolish to think so, but it was a fear Regina couldn't escape as they traveled north. Since she had exposed all her secrets and relived the pain of her parents' deaths, there had been a tangible distance between her and Cole.

He looked at her differently. Not with anger and not with contempt. She could not quite describe it except that it seemed like a reluctant understanding and a frustrated confusion. When he looked at her, there was in his eyes the anticipation of seeing someone familiar then puzzlement and irritation as though he didn't recognize her at all.

He said little and she followed his example. For two days, she tried to respect the distance he placed between them, fretting the entire time that he would simply find another mount then a suitable place to leave her.

There was still no sign of James Cross. They rode north at a steady pace and steered east when the river did. Toward Ste. Genevieve, Cole said. She herself knew a little of Missouri's first permanent settlement, still strongly French, developed early in the eighteenth century. Cole told her nothing.

They passed large openmouthed caves with the

gush and gurgle of water vibrating inside, time-worn and slicked faces of the bluffs along the river, edges of a forest thick with the green of pines, oaks, redbuds, and maples.

Cole scouted well ahead. Regina kept her gun at the ready and watched their backs. And though she didn't ask, she wondered how badly he had injured James Cross. Cole made no assumptions, covering their back ground once they camped at night, brushing out any visible tracks. They were careful to stay in water where they could and on hard rock or parched ground that didn't easily take tracks.

The second night of their trip, they slept under the stars in a clearing. On the horizon was a view of a flat silver curve that Regina knew to be the Mississippi River. Cole didn't sleep and she did only a bit, watching as he constantly searched the dark and changing shadows.

She felt safer when she could listen to the husky drag of his boot across the hard earth and the creak of his knees when he changed positions.

Both days, they stopped only for a brief lunch and to drink at a cold stream. The roofs of homes and businesses were tiny dots to the west as they passed the towns of Desloge, Bonne Terre, and De Soto. They never got close enough to be seen. And always there was the threat of Cross.

On the third night, they camped in front of another cave some miles past Ste. Genevieve, this one smelling of dead animals and rotten food and too small for even Regina to stand upright. She wasn't exactly sure where they were and Cole hadn't volunteered the information. How close were they to St. Louis? He had pushed them hard over many miles the last few days.

The night was comfortable with a breeze blowing in from the south. Still her shoulders were tight with apprehension, her neck and back sore from constant craning in the saddle to check for Cross. And Cole's steadily increasing silence flicked at her nerves until they thrummed like a drawn bowstring.

On this night, as the one before, they ate supper with only pleasantries between them and Cole left to make a thorough sweep of the area.

Regina washed her face and hands, freeing herself of the day's grime and taking pleasure in the cool water. After checking her gun, she sat down at the fire and began to brush her hair. She loved the freedom of wearing real clothes and not hiding behind the disguise any longer, but more than anything she loved being able to wear her hair down.

Cole returned, calling out a warning. "It's me."

She nodded and kept on with her brushing, noticing after a moment that he still stood on the other side of the fire. She looked up and he jerked his gaze from her, moving quickly away.

He'd been watching her. At the knowledge, a queasy feeling of excitement rumbled in her belly and shivers skipped up and down her arms. "Did you find something?"

"No sign of him." He turned away and sipped a cup of coffee, scanning the horizon. In the distance, the inky ridge of a bluff was layered with shimmering shades of silver and blue. "I can't figure it."

"What's that?" She lowered the brush to her lap, her gaze darting to shadowed bushes and dark corners.

Cole, too, stared out over the dips of hills and rocks. "We haven't heard from him. I'm just wonderin'—"

"Do you think he could be dead?"

He drained his cup and held it dangling from one finger. "I don't know, but there's absolutely no sign of him."

"Good." She watched Cole for another second, wondering if she should come out and ask him if he planned to leave her. They had covered a lot of ground in the last two days, partly, she knew, because of James Cross. Was it also to find a suitable place to leave her?

Seeing Cole in his usual position, with his back to her, waiting with taut muscles for whatever threat might appear, she went back to her hair. She pulled the brush through, delighting in the stroke of the bristles on her scalp, the luxuriant feel of her fingers gliding over the satiny thickness.

Like the flutter of stars on a cloudy night, Cole's mouth harp music floated to her. Her eyes drifted shut and her shoulders relaxed. Despite the distance he had created, she felt a connection to him.

Once again, he played "The Blue Danube Waltz." Regina felt the anticipated tug in the pit of her stomach and wondered what memories the song held for him.

The melody was still haunting, but this time with a seductive lilt. He dragged certain notes until she could feel them swirling in the pit of her stomach. Others he made wispy, breathy. They lingered over her and trailed down her body as though they were his hands on her.

The music washed over her, soothed her in ways she wished his hands would. Should she talk to him, ask his intentions? She hated to voice the thought, in case he hadn't planned it.

She sat there suspended in the cool clasp of evening air and the flow of his music, her heart and throat aching with each coaxing breath he drew. It was a moment before she realized the music had stopped.

She opened her eyes to ask him to keep playing and froze.

He stood at her back, silent, almost a shadow, but his presence tingled in her belly. Every nerve hummed with awareness of him. She could smell the remnants of fire smoke, the tang of clean sweat mixed with leather. His heat curled around her.

Every tendon strained toward him. *Touch me just once.* With sheer strength of will and some small fear, she sat without moving lest he turn away as he had moments ago.

Something floated over her hair, light and tentative. She held her breath, using all her senses to concentrate on feeling it again. It came, more sure this time, a definite caress.

His hand slid over her hair and her heart lurched to a stop.

Pleasure knotted painfully in her chest. She didn't dare breathe for fear of waking from a dream or driving him away if this were indeed real.

Slowly, as though she might dislodge his hand if she

moved too fast, she drew in a shallow pant of air. Her arms and legs trembled. Anticipation shivered up her spine. Yearning, straining toward him, her body thrummed. Tingles pricked her arms, her legs, her shoulders.

And she waited, hoping.

His fingers moved through her hair, lightly at first, streaming through the shoulder-length strands. Then his thumb brushed the skin at the nape of her neck. A tiny circle of heat exploded there, radiating out to ripple across her shoulders.

She thought she would melt from the sheer pleasure of his touch and blinked away the sting of tears in her eyes. *Please don't stop.*

His fingers splayed on her nape and slid up into her hair to cup her skull. With no thought at all, she arched her neck, tilting back so that he cradled her head in his hands. She kept her eyes closed, afraid to look and break the spell. The heady perfume of pine and cedar mingled with the sweetness of clean skin and musky male odor.

Her shoulders brushed his knees and the beginning slope of the steel-threaded muscles of his thigh, cupping her, not supporting her. Her breath shuddered out and she forced herself not to lean against him. Langorous heat wrapped around her, tingling in her nipples, drawing them tight and making her breasts heavy.

His fingers spread and trailed through her hair, moved to tenderly caress her jaw. He stroked her cheek then abruptly he was gone.

The realization didn't penetrate her dazed state for

long seconds. She opened her eyes, steadying herself with a hand on the ground. Had she imagined it all?

No, she could still feel the brand of his touch on her neck, the heat of him against her shoulders. Turning, she saw he stood with his back to her, arms folded across his chest, staring out into the night.

Her unease returned. Was he bidding her goodbye? Her nerves were ragged with uncertainty, but she stood, straightened her skirts, and walked over behind him.

With her heart beating in her throat, she spoke around a lump of emotion. "You're leaving me, aren't you?"

CHAPTER ELEVEN

His gut clenched at the plea in her voice. Leave her? He almost wished he could, but there was something in the brave defiance, the demanding words that tickled his nerves.

He read the fear beneath the steady voice and found himself wanting to turn and hold her. But he wouldn't allow it. The muscles across his neck and shoulders burned with the effort. He could reassure her and that was all.

The distance he'd kept for the last two days had been deliberate and hard won. He wouldn't risk it. Still, he was shocked that she thought he intended to leave her.

Only moments ago, he'd come close to forsaking his quest for Sutter and taking her. He'd wanted to move his hands through the thick satin of her hair and down over her body, take the surrender he sensed she was offering. Lose himself in her and put off what he knew was coming.

Tomorrow they would reach St. Louis and Sutter.

Then she would look at him with contempt. The urge for her drummed through him, dividing his mind and his will. But as much as his body burned for her, his mind wouldn't release him.

"I'm not leaving you." His voice sounded tired, even to him. "Hell, we'll be there tomorrow."

She seemed taken aback at that and paused for a moment, then said, "I know you're not going because of me."

"What?" Immediately alert at the quiet confidence of her words, his head swerved. Slowly, he turned to face her, eyes narrowed. Unease skittered up his spine.

She gripped her skirt, stepping back from him as he advanced on her. "I think you're going up there to find someone named Sutter."

Instantly his mind replayed the conversation with his brothers in the barn the day James Cross had caught them unaware. He hauled her to him, hard. A pulse fluttered at her throat and he noted the spark of fear in her eyes before she masked it. "You little sneak! You were eavesdropping."

"I wasn't sure what you'd tell them about me." She stiffened in his arms and lifted her chin, trying to pull away. He held her fast, his hands squeezing the soft flesh of her upper arms. "I wanted to be sure you kept your word."

"Kept my word?" he choked out. He fought off the black cloud of fury hazing his vision and pulled her tightly against him, skimming her breasts with the buttons of his dark shirt, pressing her thighs with the hardness of his. Burning under the anger was an ember of desire. He fought it, knowing he flirted with danger. "Honor is a strange thing when coupled with lies, isn't it?"

"You needn't act so maligned. You didn't tell all the truth either."

"I didn't figure you needed to know." His voice was abrupt and he broke her gaze to stare over her head, staving off the memories and sense of doom closing over him.

"Nor I you," she returned with a toss of her head. For a moment, she watched him then her voice gentled. "You could've told me you had business there. I would have accepted that."

"Would you?" He refocused on her face and realized with a shot of self-disgust how hard he held her. He pulled his hands away, knocking off his hat and running a hand through his hair. "The most important thing was to get you to St. Louis."

He knew he hadn't told Gage or Emmett his plans about using her, but what the hell had he said in the barn? "What else?"

"What else what?" She rubbed her arms and he felt a twinge of conscience at having held her so brutally.

"What else did you hear?" He didn't touch her, but stayed close, crowding, ready to force the truth out of her if he needed to.

"I—" She licked her lips and shifted from one foot to the other. Her gaze slid from his briefly. "I know it's caused bad feelings between you and your brothers. Between you and your whole family."

"That's nobody's business." He battled the hurt, the pain that seared his nerves. She was right. His obsession with Sutter had cost him a precious lot.

"But, Cole . . . you've been carrying this grudge for a long time. You're driven to kill this man because of hate. And at the expense of your family?"

It was no more than what he'd said to himself, but hearing it from her made it sound vicious, calculating, and lashed the pain deeper. "And what about you?"

"What do you mean?" She frowned, her gaze locking on his, searching, waiting.

"Why is what you're doin' so different?"

"Because . . ." She shook her head, confusion clouding her eyes. "I'm not tracking Wendell Cross. I'm not planning to kill him, to take a life for the one he took."

"Other people are doin' it for you," he reminded flatly.

She rubbed her forehead with the back of her hand, pausing as though striving for patience. "No. I'm willing to let justice take its course. You're . . . you're—" She gestured with her hands, struggling to convey what she meant. "You're seeking revenge."

"It's justice to me," he said flatly.

"You don't mean that. If you kill this man, as you plan to, you'll never be free. How can that be right?"

He turned away from her, needing some space. He'd thought too much about her in the last few days and the anger only brought the desire to boiling. "What about you?"

"What about me?" Once again the cool haughty tone, the flash of the nun she'd pretended to be.

"You've been locked up in that damn nun's costume since you got to Calcutta, your every move determined by the man who killed your father. Hell," he sneered, "you don't even have a life."

"Oh, and you're so different?" She moved in front of him, refusing to let him escape. "Hate is *your* prison. Your every move has been the result of something that happened a year and a half ago, that you can't let go, even when your family tried to help you."

"Leave them out of this." His voice was low and threatening. "You don't know a damn thing about it." He stepped away, intent on gaining some distance from her and the memories she had stirred up.

Her fingers curved around his forearm, stalling him. "You're right. I don't understand it all, but I do know it has to do with your wife, Sarah. She was . . . unfaithful."

His gaze sliced to her. How long had she been outside that barn? Just the mention of Sarah's name on Regina's lips edged his anger into savage fury and he clenched his fists in reaction.

If anything, she looked sorry for having said the words, as though she didn't like causing him pain. His jaws locked and he skirted the fire. He didn't want to talk about Sarah and Luke, certainly not with Regina.

"I'm sure it was very painful. Well, I mean, it's never happened to me, but I imagine it is. Oh, bother. I'm trying to say I'm sorry." She didn't follow him this time, but stood where he'd left her.

He lifted a hand in acknowledgment, her voice a dim echo in a mind now rife with old accusations and guilt. He recognized her sympathy and wished he could sort out his own emotions.

Pain and anger engulfed him. Which emotion was a legacy of Regina and which of Sarah? He stared out into the night, over the tops of frothy pines, inhaling the bitter tang of cedar resin and the scent of nearby water.

"She was"—Regina paused, seeming to search for the right word—"involved with Sutter. You were close to him?"

"At one time, he was my best friend. Didn't you stay around long enough to get that?" The old pain was a blistering knot, festering and spreading its poison through his blood. In the deepest part of his heart, Cole knew the pain was for friendship betrayed, not for Sarah.

Regina walked over next to him and put a tentative hand on his arm. "What happened to her? Did Sutter kill her?"

She died running from me. The guilt fed the anger and erupted inside him. "What do you want?" He spun to face her, his voice brutal. "You want to hear how I found them together, how she told me she was planning to go away with him?"

Regina's eyes were steady on his face, but bright with unshed tears. "What happened?"

He gave a burst of bitter laughter. His breath choked him for a moment as the scene ground over and over in his head. The despicable things he'd called her, raising his fist to her and being pulled back by Sutter.

The ugliness stabbed him, making him ashamed

and angry again. "She ran for her horse and took off. It had rained that night, enough to flood the creek and the gully, too. I yelled at her not to take the gully."

He stopped, the blood and screams and pictures of her limp body flashing through his mind. His breath panted out. Sweat tickled his neck, burned in his eyes. "She jumped. The horse lost its footing and they both went down. The mare landed on Sarah. Her neck was broken, but . . . there was blood everywhere."

His hands shook. He could no longer see Regina's eyes, but instead saw Sarah's blue ones, accusing at first, then sad. Finally lifeless. Pain cleaved down his middle, so sharp he thought his breastbone would split.

"But, Cole, it was an accident." Regina's voice was thick, as choked as his. "It wasn't Luke's fault and it wasn't yours either."

"What do you know of it?" He squeezed his eyes shut, wishing he could stop the memories. And now the words, dammed for all these months, pushed their way out. He hated it, hated himself, but it refueled his hate for Sutter and Sarah as well.

"She was hemorrhaging, losing my baby." He gritted his teeth, trying to control the surge of fury and pain roiling through him.

"No—" Her voice broke.

"Don't you see?" he growled savagely, like an animal in the throes of pain and fighting for release. "She was going to have another man raise my child. My best friend."

The images of Regina and Sarah blurred and merged. Green eyes became blue. Raven hair became gold. He wanted to kill, to squeeze the life out of her just as she had squeezed it, drop by slow torturous drop, out of him.

Fury shook him and slowly he realized that his fingers were bruising Regina's throat. It was Regina's soft voice begging him not to hurt her, Regina's soft hands clutching at him. Shock and fear blazed through him and he pulled away from her with a low moan of horror.

He drew in great gulping breaths of air, trying to calm the rage in his blood, restore some reason to his jumbled churning thoughts. His eyes burned and he closed them.

There was a sudden soft brush against his lips. His eyes snapped open. "What the hell—"

She stood in front of him, eyes glistening with sympathy. Shadows and moonlight played around her hair, gilding the ebony tresses with silver. Her words whispered against his cheek. "I am so sorry about your baby."

She stared at him, understanding giving way to desire and finally surrender in the jeweled depths of her eyes. The same desire throbbed in his gut along with fury and pain. He needed something or someone to wash it away.

Her, his body screamed.

Not her, his mind echoed. Not her. Not her.

The unspoken words throbbed between them. His refusal was as plain as if he'd spoken.

The fire in her eyes dimmed and she pulled away. Cole reached out, catching her hand in his, not able to touch her as he wanted yet not able to let her walk

away. The calloused skin of his palm met the smooth
velvet of hers. He didn't speak, but held tight to her
hand, trying to communicate his gratitude. He latched
on to her strength and worked to stem the need swirling through his body.

Heat merged through their palms, tingled up his
arm. His heart swelled for her. His body burned. Her
gaze was careful and steady, giving. A peace seeped
into his soul and soothed his battered nerves.

For an instant, it was enough. He allowed himself
to take from someone the wellspring of strength he
hadn't ever allowed himself, even from his sister,
who'd tried more than anyone to reach him.

Then Regina moved closer, gripping his hand
fiercely and turning so that she stood next to him, his
arm curving around her shoulder. He swallowed,
glimpsing the steely determination and patience that
had allowed her to wait so long for the capture of
Wendell Cross.

They stood side by side, silently taking strength
from each other. Cole's body trumpeted other feelings, other desires, fraying his willpower. He wanted
her, but knew he should keep a distance until he had
made a decision regarding her. He yearned to be con-
tent with this small closeness, but he wasn't.

The air quivered with tension and angry words.
Cole hovered on the double edge of sanity and passion; logic and possession. He should put her from
him. His hand loosened on hers as he prepared to let
her go. She turned to him, her eyes dark pools of uncertainty and apprehension and pain. She touched his
face with shaking hands.

Without thought or hesitation, he clasped her shoulders. It seemed the most natural thing to pull her close and take her mouth as he'd imagined for days, but he hesitated, reminding himself with thin control of his deal with Grand.

Not this way. He shouldn't take her this way. Not with this secret between them, the cruel callousness he'd used to get her here.

Her gaze fixed on his, her face naked with longing and an emotion he didn't want to name. She leaned up and pressed trembling lips to his.

His control shattered. Desperation and logic erupted.

His arms went around her and he hauled her full against him, raising her so that her feet came off the ground. Her breasts pressed into his chest; her leg brushed the heat between his thighs. She gasped into his mouth then wound her arms around his neck, meeting his openmouthed, hot kisses eagerly, passionately.

Her wet mouth on his drowned his conscience. His breath seemed tied to the essence and taste of her. Frenzied desire shook through him. He held her tight, edging around the low flame of the fire and making his way in a daze over to the blanket she'd spread earlier.

His knees gave and he was on top of her, never leaving her mouth, his hands skimming over the calico dress. Her breath was as harsh and raspy as his. She clutched at his shoulders, kneading, begging. Cradling her back with big palms, he held her up, trying to fumble for the buttons. She moaned at his touch and he was reminded of her injury.

"Your shoulder." He tore his mouth from hers, cursing himself for a fool for not remembering.

She reached for him. "No, don't stop."

Desperation swept through him, like a hot stinging wind. Holding her felt as if he'd found the lost part of himself. He knew he should stop, but was powerless in the face of her sweet warmth and reaching arms.

He tried to regulate the flood of heat in his blood and couldn't. His heart felt as though it were being pulled through his chest. Conscious thought withered and scattered like fallen petals. Spinning, flying, running from the past, holding off the future.

Doing this to her—with her—was insane, unfair, but she reached for his shirt, as greedy and hungry as he was. Buttons slid free under her questing fingers and she devoured him with her gaze, smoky, green, muted by the shadows of the night.

Aching, hungry for something he wouldn't name, he pulled at the buckle of his holster and dropped it to the ground in one jerky movement. He slipped the first button of his britches undone then stopped, arms shaking, as she arched toward him and pressed her lips to the hollow of his throat then his chest.

Her hair, gold-brushed ebony by the firelight, streamed across her shoulders and the blanket. His shirt slid to the ground and her quick mouth branded him. Hot kisses rained the width of his chest and up over his collarbone. Fire licked at him. Her fingers touched everywhere—his chest, arms, belly.

His arms went around her. With both hands, he cupped her firm bottom, arching her into him, letting her feel the pulsing ridge of desire between his legs. Her dress bunched between them. The smooth tautness of her belly met the tempered angles of his. Her thighs hugged his hips, her hands glided over his shoulders and back, up his neck to flex her fingers against his scalp.

Cole's reason disappeared like a puff of smoke in frigid air. He kissed her, harshly at first, wanting to go slow but unable to. She met each desperate thrust of his tongue with her own. Drowning in her heat, he gave himself up to the icy fire pulsing through his body, sharp and steady like pricks of a knife.

Heat trickled through him. Fire danced in his belly like a caged thing, begging to be released. His fingers skipped down her back and released the glass buttons. He peeled her dress away; the chemise and drawers followed as he bore her down on the blanket.

His gut kicked. Desire funneled through him, spreading, searing like molten wax. She was perfect. Her breasts were full and round, large enough for his big hands, all cream and rose in the shadows of his body.

For a moment, he stared and she whimpered low in her throat. Just looking at her made him light-headed and he was seized with a sudden piercing tenderness. His hands and lips tingled in anticipation. And the fire was there, driving him, lapping at him. He'd never seen such beauty in his life, such pure perfection, and remembered when he'd cursed it as a joke of God.

Vaguely aware his hand shook, he cupped one breast. She drew in her breath, watching him with burning eyes. He rubbed his thumb across the delicate nub of her nipple; it hardened instantly. Such intense pleasure crossed her face he thought she might swoon.

His head lowered and he drew the sweet flesh into his mouth. Her nipple beaded, succulent, ripe for his tongue. She gasped. Heat rippled out in scorching waves.

Her hand tangled in his hair to hold him there. She arched, her breasts swelling for him. Her body trembled. He played her as long as he could, fighting the frantic urge to take her now. He wanted to give her pleasure.

He circled her nipple with his tongue, laving, suckling, until she writhed against him and drew her nails down his arms. Moving down the taut skin of her belly, he flicked his tongue over smooth flesh. One hand glided low and between her legs. She was hot, wet, ready. His restraint burst. He pulled away from her and shucked off his boots.

Her voice rose, fevered, impatient. "Where—"

"Just a minute." His hands fumbled with the buttons on his pants, then at last they were free. He pushed the britches down his hips and kicked them off. He turned back to find her raised on her elbows, watching him. At the smoky passion in her gaze, he moved toward her.

Her gaze dropped to his shaft, engorged, thrusting, and her eyes widened. In a quick unconscious motion, she crossed herself.

Cole laughed, wicked and low, kneeling to lean toward her. She was priceless. "Wishin' for that habit now?"

"No," she breathed, her gaze still fixed there. Then she looked in his eyes and lay back on the blanket, opening her arms to him.

He couldn't escape the feeling that he was coming home, the sudden knowledge that this was right.

She pulled his head down for a kiss, long, lingering, their tongues stroking and gliding at a frenzied pace. She seemed as desperately eager to touch him as he was to touch her. Her hand stroked over his belly, nails raking the muscles now clenched with control.

She touched his swollen length and he grew iron hard in the velvet of her palm. He choked back a savage groan, wanting to enjoy the feeling of her hands on him and wondering how long he could.

"Cole." Her voice was a breathy whisper, flowing over him like silk and whiskey.

He leaned over her, still exercising the small restraint he had remaining. He was ready to burst, but this new relationship with her was somehow as important as the physical one.

She dragged a hand down his length and up again.

A groan rumbled out of him and he thrust his tongue inside her mouth, miming the movement he ached to make lower in her body. Her hands moved over his butt, flexing, stroking, tracing, inciting him to a fierce surging. He spread her knees with one of his, stuffing his shirt under her shoulder for cushion.

She shifted, opening her legs to him, and he slid inside. Only a little at first, exploring, readying her. He withdrew and slid again, the muscles of his shoulders and hips stinging with the effort to go easy and not rip her apart. Heat sparked and he felt her moist heat build around him.

Her breath shuddered out. She locked her arms around him, watching him with smoky eyes, greedy, urging. He moved again, deeper, and she arched into him, her lashes fluttering shut in pleasure. "Cole."

The sound of his name on her lips tightened something inside him, shifted his world. A tenderness, long dormant, stirred, but the savage need for her swept it away. Unable to wait any longer, he slid long and deep. Then he felt it, a membrane guarding the deepest core of her.

He froze, lifting his lips from hers. "Damn."

She was panting, gasping his name, sliding her body sinuously against his. The shock of her virgin state resurrected his numb mind and he tried to pull away.

In the instant of paused momentum, she gripped his hips and surged upward, taking the length of him and wresting the decision from him as well. Her membrane broke and hot tight flesh surrounded him. Friction. Spinning heat. Wet and sleek, she held him. Ragged desire clawed through him and he fought for control.

She reached for him, pulling his head down to her, meeting his lips with hungry demanding ones.

He surged, no longer capable of rational thought, only feeling, operating on her sweat-sheened skin sliding against his, the musky love scent of her, the cushion of her full breasts and hard nipples drilling his chest.

She met his rhythm, a beat behind at first then heated silk flowed over him. She bucked against him, anticipating his next move and meeting it with unerring deliberation. Cole knew only the need to release the tight coil inside him, the pressure boiling between his legs.

She pulled him in deeper, deeper, panting his name.

Sweat slicked his back, his belly where it met hers. Her gasping pants echoed in his pounding head, gentle, a seductive rhythm.

Faster and faster, a frantic joining. As though he could erase the wasted and black months of his life, vanquish the truth of what he'd done to get to Sutter.

She arched on the blanket and cried out, her inner muscles tightening around him. He waited for her repeated shuddering response then he climaxed, hot and bursting inside her.

They lay there, hearts calming. Slowly, the hiss and crackle of the fire trickled in, the rustle of leaves in a tender breeze bringing back reality.

He looked down. Her eyes were closed and her brow was furrowed. In pain? Regret? He cursed. Either way, he had hurt her.

"You sorry?" His muscles tensed as he waited for her reaction.

"No." She opened her eyes and met his gaze squarely. Hers was fervent, sincere, and completely trusting.

He started to speak then stopped, humbled at the honest need he saw in her eyes. With one hand, he smoothed her hair from her damp brow. He rolled off her and onto his side, facing her.

She smiled and kissed him, deep, lingering, sweet with a giving that even now twisted his gut. His hand flexed on her waist, curving to the delicious softness of her skin. With a smile on her lips, she slept.

Cole didn't. He didn't want her to have regrets because he had enough for both of them. He had done exactly what he had sworn not to.

Rioting emotions charged through him. Shock at how not only his body, but his mind had responded to her. Regret that he had made love to her before making a decision. Torn between the pleasure they had shared and the knowledge that it shouldn't have happened.

He hadn't expected this depth of emotion. The regret returned, the bite he had been feeling almost since the moment he had wired Abe Grand.

The fire warmed his back and she snuggled closer. He pulled the blanket over them. Stroking the supple skin at her waist, he stared down at her, savoring the weight of her breasts against his chest. His heart squeezed at the peace and trust on the exquisite features.

The dew of her flesh was still on him, binding him to her and suddenly his mind cleared. He knew exactly what he must do about Sutter.

CHAPTER TWELVE

Regina awoke to the sound of birds chattering and the sun trying to peek through a patch of fog. The scent of fire smoke drifted to her and the toasty smell of bread. A blanket covered her nude body, warding off the first chill of the morning. She stretched, feeling a twinge of pain in her shoulder and a deeper ache between her legs.

Immediately, her gaze went to Cole. Bare to the waist, he knelt by the fire, sliding a skillet back and forth across hot rocks. Bronze skin sheathed muscles as hard as stone and they flexed with each movement. Her body thrummed just looking at him. She could still feel his touch in the tenderness of her breasts, the heavy tingle between her legs, the ache of his stamp on her heart.

Perhaps she should be ashamed for so wantonly offering herself to him, but she wasn't. His pain had made her reach out to him. Her fear of never having what they'd shared had made her stay.

She pulled the blanket tighter around her body.

They were close to St. Louis now. What would happen once they arrived? Would Cole deliver her to Abe and resume his search for Sutter? Would he even stay for the trial?

Last night, there had been no soft words spoken, just a raging need quenched. No promises made, only a bond of bodies and the giving of her soul. For her part, it had begun as an instinctive offer of comfort and ended as a totally selfish act. She had needed him.

Tired of patience and stamina and this infernal waiting for everything in her life, she had taken the one night she was certain of. Cole started a fire in her, a living, breathing tongue that stroked her insides every time he was near. For once, she had thrown caution and common sense to the winds. And she didn't regret one delicious second.

Love swelled through her, sending a warm glow from her middle out to her arms and legs. She did love him, there was no denying it, but the emotion scared her. He was too much like her father, so obsessed with his goals that he excluded others.

"Morning," he said without turning around.

Startled, her eyes widened. How had he known she was awake? "Good morning," she murmured.

"Breakfast'll be ready in a few minutes." He set the skillet off to one side and placed the coffeepot on top of the center rock giving the most heat. "Pan biscuits."

She thought about saying something casual like I'm starved, but she was suddenly aware of the itch of sweat and dirt and the blatant feel of her nakedness. The scent of sex lingered on her skin. Securing the blanket around her, she sat up. "I think I'll wash first."

"Make it quick." His voice was cool and aloof, giving no hint of the savage passion of the night before.

He didn't turn to look at her and she stared, uncertainty pulling at her. Was he sorry about last night? He'd asked her the same thing, but never answered himself.

She stood, wincing as the pain sharpened between her legs and rippled through her body. Bending, she picked up her dress and undergarments and stared for a moment as she realized how wrinkled they were.

She clutched the clothes to her, remembering how she and Cole had flung them off in a mad hurried fever. Her face heated. His scent wafted to her from the clothing and she turned to the saddlebags to fetch her other dress. She had no choice but to wear her same chemise, though the musky darkness of his scent suddenly unsettled her.

Taking a cloth, strong lye soap, and a towel from one of the bags, she made her way down a slight rise to the creek. Water pooled in a quiet eddy to the right under a bush, and she quickly dropped the blanket. The first touch of water was frigid. She gasped, her muscles drawing taut at the shock, but she continued on.

The water came only to mid-thigh. She hid just behind a bush for some privacy. She draped the towel over the bush and dipped the cloth into the water. The initial coolness shriveled her skin, but she soon warmed as she scrubbed. She lathered her breasts and arms and worked the rag in soothing circles, washing away the sweat and grit and Cole's scent. In her heart, she held close the memory of his touch.

She tried not to think of last night and what they had shared. Instead she tried to quiet her mind. Her gaze drifted to the clear water tumbling over rocks and fallen branches, sparkling like a ribbon of transparent silver. Across the stream, a mother blue jay scolded her chicks. A frog stared goggle-eyed. The underbrush crackled then revealed a covey of spotted quail waddling past.

Always at the edge of her thoughts was Cole. Her rag caught on a leafy branch of the bush and she worked it free, glancing down at her body. She paused, her heart clenching tight. A smear of blood stained the pale skin of her inner thigh and the hollow where her leg and hip joined.

With bittersweet joy, she ran a light finger over the spot. Her breath shuddered out. She would never forget last night, but where did they go from here? She couldn't live with his obsession for Sutter and neither could she ask Cole to give up his search. She loved his intensity, but was also aware it neglected everything, and everyone else, in his life.

She finished washing and climbed out of the water, rubbing herself dry. The sun had burned off the fog and glowed full force, heating the air around her. Still damp, she slipped into her chemise and drawers now toasted by the sun.

Cole was too much like her father and Regina didn't want to think the best things about Cole. She wanted to forget the way his eyes burned like black fire when he looked at her, his unexpected patience in teaching her the mouth harp, his immediate attempt to withdraw when he'd found she was a virgin.

She couldn't allow herself to dwell on how complete she had felt last night. Even though their joining had been fevered, greedy, aching, it was what she needed. She was hurt at his sudden aloofness, but she wasn't sorry for what had been.

"Regina?" Cole's voice came low and unexpected behind her.

She stilled and stared blindly at the gurgling stream, squinting against the mirror-sharp prisms of light bouncing off the water. She clutched the dress to her, painfully aware that she stood in only her thin undergarments, which stuck to her damp skin. She couldn't make herself turn around. "Yes?" The word was breathy, caught between hope and startlement.

"I came to see if you were all right."

"Yes. I'll be there in a moment." She didn't loosen her grip on the dress, just pressed it tighter to her breasts and wished she could cover herself. His gaze was hot on her, as tangibly heavy as the weight of a hand. She could feel it in the tingling skin on her back, the prickle of hair on her neck and arms.

"Look, about last night. I'm sorry—"

"I'm not." Lifting her chin, she blinked back the sudden sting of tears. She had hoped he had needed her as much as she had needed him.

"No, I don't mean I'm sorry it happened. I'm sorry about—" He paused, words hanging in the air between them, pulling some invisible cord of tension from her to him. "It was your first time and I wish it'd been better for you. Inside, on a bed. And I shouldn't have rushed you."

"You didn't," she put in quickly, anxious that he·

understand the decision hadn't been taken away from her. "I wanted it as much as you. I'm glad you were the first."

"It was so fast. I felt . . . like an animal."

She heard the apology in his voice, the near shame. Hope blossomed at his words, but she battled it. She was too uncertain of him, of them.

Reaching deep for strength, she turned to him and managed a gentle smile. "Nonsense. We both had a need and I'm not sorry for how it happened."

It had been a mistake to turn around. His eyes, hot, blazing, seared a path over her partially clothed body, but it was his face that tugged at her heart. Need flitted through his eyes before he masked it. His gaze made one more wary track down her body and he nodded, pivoting sharply to head back to camp.

In that instant, Regina knew Cole *had* needed her. Triumph then warmth filtered through her and for some unfathomable reason, she thought of Sarah Wellington. Even as the words jumped out, shock jarred her brain. "You didn't love her."

He froze, the muscles in his neck cording with lean tension. "What?"

She knew he understood and waited for him to answer, not really believing he would. The sun heated her back; water trickled lightly behind her. Her heart rushed like wind through a tunnel. The suspicion that Cole hadn't loved his wife had somehow been proved to Regina last night. Her heart knew in that mysterious intuitive way women sometimes have with a man who's known their body. But she wanted to hear him say it.

Long minutes passed, punctuated only by the sound of Cole's harsh breathing and the gurgle of the creek. With sharp disappointment, Regina decided he wasn't going to answer and lifted shaking hands to pull on her dress.

"I never should've married her." His voice was hoarse, the words labored. "She was Luke's from the time we were fifteen."

"Then why—"

He strode for camp, his voice terse over his shoulder. "If you want breakfast, it's ready."

She stared after him, not pleased to have had her suspicions confirmed and stunned by the scope of what he'd revealed. His vengeance for Sutter was spawned by betrayal, not love. He wasn't, as her father had been, motivated by a need for justice or protection or even adventure, but by bitterness and hate.

She loved him anyway.

She pulled the dress over her head and struggled to fasten the buttons. She thought of the fierceness of his face as he lay atop her last night, the intimidating coldness of his eyes as he talked about Sutter, the frightening rage that had distorted his features into someone unfamiliar.

Cole possessed the same intensity as Worth Harrison, the same narrow vision that neglected others. Not out of malice, but complete unawareness.

Cole's life was his to command, as was hers. She could no more ask him to give up something he felt strongly about than she could turn her back on what Wendell Cross had done.

Her love for Cole battled with a harshly learned

need for self-preservation. She had been hurt by her father's absences, his infrequent visits home. Not deliberately, but hurt just the same. Cole's sudden brusqueness hurt, too.

For her peace of mind, she had to think only of what lay ahead and not the distance that lay between them.

She was driving him crazy. Cole didn't know what he wanted from Regina, but this wasn't it.

She threw him off balance. At his deliberate distance, she exercised a quiet control that was slowly eating away at him. There had been no demands, no tears, no cold shoulder. It made him itch to get to Abe Grand as soon as possible so he could tell her—

Tell her what? That you love her? He started at the thought, flinching as though a gun had gone off close to his ear.

No, it wasn't love, but there was a bond of some kind. She had helped him last night, whether she wanted to or not. He had needed someone—her—to staunch the pain and she had.

Even so, he couldn't stop thinking about what it had been like between them, couldn't make himself halt the image in his mind of peeling away that damn high-necked blue dress she wore today and kissing every inch of velvety flesh.

Nor could he dismiss the subtle difference in his own mind, though he had neither the time nor the inclination to name it for what it really was. But in his soul he felt it.

Even through the frantic hunger of their mating last night, there had been a sweetness to her abandon, a depth of trust in her surrender that even now sent sparks of warmth licking along his nerves.

He wanted to hold her, tell her that last night was the most undeserved gift he'd ever received. The idea was not altogether unpleasant, but definitely uncomfortable.

His decision to get to Grand and call off the deal regarding Sutter was right. He didn't regret that. He just wanted to get it over with.

CHAPTER THIRTEEN

Framed in the fiery red of sunset, St. Louis was a spasm of motion and noise, a bustling city ever poised on the edge of expectancy. Cole and Regina had passed through the rapidly expanding city of Carondelet and kept east, close to the river.

Since they had entered St. Louis, Cole had felt someone following them. How he could divine anything in this chaotic mass of movement, he didn't know. But he'd learned long ago to trust his instincts.

Saturday was the day most people made their weekly trip into the big city and he watched them all with a wary eye. People hurried down streets and sidewalks, clustered next to the doors of groggeries, boardinghouses, and refineries.

An endless undulating sea of bodies surrounded him, closing in and stripping the air. The sense of suffocation spawned an urgency to get Regina somewhere safe and finish his business with Abe Grand. Now that Cole had made the decision, he couldn't shake the apprehension that something would happen to stop him.

The crush of people did nothing to reassure him and was one reason he didn't like coming to the city. Noise was the other. The low wail of steamboats, the constant buzz of people, the squeaky wheels, and the dull yet shrill blow of the train coming across the Eads Bridge collapsed in on one another, swelling in his ears until he could barely hear himself think. He kept close to Regina, his nerves strung taut with anxiety and worry.

A horse-drawn street railcar braked alongside them, its wheels screeching on the track. Since the inception of Erastus Wells's Missouri Railway Company in 1859, eight other companies had joined the city's street-railway network and their five-cent tickets were interchangeable on any line to any part of the city.

For a moment, Cole wanted to board one of the railcars and disappear among its passengers, but he needed the mobility of the horses if something happened.

He shut out the noise of horses, people shouting orders and greetings, the *eeeek* of metal on metal, but he couldn't shut out the sudden grinding sense of dread, the kind that pushed up under his ribs with the punishing blow of a fist. Every hair on his neck prickled at full attention.

Shifting in the saddle, his knee brushing Regina's thigh, he turned. His shoulders drew tight as his gaze skimmed the crowns of bowler, Stetson, and top hats, slicing to every man, woman, and child who jostled and bumped their way to another destination.

He looked twice at a man whose conspicuously large size reminded him of Sutter. Two women selling pastries and nuts pushed their way between Cole's and Regina's horses, jerking the reins from her mare. He swiftly snagged them and glanced at her. She returned his stare calmly, though her features were tight with apprehension. She took the reins from him, her knuckles white.

The city was the same as Cole remembered from his last trip of two months ago, but somehow it seemed sinister. The abruptly curving streets were a limitless refuge of invisibility. The alleys, tucked away from the gaslight of well-traveled routes, provided a welcome source of darkness. A perfect place to observe unobserved.

Again, he peered over his shoulder. A faint rosy line at the horizon remained of the sun. Dusk drifted over the city like a blanket of ash. Men dressed in the black uniform of the St. Louis Gas Light Company walked the streets lighting the gas lamps.

People went about their business, presenting no threat, their numbers thinning with the advent of darkness. Still something nagged him. Because of Regina, he saw a threat in every man's second glance at her beauty. He kept close to her, shielding her body with his, his gun loose and ready in his holster.

Time was on their side, he assured himself. They had arrived a day earlier than he'd told Grand in the telegram. Cole was glad now that he'd pushed so hard, though tomorrow the traffic in town would have been considerably less.

He'd searched every face they'd passed, but there

had been no sign of James Cross. Cole knew only death would've kept the outlaw from pursuing Regina and was fairly certain he'd mortally wounded James. But there was a threat from somewhere. He could feel it.

They halted their horses at the corner of Fourth and Carondelet to wait for a railcar to pass, and he turned to Regina. "Is there a hotel close to Grand?"

She waited for the car to clatter past then answered. "Yes. We can go straight there. It's close to the river, not far from here."

"I'd rather get you settled in first. Then I can tell him you're here."

"You?" Her eyebrows arched in surprise. "No, I want to go. He may not be here yet with—" She paused, waiting for a man to pass behind their horses. ". . . Wendell. Anyone at the agency would know me or my name. They wouldn't know you."

Cole tamped down his impatience. He hadn't thought he would have problems with her. He couldn't very well lug her in there and tell Grand he'd changed his mind. Fighting for time and the chance to undo what he'd done, he used the only argument sure to work. "We still don't know about James Cross. I think it would be better if you were somewhere safe. I'm sure Grand would agree."

She studied Cole for a long moment, her face blank. Then she nodded. "Barnum's Hotel is on Second Street, close to Abe's office, but it's expensive."

"That'll do." Cole shifted in the saddle, glancing again over his shoulder, dread still pinching his gut. Shadows shifted. Brick and stone buildings loomed.

He passed a hand over his neck, his gaze probing the darkness.

They wound their way further into the city, past the U.S. Arsenal, coming upon Fourth Street with its "Veranda Row" ladies' shops, the center of the retail trade. They turned east and he could see the roof of the Federal Customs House and post office on Third, standing where the St. Louis Theatre once had before being razed by the federal government in '51.

He made mental notes of their location, but his main concern was the growing certainty that someone followed them.

They passed the county courthouse, one wing facing Fourth, Fifth, Market, and Chestnut streets. Cole whistled in appreciation. "That is some building."

"It's beautiful inside, too."

This time he felt it, a presence behind them as tangible as his own. He turned the mare full around, the sharp movement causing her to dance on her hind legs to keep her balance. An elderly gentleman strode past, then a group of workers, dirty and grimy from a long day. They spared Cole only a cursory glance. He scanned the black pockets that were the alleys they'd passed, the jagged curve of the street.

Though he couldn't catch even a shadow, Cole knew someone followed them. Possibly Pat Cross? He had no doubt the other Cross brother would be close by for Wendell's trial. Perhaps it was Grand? Had the shrewd detective seen them enter the city?

Perhaps his nerves and the prospect of calling off the deal with Grand were making him itchy. He told himself that, but he didn't believe it.

After half a block, Regina pointed. "There it is. Barnum's."

Cole reined up and his eyebrows lifted at the towering structure. "That's some place."

"We can go somewhere else if it's too—"

"Nope. This'll be fine. It's close to Grand and the courthouse."

"All right." Regina dismounted without waiting for assistance from Cole, just as she had done the other time they had stopped that morning.

He hated this distance between them, but soon he'd be able to go to her with a clear conscience. He swung down from Horse and looped the reins over an ornate iron hitching post in front of the hotel then craned his neck. "That thing must be seven or eight stories tall."

"Six," she corrected with a smile. "It was the biggest, most plush hotel in the city for a while, but there are others now."

While Regina looped her own reins on the hitching post, he took a better look. Wrought-iron lamps, dripping with globes six deep, flanked the sidewalk in front of the hotel. Soft light flowed over the dark dirt of the street and up to the building, illuminating the imposing structure in a proud glow.

The stairs, an ivory stone marbled with a deep tan color, were polished to a glass sheen and led to two massive walnut doors fitted with brass handles and etched glass. Another lamp stood to the left of the doors.

To the right stood a black man in a crimson uniform, resplendent with brass buttons and a high crowned hat. White gloves glowed in the dusky light.

He was crisp, painstakingly clean, and put together as precisely as a soldier.

Suddenly, Cole felt Regina's body slam against his and her hand gripped his thigh. "Cole?"

Her voice was shaky, hoarse with fear. His hand went automatically over hers and he turned, his gaze following the line of her vision to a corner across the street. A beer garden bustled with activity. Crowds of men, some in expensive tailored clothes and some in tattered homemade, mingled together. But only one man caught and held Cole's attention.

There, holding a tankard of beer and standing next to a street lamp with brilliantly lit globes, was James Cross.

But even as Cole pulled Regina tighter into him, his mind refused to register the man's face as that of James Cross. It was the other brother, Pat.

The nose and forehead weren't as broad as James Cross's, but there was an eerie resemblance. The man glanced up and down the street, but not at them. Cole grabbed the saddlebags from Horse.

Taking Regina by the arm, he edged back to the front steps, intent on getting her inside as quickly as possible. "Shhh."

A streetcar rumbled past and Cole took advantage of the cover, moving her up the steps.

Next to him Regina trembled, but said in a stunned voice, "That's not James, is it?"

"It's Pat."

She sagged for a moment then visibly gathered herself and continued walking. "I can't believe how similar in looks the three of them are."

"Kind of eerie." Cole spared her a glance and walked leisurely up the steps, trying not to attract attention. He was concerned at Pat's presence, but the man obviously hadn't been the one following them through town. "You okay?"

She looked at him finally, her hand gripping his tightly. Her face was blanched white and her eyes a little frantic, but she nodded. He ushered her through the double doors held open by the black doorman.

Once inside, she released Cole's hand quickly as though only now aware she'd held it. They continued across a slick-looking floor of black and white squares to the front desk. A man in a white coat, with a thin high-carved nose, greeted them from behind an ornately carved glossy desk. He fingered a droopy mustache and twitched his nose as though it itched.

Keeping his body turned so he could see the door, Cole requested adjoining rooms. Regina didn't even protest. She didn't turn around, but kept up a nice stream of pleasantries with the man.

Cole paid for two nights in advance, glad she was keeping the desk clerk occupied so he could watch the door for signs of Pat Cross. There was a newfangled electric riding car that would take them up to their rooms on the fourth floor, but Regina frowned and shook her head. Cole refused the offer of help from a bellboy, giving him a coin for the missed job.

He and Regina walked up the sweeping staircase covered with a plush carpet of burgundy, gold, and ivory. He stayed close, but was careful not to touch her. She glanced over the banister when they rounded the corner, looking, as Cole was, for any sign of the third Cross brother. They reached their rooms in relative silence, going into hers first.

Once inside, Cole searched methodically. Under the four-poster bed, behind the heavy gold draperies, in the sprawling wardrobe, and finally in the separate water closet.

She paced the width of the room, touching the moss green satin coverlet, the brass bed knobs, and the small vanity built into the wall. Her voice was quiet, low with unvoiced suspicion and apprehension. "Why do you think Pat Cross is here?"

"For the trial." Satisfied that the room was empty, Cole faced her. "The good thing is he didn't recognize you."

"And the bad thing?"

"It won't take him long." Cole took off his hat and ran a hand through his hair. "I'll go check in with Grand and be right back."

"I'm coming with you."

"Regina, no." The words were brusque and commanding. He gentled his tone. "If that man out there doesn't know yet who you are, let's put it off a little longer. Once the trial starts, everyone in town will know your face."

"I know you're right, but I'd feel better if I were with you. And if I could see Abe for myself."

"It's better this way." Cole waited, muscles tensed in his neck and shoulders, gut clenched in hopes she would grant him this tiny space of time to undo what he'd done.

After a long pause, she nodded. Folding her arms over her chest, she studied him, eyes wary. "You'll hurry?"

"Shouldn't take long."

She reached in her dress pocket and pulled out the revolver Cole had purchased for her in Calcutta. "I've got this and I'll keep it right here."

"Good." He walked to the door, suddenly rocked by feelings of guilt. A tiny sliver of panic edged in and he wanted to reassure her as much as himself. Opening the door, he checked the hallway. All clear. He turned to her. "I'll be back soon. Don't open the door unless it's me."

"All right." She stepped toward him, her gaze solemn with unasked questions. There was also a flash of yearning in her eyes, a longing that tugged at the part of his heart she had invaded last night.

Answering her need as well as his own, he reached out and cupped her nape, pulling her to him. His head lowered and he kissed her gently, his heart filling with the essence of her.

Her fingertips rested lightly on his chest. She didn't move away, but neither did she respond. As if it were his own body, Cole could feel the battle of desire and uncertainty within her.

He heard the click of the door and the wrenchingly familiar voice at the same time. "You're gettin' careless in your old age, Wellington."

Cole went for his gun, an automatic motion rehearsed hundreds of times over the last eighteen months. The thought flashed through his mind that Sutter had been the one following them through town.

Cole spun, only to find Sutter with his revolver already leveled at him. Sutter, a good two inches taller than Cole, looked haggard and kept wary bloodshot eyes on him.

Regina moved out from behind Cole, but stayed close as she looked at the big man now standing in the room.

With a flash of the old devilry in his eyes, Sutter swept off his hat. The dark hair, a shade less than black, was longer, still wild. Red-rimmed blue eyes tracked over Regina. "Evenin', ma'am. I'm guessin' you'd be Miss Harrison."

"Who are you?" Regina drew herself up sharply, shock and confusion chasing across her features. "What do you want?"

"Mr. Grand sent me, ma'am." Sutter tipped his hat.

"Regina." Cole moved forward, torn between squeezing off a shot and grabbing her.

"Abe sent you?" She glanced at Cole, a small frown puckering her brow.

He wanted to pull her to him, tell her now while he had the chance, but it was too late.

"Aren't you going to introduce us, Cole? Seein' as it was you who set up this little meeting." The words flowed from Sutter like sap from a tree. His smile froze in his eyes.

"Cole, what's going on?" Regina stepped up, touching his elbow.

He reached for her. "Regina—"

"Luke Sutter, ma'am. At your service."

She went as still as a hammered plank and Cole's hands dropped.

The air in the room evaporated. Her voice was coarse and crinkly like singed paper. "You're . . . Luke Sutter?"

Sutter's gaze sliced to Cole, speculation sharp in the tired eyes.

"Regina, listen—"

"No."

Cole moved in front of her, his heart kicking his ribs. Her face had crumpled, desolate, waiflike, but her eyes tore at the most tender part of him. They were dead, dull, completely empty.

The words he'd planned to say died on his tongue. He had never denied coming for Sutter, but for her to find out how he'd planned to get him—

She swallowed and winced as though it hurt her throat. Twin flags of color finally warmed her ashen cheeks and she lifted her head to look straight through him. "You arranged this. While I was lying in your bed . . . bleeding."

It was a flat statement, laced with horror and disbelief. As though by saying it out loud she could make it untrue.

Sutter frowned and stepped closer. "Ma'am?"

Cole sent a glacial stare at him and turned back to her. "I don't deny that, but—"

"There are no buts." Her gaze dropped from him and focused on some faraway vision. He felt her withdrawal as though it were the warmth of a blanket leaving him on a frigid winter morning. "There never were. You *used* me to get to him. That's the real reason you came to St. Louis."

His gut clenched. Pain erupted in his heart, igniting steel-hot shards through his belly, arms, and legs. "I thought I had time to get to Grand, that I could call it off." He turned to Sutter, who watched the whole thing with a kind of confused wonder. "Get the hell out. I'll bring her myself."

Sutter, his eyes deep with pain, looked from Cole to Regina then slowly holstered his gun. He reached for the door.

"No." The word lashed through the air. Regina's voice shook and she looked at Sutter. "I'm going with you."

"The hell you are," Cole exploded, reaching for her.

"Don't touch me!" she hissed. She jerked away, her face tight with control, her eyes shooting emerald fire.

Lightning quick, Sutter moved away from the door, his gun on Cole once again. "I'm prepared to take her, Wellington."

"Try it." Cole cocked his gun. "And we can settle this now."

"You can stand here and kill each other for all I care, but I'm leaving."

Old pain and new ripped through Cole. First Sarah. Now Regina. Shooting Sutter wouldn't make her listen to him. There was nothing he could say in his defense that she would listen to. Because the horrible truth was she'd found out how calculating, how devious he'd been.

But I didn't care about you then.

The words came from nowhere and Cole bowed his head against the weight of realization. That declaration would most certainly be flung back in his face and he wouldn't blame her one bit. He clenched his fists to keep from touching her, knowing full well the betrayal she felt. He'd felt the same when he'd found Luke with Sarah.

Her gaze scraped over Cole, the light of emotion—hate—coming into her eyes for the first time since Sutter had walked in. She saw the revolver Cole still held leveled. "Are you going to use that on me?"

"Of course not."

"Put it up." She picked up her bag and turned to Sutter, who watched it all with grimness and a strange light in his crystal blue eyes.

Those eyes told Cole that Sutter knew what was between him and Regina, though Cole barely knew himself. He only knew he needed her, had wanted to forsake his deal with Grand for her, and now she was planning to go off with Sutter.

Regina walked to the door. With a pained grimace, Sutter opened it, watching Cole for some sign of movement, waiting for Cole to stop them.

But Cole was slowly dying, his insides crumbling like charred wood. Even so, the words were labored, eeked from his very core. "Regina, I'm sorry. I can only say I realized too late—"

She turned and his words jammed. Her face was powder white, eyes glimmering like heated stones. Her voice was steady, but a lone tear trembled on one eyelash. "I never thought *you* could do this."

The words twisted Cole's heart. She walked into the hallway and Sutter followed, closing the door softly. Cole stood stunned, feeling as though he had been lashed then rinsed with brine water.

He'd lost Regina and now he'd lost Sutter, too. Trying to hold on to his shredding self-control, he took a deep breath, clenching his muscles at the pain that spread through his body like fire. He had tried to do the right thing, but he hadn't been quick enough. She had left with the man who had once been his beloved friend and was now his devoted enemy.

She had left with Sutter just as Sarah had planned to.

Regina moved in a haze. Sights and smells around her distorted, even the most commonplace things swelling, gaining brutal strength. The soft white gaslight of the city blinded her, making her eyes sting, her head throb. Pain funneled through her, each shot more potent than the last. She understood now Cole's distance from her since their lovemaking.

He had intended to trade her for Sutter!

Even though she knew the words were true, part of her refused to accept it, refused to be angry. As though she could feel nothing and watched everything from a balcony far away. She allowed Luke Sutter to take her arm, vaguely aware that he guided her out the back way and into a waiting carriage. She didn't care where they went as long as she got away from Cole.

Even the pain of losing her parents hadn't been so completely devastating. She'd naively believed her whole life was ahead of her and that Wendell Cross would pay. Even though she hadn't really believed she would have a life with Cole, it hurt to realize that it had never been a possibility.

She had so hoped that something might work out. *You fool. You stupid fool.* He's never felt for you what you felt for him. He never pretended to. You saw things in him that weren't there. You knew it and yet you let yourself be coaxed back into believing the best about him.

She struggled to summon the anger, but all she felt was the sharp ripple of neverending pain. The betrayal had pierced her heart like the cold steel of a newly whetted knife, a sting at the first cut, then the deeper reaching relentless pain as the flesh of her soul felt it.

Through the trip Sutter was silent, as though he sensed one word from him would send her screaming into the night.

"Miss Harrison?"

Regina stared blankly at the hand he offered, realizing the carriage had rolled to a stop. She stepped down and Luke ushered her silently through the distantly familiar foyer of Abe Grand's ornate residence.

She wished she could disappear, melt into a puddle beneath the Aubusson carpet in Abe's sitting room. Her body shook, each part feeling like a separate joint that at any moment could blow apart and scatter into the night.

"Hello, my dear."

She submitted to the hug from Abe, but she

couldn't focus on the wrinkled patchwork face of her father's old friend.

Emily, Abe's fiery-haired wife, enveloped Regina in a warm hug. "You're so pale, Regina. Let me get you some tea."

"No, thank you." Still numb and feeling the need to escape, she croaked, "I think I'd like to lie down."

"Of course." Emily hugged her again, steering her to the stairs. "You'll feel better after you've had some rest."

Regina wasn't aware of walking up the stairs or into the bedroom provided by her friends, but a few moments later, she stood there with Emily.

The older woman frowned. "Please ring if you need anything."

Regina nodded. With one last concerned glance, Emily walked out and softly closed the door.

Still wrapped in the cold, protective, numbing shell, she lay down on the bed without removing her clothes and closed her eyes. Sometime later, her cheeks burned as though chapped. She touched them and was startled to feel the wetness upon them. A hoarse sob echoed in the room.

She'd gone, just like Sarah. And there wasn't a damn thing he could do about it.

He should be glad to be rid of her. Now he could get on with his business about Sutter. He should be glad, but he wasn't.

A roar built inside his chest, expanding, forcing its way past his tight throat. He threw his head back, struggling for breath. His ribs seemed to swell, pressing into his heart, his lungs, smothering the air there. A low moan of pain escaped him.

He kept seeing her eyes smoky with passion, felt the smooth satin thighs pulling him deeper into her, reliving the instant when his heart had opened for her. Memories that should've warmed him, but instead drove through him like a spike.

She'd cost him Sutter. Cole tried to focus on this fact, lay the blame for what had just happened on her. He kept seeing her face, impassioned as they talked about their different ways of gaining justice, sweet with surrender as he took her body, hollow with the yearning for reassurance moments ago.

Fueled by anger and a desperate need to wash her image from his mind, he slammed out the door and down to the front desk. He brought the bottle of whiskey, aged in a Georgia cellar for fifteen years, back to his room.

He was good and well drunk inside of two hours and didn't give a damn.

He didn't know when he fell asleep, but when he opened his eyes, the sky was the gray blue of a pigeon's belly and the sun a pink disc on the horizon. His head felt as though it had been split and stuffed with burlap. His mouth tasted like whipped dirt. He squinted against the pale first light of day and groaned at the shaft of pain that sliced through his head.

He tried to summon up Regina's face and her features were blurry. But the guilt was there. And anger. And panic. He had to reach her. Where had Sutter taken her?

And where was Sutter? Regina would be in town for the trial. Sutter could already be gone.

Cole knew it was his fault he'd lost her. He had to get to her and try to explain, even though the words wouldn't be worth a tinker's damn. But, as much as he wanted to go to her, he knew his business with Sutter still stood between them.

It would take only a short time to settle the score with Sutter, then Cole could go to Regina free of the past.

"Any luck?"

"No." Pat Cross shook his head in answer to his brother's question about seeing Regina Harrison.

"No detectives either?" Wendell gripped the steel bars that separated him from his brother. "Not even Sutter or any of the others who brought me back from Mexico?"

Again Pat shook his head.

The pair of them spoke low and guarded their words so as not to alert the four sentrys in the room. Pat glanced over his shoulder at the closest guard, who watched them with slitted eyes.

"That girl's here, I know it. If there's a trial . . ." Wendell hissed the words, letting the urgency and venom color his voice.

Pat stepped up and whispered, "If it gets to trial, she'll be there. Then she's dead for sure."

Wendell knew his brother had something more to tell him. The look of suppressed rage and deep-reaching loneliness in Pat's eyes alerted him.

Wendell said one word, but asked a wealth of questions. "James?"

Anger tightened Pat's features and he shook his head. "He's dead."

"You're sure?" Wendell's voice shook with sadness and shocked anger.

"I found him in the cave."

Wendell put a hand on his brother's shoulder and squeezed. *Get me out of here.*

His brother understood as though he'd spoken the words.

CHAPTER FOURTEEN

Where had Sutter taken Regina? How was she? Had she slept? Or, like him, had she not even tried? The questions hammered at Cole as they had all night. He couldn't drown them with whiskey nor could he drown the guilt. As long as he lived, he would never forget the hollow abandoned look in her green eyes.

Past the tendons and marrow, deep in a secret place he'd thought dead long ago, his body ached at what he'd done to her. How was he going to fix it? Had he lost her for good?

He told himself to head for the east end of town and start looking for Sutter. He found himself, instead, at Third and Washington, staring at a small brick building sandwiched between a tailor that boasted international renown and an insurance office.

Half-closed shutters lent an air of discretion and camouflaged the bars reinforcing the windows. The place was distinguished and subtly elegant. A brass door plaque quietly announced to visitors the offices of the Abe Grand Detective Agency. He didn't expect to be greeted warmly or even get answers, but he was going in.

Several people ventured inside; few came back out. Exiting, he supposed, by a back door. Cole waited, noting belatedly that there was no sign of Sutter here.

He wanted Sutter, fiercely enough that it tasted like bile on his tongue, but Cole had to know how Regina was.

The sun played tag with a clump of clouds and the air was thick and flat. He weaved his way across the street, dodging a railcar and a stagecoach and spooking the team of a milk wagon. Curses from the driver of the milk wagon followed him, but Cole didn't look back.

He deliberately left his gun loose and in plain sight as he walked up to the door. It was made of solid mahogany, with three brass locks and thick glass that distorted the view inside. His gut clenched and his hands were clammy on the brass knob as he pushed open the door. It opened easily, silently.

His nerves splayed like drawn fiddle strings across his neck. The bitter tinge of cigar smoke hung in the air. Two desks bracketed either side of a room bordered with oak cabinets that stood at precise attention.

No bell jingled to announce Cole's arrival, but suddenly there was a voice behind him.

"May I help you?"

Cole turned, recognizing the clerk he'd tried to "persuade" with his Smith & Wesson regarding information about Sutter a couple of months ago.

"You!" The anemically pale man recognized Cole as well. Dark eyes widened and anger replaced surprised dismay. Slender reed-thin fingers dipped into a spotless black sack coat reaching, Cole knew, for a gun.

He didn't blame the man, but he also didn't want any trouble. Cole fingered the butt-end of his revolver. "That won't be necessary. I just came to talk to Mr. Grand."

"If you intend to use the same method you used on me, I think I'll need this." The clerk withdrew a small derringer.

Cole spread his hands in a show of peace. "Look, I don't want any trouble. Just to talk to Mr. Grand."

"It's all right, Hutchins." A battered gravelly voice came from behind Cole. "I'll talk to the man."

Cole arched an eyebrow at Hutchins, silently testing the wisdom of turning around. The clerk lowered the gun, but kept it in plain sight.

Cole turned and faced Abe Grand. Small pillows of smoke curled from a stubby cigar. The man was a full head shorter than Cole, dressed in a baggy brown sack coat, rumpled shirt, and wrinkled trousers. "Abe Grand?"

"Yes." The older man had a kind voice, matched by kind brown eyes until they tracked over Cole. With surprising swiftness, the eyes hardened, became frosty, unyielding. Cole suspected the man had an intuitive nature and acknowledged a silent respect even as he also recognized that Grand perceived him as a threat.

He stared at the man, taking in features that seemed to be all loose skin and mismatched parts. The face was not unpleasant, but arranged almost haphazardly.

Even as Cole stared, the features changed. Though the right side of Grand's face sagged, the features meshed together in an implacable mask. Impressive and intimidating.

But it was Grand's eyes that had Cole mentally checking the number of cartridges in his revolver. The deceptive loose-limbed movements, the intelligent eyes that could turn ruthless in a millisecond, told Cole that here was a shrewd, complex, and potentially lethal force.

He stuck out his hand. "Cole—"

"Wellington," Grand finished, his voice pleasant, almost conversational. The eyes were hard and probing. "I'd like to arrest you. What you did could amount to kidnapping."

So, Regina had told Grand the story. The muscles across Cole's neck knotted. "She came with me of her own free will."

"Perhaps." Speculation and anger gleamed in the brown eyes. "That girl is special to me. Despite risk to herself, she helped my men immensely, just as her father did."

Tension pulsed from the man in front of him. Cole thumbed his hat back on his head and spoke evenly. "I only want to know if she's all right."

"As you can well imagine, Mr. Wellington, you're not a person to whom I'm inclined to give that information."

"Yes, I understand." Cole didn't offer any explanation about what he'd done. That was between him and Regina *and* Sutter. But he needed to know how she was and Grand needed to know there was a real threat to her safety. "Pat Cross is in town. Saw him last night over by Barnum's."

"Yes, I'd heard." The words were calm and dismissive. Probing eyes speared Cole.

He knew he would get no answers by pussyfooting around. He also doubted he would get any by a direct question, but he decided what the hell. "You've seen her?"

Grand stuck one hand in his trouser pocket and shifted to rest one hip on the desk behind him. "I have."

"And?" Cole struggled to keep the impatience out of his voice, but the uncertainty drilled into him like the blunt end of a spear. "Damn, can't you just tell me she's all right?"

"No, I can't." Grand's voice hardened to flint. The brown eyes burned black with fanatic fever. "She's . . . hurt."

His tone left no doubt that he blamed Cole for that.

Cole's chest caved as though he'd been poleaxed. He clenched his teeth and strove to keep the pain from his face. If only he'd realized how wrong he'd been to use her to get to Sutter!

Hutchins perched behind him, silently waiting. Cole fought the urge to rub his neck and allowed a bitter smile to twist his lips. "You won't tell me where she is?"

"She's no longer your concern."

Grand was probably right, but it wedged like stray shrapnel in Cole's chest, heavy, cold, piercing. First,

Sutter had protected her from Cole, and now this disheveled hawk of a man was doing the same. It was too much. "I'll find her."

"Not with my help." *And over my dead body*. The words were unspoken though clear in the tight voice. The eyes were still guarded, but there was a subtle light of speculation in them as he watched Cole carefully.

Inwardly, Cole cursed. He'd known he'd get nowhere here. He'd thought perhaps—What? That she might want to see him, even if only to give him the tongue-lashing he deserved? "I'll be at the trial."

"It's open to the public." Grand didn't give an inch even though Cole thought he detected a grudging respect in those eyes.

He turned to go, his insides aching, churning with the need to know she was all right. She had looked so hurt, so lost, and it was his fault. Was she raging or was she reacting as she had after they had chased James Cross away from the cave, trying to bear up, but crumbling inside?

He opened the door and noises from the street drifted in—the hustle of morning business traffic, jingling keys, the flutter of oilskin shades being lifted to begin a new day. Coal smoke from a sugar refinery down the street laced the air and was underlined by the faint hint of unwashed bodies.

He stood at the edge of Third Street, hesitant for the first time in eighteen months. Thoughts of Regina tortured him. Memories of the pain in her eyes haunted him and the disbelief in her voice wrenched his insides. His chest tightened and his body screamed for him to go to her, but where was she?

He'd gotten no answers from Grand about her, seen no sign of Sutter. What the hell was he going to do?

His gut churned with the impatience and desire to search for her now, though he knew things wouldn't be different between them until he'd had a chance at Sutter.

His heart and logic split, unraveling like strands of a frayed rope. The aching pull between desire and vengeance made him feel impotent and almost hopeless.

Heat prickled in his throat as he made his decision.

On his way to the jail, Cole sent a wire to Leah, explaining to his sister the truth about Regina and that she was a witness in a murder trial. He arrived at the jail to find a crush of newspapermen milling about the doors, but he managed to slip inside without drawing their attention.

Sutter wasn't there. Cole did catch a glimpse of Wendell Cross and learned the trial would start Tuesday. Which gave him less than two days to find Regina and talk to her. He tried to shut his mind off from thoughts of her. He combed the city, telling himself the entire time that he would find Sutter then go to Regina.

His eye searched for Sutter's massive frame, but in his mind, Cole saw a tall slender woman. He scanned the crowds for a dusty limp black hat topping ragged dark hair and saw instead the surprising fall of black satin in a livery in Calcutta.

He wondered where Sutter was hiding. Was Regina with him? Cole wondered if Sutter watched him. If Regina thought of him. Did her body ache to feel Cole's heat as he ached to feel hers?

He traversed the length of town from the elegant residential street of Lucas Place, between Thirteenth and Jefferson, to the poverty pockets on the northwest fringes of downtown. Areas named "Wildcat Chute," "Clabber Alley," and "Castle Thunder" were inhabited by what respectable people called "vicious characters." At Clabber Alley, Cole narrowly escaped a knife fight.

There was no sign of Sutter anywhere. Cole was starting to wonder if he had already left town on another assignment, though Cole couldn't imagine him not staying for the Cross trial.

Exasperated that he was no closer to finding Sutter, Cole gave free rein to the impulse that had scratched at him all day. He was going to look for Regina, and he would start at Abe Grand's. It was pure hunch, but he had nothing to lose.

"I'd like to get my hands on him for just one minute." The heated words only served to whet Regina's temper. She wished for something to hit, namely Cole Wellington.

Sunlight, harsh and draining, baked her through the clear glass of the double doors leading from the room to the veranda. She was weak and wounded and part of her ached to close herself off from everyone. But the rage was stronger.

Since she'd woken this morning, the fog had faded

from her mind, the disbelief and vague realization that
Cole had used her to get to Sutter. Anger burned deep
and fervent, needing nothing more to stoke it than
words or even a stray thought. Sorrow underscored
the anger, and, hate it though she might, a frantic need
to understand. .

Luke Sutter sat in a deep burgundy leather chair
across the dark paneled library. Cole's friend-turned-
enemy was as handsome as Cole. And to Regina, there
was a slight resemblance though Sutter was two or
three inches taller.

His shoulders were as broad as a door frame and
she suspected many a woman had leaned on them.
Brawny arms and a wide muscle-planed chest testified
to a Goliath-type strength. He was the biggest man
she had ever seen.

His long ragged hair was black, like Cole's, but his
eyes were a clear spring blue. Friendly, yet they could
also be piercing and haunted.

Since last night, he hadn't been further than ten feet
from her, standing watch outside her door and keeping her company since breakfast.

Two black mastiffs, each as large as a small pony,
lounged at Luke's feet. The dogs' heavy-lidded eyes
stretched open occasionally then closed again to be
followed by soft snores. Luke watched Regina with
equal parts wry amusement and puzzlement as if he
wasn't quite sure how serious she was about wanting
to hurt Cole.

She was very serious. Memories taunted her, gentle
unwelcome ones slipping in among painful ones. He
hadn't lied when she'd asked him directly about Sut-

ter. Still, her heart burned as though he had. She had known he would do whatever he deemed necessary to get his enemy, but she certainly hadn't thought that would include using her.

Especially not after what they'd shared on the trail. Even now her blood steamed at the thought of his body entwined with hers. A telling tingle started low in her belly and she closed her eyes until it passed.

For every curse she wanted to utter, another memory would float to the surface. How his hands cradled her while they made love. The way his lips, hard and demanding, ignited a flame deep inside. The lonely refrain of "The Blue Danube Waltz" echoed in her mind and her heart twisted.

She didn't want to remember those things, only the bleak realization that he had used her, the surprise and guilt on his face when Sutter had showed up at the hotel last night.

"You're in love with him." There was no surprise in Sutter's voice, only a soft understanding.

Regina shot a glance at him and fought the urge to cover her burning cheeks. She wanted to deny it and couldn't, so she said nothing.

"Have you told him?" Sutter pushed himself out of the wingback chair, unfolding his massive frame. He towered in the room even with its high molded ceiling.

She bit back a bitter laugh. "There's no need. I can't accept what he does."

"You mean chasing me?" The big man stepped in front of her, drawing her gaze up the neatly pressed blue-checked shirt and to his face. Blue eyes smiled warmly at her.

"Yes."

"You don't even know me that well." He smiled gently, teasing.

"Well enough," she quipped then sighed. "He can't let go of the past and move on. I've spent all the time in the past that I want to."

"Yeah, but what happened to him was—" He paused, a frown knotting his brow. "You do know what happened?" It wasn't a question as much as a solemn confirmation.

She nodded.

"That would be hard on any man."

"Is it true? Were you going to run off with his wife and raise his child?" Asking the question raised a new welt of pain on her heart, for Cole and for Luke, but she had a desperate need to know.

Sutter looked down at the smooth, polished floor. With the toe of one scuffed boot, he lifted the fringed edge of the Aubusson carpet of gold and cream. His jaw worked and when he met Regina's gaze, a shaft of pain shot through his eyes. "I wanted to."

"But you didn't?" Some of her own pain was forgotten as she tried to grasp what he was telling her. "He said he never should've married her, that she belonged to you. What did he mean?"

Her voice was gentle, almost a whisper. In a way, she felt as though she were trespassing, but she wanted to hear Luke's story. Perhaps it would help her understand why Cole couldn't let go, why he had used her the way he had.

Luke stared at her, eyes haunted and dark, reminding her for a split second of Cole. It was the intensity of his gaze, the shadowed pain, and her heart ached. He gave a crooked smile, but it didn't cover the hurt in his eyes.

"I was betrothed to Sarah. We'd had an understanding since we were fifteen. Cole and I went off to university and I got involved with detective work. Allan Pinkerton." Luke turned and walked over to a bookcase that stretched from floor to ceiling, running his finger along the gleaming wood. "Anyway, when we graduated, Cole came back to Calcutta. I stayed on in Chicago with the agency. I made good money and planned to marry Sarah the next spring. Then the war came."

The words tugged at her, hinting at some deep hurt she was about to witness and shouldn't. "Did you and Cole fight together?"

"No. He was with a Missouri regiment at the time, fighting for the Union. I was further south, posing as a Confederate soldier and working for Pinkerton. Allan didn't do so well during the war. His methods weren't cut out for the military so he withdrew, but I stayed on with another outfit. One night, during a raid"—he paused and muttered "—it was stupid to go, but we did.

"Anyway, I was caught. They discovered I was feeding information to the North and they were going to kill me. I managed to escape across the border into Illinois. My commanding officer thought it would be better if Luke Sutter disappeared, so I was listed as dead."

She drew in her breath, stunned at what she was

beginning to understand. "Cole thought you were dead?"

"Sarah, too." He paused, his jaw working and he rubbed his forehead as though to erase the memories. "By the time it was safe for me to come back, Cole and Sarah were married. There was nothing for me at home anymore, so I came to St. Louis. Started working for Grand."

"But what about Sarah? Cole thought she was, that you and she were . . . together." Luke's gaze sliced to her and Regina blushed, wishing she had eased into her question, but he didn't seem offended.

"I was angry at both of them. If I'd come back . . ." He shrugged. "Everyone was picking up their lives, moving on. I worked out of St. Louis, traveled a lot, and came home to visit my parents a few times. It was on one of those trips, when I heard about my mother's death, that I saw Sarah. She found me in the family cemetery."

His hands clenched on the red-toned wood of the bookshelf. "I knew it was wrong, that I shouldn't come back, but I couldn't help myself. It felt so good just to talk to her." His head whipped around and blue eyes burned through Regina. "We met several times, but I never touched her. Never. Not until that night."

"The night Cole found you?" Regina's heart ached, swollen with pain for the man in front of her and for Cole. Luke had stayed away because he thought Cole loved Sarah. Regina knew Cole hadn't and the knowledge nearly drew a moan of pain from her. She hoped Luke never found out.

"All I did was hold her at first." Luke puffed out a deep breath, his voice shaking. "I didn't know what plans she'd made. When she told me she wanted to go away, that she was going to tell Cole, I was stunned. I said no, but I wanted to. Lord, how I wanted it."

His jaw clenched. Guilt ravaged his face. "I thought about it, too. Hard enough to count my money and try to figure out where we'd live. But I couldn't do it. I couldn't ask her to live like that and I couldn't do it to Cole. He was like a brother to me." Luke paused, a sad smile ghosting his lips. "We shared blood in grade school, in a secret pact."

The memories faded from his face and his voice cracked. "I wasn't going to do it. I told her so. I told her I was leaving and not coming back," he said vehemently, as though even now Sarah would hear him and believe.

Regina's throat tightened. The truth was so horrible, yet so compelling, she had to know. She forced out the question. "And Cole found you then, didn't he?"

"Yes." He hung his shaggy head between giant shoulders, looking defeated and so forsaken that Regina wanted to touch him, offer him some sort of shelter from the pain. "It was horrible. He nearly killed me and I nearly killed him. In the end, it was Sarah who died.

"She lost the baby, you know?" Luke turned to Regina, eyes hollow with guilt. "He blames me." His eyes faded to dull slate-blue, focused on his private hurt, so reminiscent of Cole that fierce pain stabbed Regina's heart.

"Luke, it was an accident. I told Cole that and I'm telling you." She touched his arm, aching to offer some sort of comfort. "You've got to know that's the truth. This has almost destroyed you and Cole. You've both lost so much, but you lost the woman you loved, not once but twice. I'm so sorry."

His gaze met hers, wet and piercingly blue. Faint color tinged his cheeks and he offered a self-deprecating smile. "What a mess. I'm sorry you're in the middle of this. I wish I could help you."

Luke's story didn't fit with Cole's. She struggled to understand, wondering if Cole had lied about his wife and best friend. "You weren't ever with her?"

"What?" Luke looked at her, eyes dazed and bleak.

"Cole thought she was unfaithful, with you."

"No. Only in my heart. I loved her. He knew that."

"Did you ever tell him the truth?" Her voice rose even as she tried to smother the hope that she could help both Cole and Luke find some peace.

He shrugged. "Sure I did. But he didn't believe me."

"Of course not." She turned away, her heart sinking. Cole hadn't believed Luke eighteen months ago. Why would he believe Luke now?

"He's not an easy man to love, Regina."

"Amen!" she snapped, her anger simmering again. Hearing Luke's story brought home how much Cole was ruled by his past. The thought made her clench her teeth.

She walked to the fireplace and stared down at the clean hearth. Part of her wanted to go out and find Cole Wellington, give him a piece of her mind. But part of her was afraid. She was too connected to him, could still feel his body melded with hers and those thoughts gave him an unwelcome power over her.

Sutter spoke behind her, his voice soft with remembrances. "You should've known him then. He was a real charmer. He was never much of a talker, but he could get us out of almost anything."

"I don't doubt it," she muttered, thinking of his boldness and devilish charm when he'd thought she was a nun. "Why are you defending him?"

Luke was silent for a moment. "I've had a lot of time to think. In his shoes, I don't know that I would've done any differently."

"He's looking for you."

"I know. He's never made any secret of it."

"You shouldn't be here."

The big man shrugged and his eyes twinkled with the light she was coming to realize didn't dim easily. "I'm going to watch you put Wendell Cross behind bars. His brother won't be far behind. We've been gathering evidence on their little operation for a long time. While Wendell's been on the run, James and Pat have been robbing trains and stagecoaches. Besides, I don't think they'll let him take the blame alone."

She frowned. "What do you mean? Won't they be caught if they try anything? Abe's men are everywhere."

"They're a close family."

Regina found the idea foreign, but she probably shouldn't. There was no doubt a code of some kind even among killers and thieves.

"Plus, if James is dead . . ."

"Do you think he is?" She knew Cole did, but she wasn't sure.

Luke nodded. "If he weren't, he'd be here. You could set the clock on it."

She shivered, thinking of meeting Wendell in court as well as his brother Pat. At least James Cross didn't seem to be a threat anymore and Regina knew she should be grateful to Cole for that.

Abe appeared suddenly in the doorway, a smile crinkling his shaggy face. "Afternoon, you two."

"Abe." Luke glanced up then turned toward the door.

"Hello, Abe." Regina walked over and placed a kiss on the weathered cheek. "Where's Emily?"

"Gone to help at the hospital for a while." He patted her shoulder and grinned, softening the awkward angles of his face. "I've got something for you." He held out a piece of paper.

Regina took it then blinked. "It's a bank draft. For five thousand dollars. Why?"

"It's the reward money offered for Cross."

"But I didn't find him, you did." She pushed the check back at him, but he refused it. "I can't take this."

"You can and you will." Abe leaned over and kissed her on the forehead. "Without your help, we wouldn't be able to put him in jail."

"Don't you want to wait and see if that happens?"

Abe's eyes softened. "It's for your father, too."

"But you already sent me his back pay. A long time ago."

"It's yours, Regina. You might as well take it."

"But what will I do with it?" She looked from him to Luke, stunned and feeling a curl of joy.

"Whatever you want." Abe hugged her, his smoky jacket teasing her nostrils. He spoke over her shoulder to Sutter. "Could I see you a minute?"

"Again?" Regina smiled. "You are a busy man, Abe."

"No rest for the wicked, my dear. You know that."

She hugged him, bid Luke good-bye, and walked to the stairs. The check in her hand felt foreign, strange. A hand on her arm stopped her and she turned.

"Don't give up on him, Regina." Luke stared up at her, his eyes fervent with a plea.

Her eyes stung, the check forgotten. "I don't know if it matters anymore."

"It does. Believe me." He squeezed her arm and followed Abe to the front door.

Anger still burned, but she couldn't stop Luke's words. The whole story was so tragic and set her teeth on edge. What Emmett Wellington had told Cole was true. Cole perceived that Luke had wronged him, but he had taken the memories of their friendship and his relationship with Sarah from himself.

Was there any way to make him put the past to rest? Could she do what his family had been unable to? Pain and anger and sorrow throbbed in her breast.

After what he'd done, why should she want to try? Because she loved him, even now.

The answer was a sharp, bitter-edged reminder that

she hadn't given up on him yet. *And for that, Regina Suzanne, you're a fool.*

He'd been to Lucas Place once today, but at night it was even more impressive. The owner of the tailor shop next door to Grand's, a Monsieur DuBois, had been more than helpful in volunteering Grand's home address. DuBois had been invited to Christmas dinner last year after his wife's death and he wanted his driver to take Cole there himself. He finally settled for giving Cole directions.

Now, standing across the street that glowed like milk in the lamplight, Cole stared over at the mansion. There was no other word for the house. The detective business must be very lucrative. Grand's home was a two-story affair, so tailored and opposite the rumpled man that it brought a half-smile.

The residence was understated and elegant and surrounded by a twelve-foot-tall wrought-iron fence. Cole slipped across the well-lit street and through the open gates. The house, ablaze with light, was of mellowed stone and gilded to a pearly gold by surrounding lamps. Slender columns marched across the porch and supported the second-story veranda.

As Cole drew nearer, keeping close and low to the shrubs that lined the drive, he could make out doors on the second floor. All led to the veranda. Did one of those rooms belong to Regina?

His heart ached. Anticipation and apprehension prickled his neck at seeing her.

Lamps glowed from the two rooms on the end, the

other three were dark. Cole edged closer, trying to figure a way to get on the veranda without being invited inside.

Then he saw a tiny staircase at one end of the house, flush with the stone wall and leading to the second story. He stepped into the shadows of a magnolia tree and headed for the west end of the house, his heart thudding like the heavy strike of a hammer on an anvil.

I can only say I realized too late. Like a repeating chord, Cole's words of last night echoed in her head. What had he meant? Realized what?

Regina rubbed her temples, trying to vanquish the words just as she had tried all day. She didn't care. She shouldn't care. He had betrayed her. He had intended to trade her for Sutter, used her callously for his own ends.

She had known he was driven, relentless in his pursuit for revenge. She should be able to believe by now what he'd done to her. Hadn't he pushed away even his own family?

The dogs stayed outside her door as they had last night. She walked into her room, barely noticing the fluffy high bed, the cozy game table and two chairs in the corner, the long mirror attached to the wardrobe.

One of the servants had lit the lamp in the corner next to the bed and shadows capered along the wall. The air was thick and moist, the room suddenly crowding. She changed clothes, putting on a borrowed nightdress and wrapper that rode two inches above her ankles.

The clothes were cooler, but still stuck to her sweat-dampened skin. Her anger, like the summer heat, hadn't dissipated even with the descent of darkness. She opened the doors that led to the veranda.

The air moved freer here though still warm. She stepped outside, too wrought up to think about going to bed. Her conversation with Luke replayed in her head. Why couldn't Cole believe the truth? Probably because he'd been hurt at the time.

Stop it. Do not find excuses for him. Luke was his friend and Cole should've believed him. That thought joined others in making her blood boil.

She paced from her door to the stone banister, the veranda warm beneath her bare feet. If she ever saw Cole again, she would tell him exactly what she thought and say good riddance.

"Regina?"

She froze, trying to discern if she had really heard the voice or just imagined it.

It came again, urgent and closer this time. "Regina."

She whirled, her heart stuttering to a stop before picking up a sporadic beat. He stood only a foot away, close enough for her to touch him. Though half-shadowed by darkness, she could make out the angled features of his face, the glitter of devil-black eyes, the latent power in his stance.

Her lungs swelled in an instant of joy. Then anger flooded her at his gall, at the betrayal, at the traitorous leap of her senses on seeing him.

Acting on pure reflex, she drew back her hand and

slapped him across the face. Then she launched for the door.

In a blur of movement, he shot around her, slamming the door and pressing his body against it while grabbing her with both hands.

"Let me go," she hissed. He held her arms immobile, but not her feet. She twisted and writhed and kicked him. It hurt her more than it did him, but she didn't care. "Let me go. You are despicable. I can't believe you had the nerve to come here. If Abe finds you—"

"He knows I want to talk to you."

"I have nothing to say to you." Hard hands bit into her arms, bruising in their strength, but still she struggled, desperate to get away from him. Even now a tiny part of her heart wanted him and the realization only made her more furious. "Get out of here."

"Not until I've seen how you are."

"You've seen. Go or I'll—"

"Scream the house down?" His voice was silky with the certainty that she wouldn't. "You could've already done that." His eyes glittered like black diamonds, honing in on her like a hawk.

She lifted her chin, hating herself for not screaming and him for pointing it out. Anger and hurt boiled inside her. At that moment, she became aware that her breasts teased his chest. His thighs bracketed hers. He smelled of warm male and midnight. Danger.

Her feet stilled and she stiffened, trying to hold herself away from him. She didn't want to feel his warmth or smell the musky scent of his flesh. "What do you want?"

"To talk to you."

"I don't know where Luke is."

"That's not what I want." Pain flashed through his eyes, and regret. "I'm sorry about that."

She glared at him, her lips pressed tightly together, her jaw aching from the control she was trying to exercise. *Just hear him out and he'll leave.* She held onto the words as though they were her sanity hanging by a gossamer thread.

His hands loosened on her arms and dropped away. The words came slowly, testing. "I came for you."

Her heart shifted in her chest and pain showered through her. "Then you came for nothing."

"I want to apologize."

Regina let her suspicion and distrust show on her face. The sadness and loss in his eyes could not be stronger than what she felt. Nor the fresh rip of betrayal at his presence. She moved away, angling for the door, seeking some sort of support and distance from him.

His gaze stroked over her, taking in the unbound hair, the wrapper that had come loose during their struggle, the nightdress that skimmed her ankles. He wanted her. Even the darkness and pain couldn't hide the fact.

"Stop it." She drew the wrapper together and yanked the tie into a knot. Her next step toward the door was automatic.

"Don't go." He swept off his hat and crushed it against his thigh. His breath came out on a ragged sigh. "I'm not doing this very well, but I want to apologize. For everything."

She refused to let her heart soften. He only wanted something from her and she wouldn't give it to him. She watched him, reminded of how dangerous she had once thought him.

He looked uncomfortable and awkward, but sincere. She ignored that observation and turned for the door.

"From the very beginning. I never should've used you the way I did, but the opportunity seemed a godsend." He gave a wry laugh. "No pun intended."

She stiffened, torn between wanting to run and wanting to turn and punch him until she cried. Her chest swelled like raw skin stretched over a wound.

"When I discovered you were an indirect link to Sutter, I had to take it. I just never counted on—"

"What?" His words drew across her ragged nerves like glass on a boil and she nearly screamed. Her entire body shook with anger and apprehension; her slight hold on control snapped. "You never counted on my being so gullible, so drawn to you?"

She spun to face him, letting her own pain show in her eyes, wanting him to know how he had hurt her. Rage washed through her in a scalding flow. "You knew that, of course. Knew I wanted you even though I was supposed to be 'above' such things."

"Damn it, I never counted on caring about you." His voice was harsh and loud, urgent. "I never meant to hurt you. It wasn't supposed to happen like this. I had already changed my mind and planned to meet with Grand, tell him I couldn't go through with it. Sutter showed up before I could."

"Why couldn't you just tell me? Why did you have

to let me believe you came to St. Louis out of concern for me?"

"I did, damn it! I'm telling you now."

"Please." Her voice shook and tears burned her eyes. "Please, don't lie to me anymore."

"I'm not. What I felt—feel—for you is honest. I was a blind stupid fool. I thought I could fix what I'd done before it was too late. I care about you. I wronged you and that hurts me more than I ever thought it could." He paused, his chest heaving, his breath jagged and shallow. "I was after Sutter. No one else was supposed to get hurt."

He cared about her? She wanted to put her hands over her ears, block out the words she had once prayed to hear, but she couldn't. Her body tingled then numbed. Why did he have to say them now, after what he'd done?

Damn her traitorous heart for softening! She ached to feel his arms around her, his face in her hair. The thought sent a cold slice of fear through her and she pressed toward the door. If she stayed, she would do something stupid, like go to him, and she would hate herself.

"Don't go. I came here to tell you how I feel." His words tore at her heart, telling her he felt lost and all alone in the world. She knew how he felt because she'd felt it herself the day before. "Regina, haven't you heard anything I've said?"

"Yes." She tried to gather her voice, but it was rusty, thick with suppressed tears and rage. "But it really doesn't matter now."

"You don't mean that. I know you need time, but—"

"No, Cole. Don't you see?" She couldn't look at him. If she did, she would see those eyes, drawing her in, urging her to lose herself in them, and she couldn't bear it. "It won't work."

He stepped toward her, his face harsh in the drifting light of the house. "I needed you that night. I still do."

"For what?" she cried, her stomach knotting in pain. "To prove you're alive, that you can feel something?" She gasped for hard-won breath, hating herself for saying the next words. "To remind you of what you lost?"

His face paled, white-gray in the shadows. A muscle flexed in his jaw. "This has nothing to do with any of that."

"Yes, it does." Her voice cracked. "You made it that way."

Fists clenched at his sides. His voice lowered, though still shaky. "We won't be here forever, Regina. Soon we'll be home and then—"

"Would you give up your search for Sutter?" She forced herself to look at his face, to store away in her memory the disbelief and embers of anger in his eyes. "Can you come to me free of the past, free of the hate?"

His throat worked. Reluctance and fervor and a plea rushed through his eyes. Indecision flirted there, but the words she wanted didn't come. "I thought you understood. You know what he did to me."

"Yes. I remember what you said." Her words

sounded hollow, echoing round in her mind. She braced herself for his reaction. "I also know his side."

Pain flared in his eyes and his face hardened. "Well, you've been busy."

His words lashed her as he'd meant them to. She gripped the stone wall of the house, blasted tears blurring her vision. "I'm not asking you to give up your search for Sutter. I'm asking if you could."

Long seconds ticked by, swollen with regrets, pain, hurtful words. His voice was hoarse. "I'm not asking you to give up Cross and your father's memory."

There was her answer. She studied his face, knowing the image would have to last the rest of her life. She memorized the small sun wrinkles around his eyes, the weathered creases in his cheeks, the firm unyielding mouth that had given her so much pleasure, the late day growth of beard. She nodded, her heart rending.

When she would've turned to go, he reached out and captured her hair with one hand.

Guarded, muscles tense, she simply stood there for a moment. He wound his fist in the silk of her hair and pulled her toward him. Panic edged in.

Gently yet ruthlessly he pulled her and his gaze never left hers. The black depths burned with the secret of what they'd shared and what he wanted to do to her. The blatant desire in his eyes stripped her breath.

"You want me as much as I want you."

She couldn't tear her gaze from his nor could she staunch the tears that sprang to her eyes. "Don't do this."

"You won't be able to forget what it was like with us. I'll be there when you wake in the middle of the night. I'll haunt your dreams. Your mind will take me over your body and inside—"

"Stop it," she burst out. She tried to pull away from him, frightened and desperate to escape. "I can't live like that. As an afterthought, a place for you to rest and recoup between the daring and the hate and the bungled searches. That isn't what matters here. We're past that, can't you see?"

Frantic to convince him, her words tumbled out. "I know you think you need to go after Sutter. I'm not asking you to quit. But you can't ask me to live with it." Her voice was thick with panic and unshed tears. She had to get away from him, but he had to let her go on his own. She didn't know why it was so important that he choose to let her go, but it was paramount.

Black fire sparked his eyes and he lowered his head to hers. She didn't try to avoid him, but looked at him with sadness and determination. Tears trickled down her cheeks. His lips stopped an inch away from hers, his breath feathering her sensitive skin. Her heart twisted.

He untangled his hand from her hair and freed her. Pain and anger fired his dark eyes. She took a step back, groping behind her for the door. Another step and she touched the knob.

"Regina." His voice grated out, full of the same loss she felt. "Say you understand that I tried to do the right thing. Forgive me." The words were hoarse, raw with undiluted hurt. "Give me some peace."

While disguised as a nun, she'd heard the words

before, always from some dying man or a patient of Doc Warren's caught in the last throes of fever, but never had it touched her as it did now. The simple plea in Cole's voice snatched her breath and nearly destroyed her willpower. The hurt lanced through her, lethal, potent.

If she'd been damned to eternal hell, she couldn't have said the words. She fled into the bedroom and locked the door behind her. Broken cries shattered the silence of the room and she realized they were hers.

CHAPTER FIFTEEN

The pain soaked into her pores, her soul, like a slow-spreading poison. Would it ever stop? Even though Regina had known by the torture on Cole's face that his apology was sincere, his manipulation of her wasn't something she could easily forgive.

She hadn't been able to tell him so, but there was a part of her that did believe he hadn't meant to hurt her, that he had intended to call off his deal with Grand.

She didn't want to believe it, didn't want to understand or reach out to him. The pain inside went deeper than her knife wound ever had and refused to ebb.

Cole was a dark man, driven by demons and vengeance. She should be well rid of him, glad of the chance to have a life apart from him.

But she wasn't.

She spent the next day in a jumbled haze of anger and pain and aching frustration. It came as a shock to her late that afternoon to realize the trial would start tomorrow.

She had spent eighteen months of her life waiting, praying for this day and had completely forgotten about it in the last twenty-four hours.

Memories tumbled back. She tried to focus on those of her family and not on those of Cole or Leah and her early days in Calcutta. Good and bad pictures merged together, vying for domination.

There were warm memories of reading Shakespeare with her father, challenging him at the spelling game they played when he was still headmaster at the school. The later memories were bitter, the Christmases he'd missed, the extended illness of her mother without the comfort of a husband.

At first, she latched on to the memories almost eagerly, anxious to have something to take her mind off Cole and his disturbing visit of the night before. But other pictures crept in.

Images of Cole kissing her behind the orphanage. His gentle hands on her, doctoring her wound. The sweet sound of the mouth harp. The rending pain of betrayal when Sutter had found them at the hotel.

The tide of her thoughts turned, shifted on an ugly edge. She saw her father's blood and felt it on her hands. Saw Wendell's leering face leaning over her father and heard her screams.

Would the jury find him guilty? Could she remember everything? Would they believe her? They had to.

Memories crowded in on her from every angle, pressing, squeezing until she had nowhere to turn. She couldn't bear thinking about the horror of the crime she'd witnessed nor did she want to remember Cole.

Another memory tugged, folded out before her in a frustratingly clear realization, like something she'd searched for and finally found in the most obvious place.

Her father had always explained his job as a detective to her. Though he couldn't give her details, he tried to tell her how to reach him if she ever needed to. Before each new assignment, he would leave notes for her and her mother. Why hadn't she remembered that before?

She realized now that she had held on so long to the hope of getting Wendell as a way to also hold on to her resentment about her father. Or perhaps it was just her way of keeping a piece of him. She'd always hated his leaving, cold with the fear that one day he wouldn't return. One day, he hadn't.

With a start, she admitted she no longer resented his time away from her and her mother. Wendell's conviction would be Regina's way of finally saying good-bye.

Even as worried as she was about seeing Wendell Cross again and the outcome of the trial, she couldn't completely escape Cole.

She woke in the middle of the night, drenched, her body throbbing for his touch, just as he'd said she would.

When she slept again, the dream was different. It was mixed with floating images of Wendell's laughing face and streaks of her father's blood.

*   *   *

Could you give up your search for Sutter? He'd wanted to tell her what she wanted to hear, but he couldn't. Cole tried to think the words now and still he couldn't. Even sitting here in this courtroom, waiting for her, his hands itching to touch her.

Anger, resentment, a desire to hold her all coiled in his chest and cut his breath. He fought the anger, knowing she had been as hurt as he. Staring around the room, he tried to control his ragged breathing.

The courtroom was as impressive inside as out. Stately carvings of the scales of justice edged a two-story vaulted concave ceiling. The sun streamed through high polished windows, slanting light across the stone-tiled floor.

Rows of wooden chairs filled nearly half of the salmon-colored room. Twelve highly polished chairs squatted to the left of the judge's seat which resided behind a high desk of the same mahogany. Devoid of any decorations, it was commanding in its starkness.

Wendell Cross sat at one of two tables facing the judge. Cole had chosen a seat in the second row, betting that Regina would sit with Abe Grand in the first row. He wanted her to know he was here. For her. Part of him wanted to be out there searching for Sutter, but Cole wasn't going anywhere. Not today.

He remembered her words about her father never being there. Did she think of Cole that way? She had said as much. Regret ached in his throat. He hadn't been able to promise her what she wanted, nor to convince her that he cared for her deeply.

Anger still nudged him occasionally. He had all but bared his soul to her and she had rebuffed him.

If she cared about him, she wouldn't have asked him to give up Sutter. He told himself that several times, but then he would remember that she hadn't asked him to give up Sutter, only if he *could*. And, damn his blasted hide, he hadn't been able to say the words, not even to hedge around them or lie.

He'd spent half of yesterday trying to talk himself into doing what she wanted and half of it looking for Sutter.

He shifted on the hard chair, scooting to the edge and dangling his hat between his legs. Masses of people clamored into the room, shuffling and scraping rough-shod feet along the gleaming floor. Cole shut them out. What a pair he and Regina were! He couldn't change his mind and she wouldn't change hers.

He didn't want a future without her and at the same time, he didn't see how they were going to have one. The thought speared cold fear through him. There had to be a way to make her understand that he must finish with Sutter. And convince her of his feelings.

She claimed Cole wanted her because she made him feel something. Partly that was true. She made him feel more alive than he did when facing down the barrel of a gun, but he also admired her courage, her patience, her determination.

He knew he had hurt her and he had to find a way to make her believe he cared.

His gaze fixed on Wendell. The burly man lounged

in the chair, one knee bent, one leg stretched straight out in front of him as if he were enjoying a glass of fine brandy and not about to face a trial for his life. Even when Cross turned to stare over the courtroom, his eyes were quick, observant, but not concerned.

Cole's eyes narrowed and the hair on the back of his neck prickled. Wendell was too nonchalant. Cole turned, scanning the room for Pat Cross, but didn't see him. Unease pricked. With his oldest brother going on trial, Pat would surely show up.

A short knot-muscled man with prickly blond hair leaned across to speak to Wendell. His lawyer, Cole supposed. Where the hell was Regina? Shouldn't she have been here by now? Had there been trouble?

Perfumes and hair oils teased the air. Underneath hung the smell of dirt and unwashed bodies. He shifted again, tamping down the urge to bolt from the overcrowded room. Sound erupted behind him and he turned toward the doors. People churned in a swollen mass, all moving toward the same place. Was it Regina?

The prospect of what she faced stretched the muscles across his chest, staunching his breath. His throat dried up. He wanted to go to her, hold her, help her through it, but after the other night wasn't sure he'd be welcome. He curled his hands around the edge of the seat, squashing the urge.

He strained, trying to see over the dozens of heads blocking his view. Slowly, the clot of people parted. Two men, both in policemen's uniforms, opened a narrow path. The wrinkled face of Abe Grand appeared, sans cigar. And right behind him, Regina.

Cole's breath jammed. She was beautiful though subdued in the blue dress he'd bought her. Her hair was braided and tucked into a smooth knot, emphasizing her slender neck and shoulders, making her appear fragile.

His gaze devoured her, taking in the chalkiness of her skin, the purple shadows under her eyes, the stiffness of her movements. She wouldn't show it, but he knew she was frightened.

A swarthy man, about Cole's height, followed close behind with his hand on her elbow. Slowly, the party moved down the aisle and through a waist-high swinging gate. The dark man guided her into a chair and motioned to Abe.

Grand's gaze fell on Cole as he walked around the table to meet with the other man, and Cole thought he saw a flash of approval. He didn't care. He wanted Regina to look at him, to know everything was going to be all right.

She didn't turn, but sat with stiff back and neck, twisting her hands in her lap. The court clerk came forward and announced the judge. Cole stood, along with everyone else, but never took his gaze off Regina.

Abe Grand was the first witness called. He testified how Worth Harrison had worked for months to expose a corrupt sheriff named Wendell Cross for robbery and bribery. Regina's father had come to Abe's office on a February night about eighteen months ago. "Worth was outside when I heard a scream."

The state's attorney, Aurelius Fletcher, paced in front of Abe. "The person screaming was Miss Regina Harrison?"

"Yes."

"She witnessed the entire incident?"

"Objection!" This from Plunkett, Cross's attorney. "Calls for speculation on the part of the witness."

"Sustained. Continue, Mr. Fletcher."

Cole heard the testimony, but watched her. Her shoulders were blocked in rigid lines and he saw a muscle work in her jaw. He ached for her, for all the memories dredged up, for what he'd done to her, for not being able to hold her now. *Turn around, Regina. Look at me.*

Stop looking at me. Regina could feel Cole's gaze stroking her, urging her to acknowledge his presence and believe he was here for her. Was he, or had he come hoping to find Sutter?

She struggled to keep her mind on Abe's testimony. Soon she would be called to testify, and she would have to face Wendell Cross for the first time since she'd escaped him. The thought was both exhilarating and intimidating.

Her palms sweated; her back ached with the effort to remain rod-straight. It was due to the man behind her as much as it was due to the trial. She had seen Cole from the corner of her eye as she was led to a chair even though she didn't have to look to know. He overpowered the room, his presence lethal, immediate, commanding. And despite what had happened between them, having him close was strangely comforting.

She realized he was probably here to find Sutter and felt a sharp stab of disappointment. If Cole had come for Luke, he was out of luck. Luke would not be coming to the trial. He was lying in wait for Pat Cross. She tried to put all thoughts but those of the trial out of her head.

On the second day, Cole was again seated behind her. She tried to overlook the significance of that and couldn't. Instead, she took strength in the fact.

Had Cole changed his mind about Sutter? Was this his way of telling her? Or was he merely lending support? She had been surprised to see Cole yesterday, but now found herself grateful for his presence.

The tension of the trial and the clamor of newspapermen around her had drained every dreg of emotion from her. Now she felt shut off, as though she witnessed everything from behind a canvas screen. Even the shock had dulled. Last night she had dreamed of her father's death, a dream she hadn't had in over a year.

As the time neared for her to take the stand, Abe covered her hand with his. She knew if she turned, Cole would be there. And strangely it was that fact that made her feel something other than a seeping numbness.

"The prosecution calls Miss Regina Harrison."

The words ricocheted through the still courtroom, snagging the crowd in a pall-like silence. Regina's heart thudded and she swallowed hard.

Memories, old feelings bubbled to the fore. Guilt and sorrow at the death of her father, resentment at his absence when her mother had died. Cold fear clawed through her belly at the prospect of facing Cross again as she had that night her father had died.

Her breath stalled in her chest and she gripped the warm wooden arms of the chair. Tremors rippled down her spine; her knees wobbled. Her lungs grew tight as though her heart had grown too large for her chest. Suddenly she felt a strong familiar hand on her shoulder. Cole.

Her muscles relaxed and, for a moment, she let herself lean into the comfort of his touch. Warm hard palm melded to the bone and flesh of her shoulder, squeezing, massaging, pulsing courage into her. She wanted to feel his thick arms around her, holding her close as he had the night they made love.

The band constricting her lungs loosened. She drew a steady breath, trying to squash the flutters in her stomach, the feeling that she had just lost her footing on thin ice and was sliding headlong into an embankment.

Abe's hand was on her arm, helping her up, and without conscious thought, she turned to meet Cole's gaze.

As though they were alone in the courtroom, he rose with her, his hand on her shoulder, his gaze never leaving hers.

I'm here. His black eyes were steady, reassuring, fierce with caring.

Her eyes burned at the tenderness in his and she silently thanked him. Then she turned and walked to the stand.

She made herself look at Wendell Cross. At first, her breath locked in her lungs. Her chest ached; sweat itched her palms and between her breasts. As she watched, he glared at her and with a lazy, almost careless motion, drew his index finger across his throat.

A gasp rose from the courtroom. Fear chilled her, but at the same time a new certainty unfolded. She had done the right thing. The jury would find him guilty.

After all the waiting, biding her time, fighting the lies, she was going to vindicate her father's death.

Mr. Fletcher began the examination. With her gaze on Cole, she answered the lawyer's patient questions and related the story to the jury. Plunkett tried to challenge her certainty of identifying the correct man in the darkness, but she stood firm. Wendell Cross had been directly under a street lamp and less than a foot away. She hadn't made a mistake.

Finally, she was allowed to return to her seat. Her stomach still jumped nervously, but an easy calm inched in. She had done it.

Other witnesses followed, one an undercover detective who had seen Wendell running from the scene. It was mid-afternoon when closing arguments were given and the jury dismissed.

They took less than fifteen minutes to return with a verdict of guilty.

An exultant noise burst from the crowd. Regina closed her eyes in relief, then was swallowed up in a hug by Abe. She even welcomed the musty smell of cigar smoke in his wrinkled jacket. At last justice would be served. She wanted to laugh and cry at the same time.

Turning, she found Cole's gaze on her and he smiled. With her heart bursting, she smiled back.

*   *   *

"Wendell Cross, you are hereby sentenced to hang by the neck until dead."

At the judge's words, the courthouse exploded in a melee of movement and sound. The hordes of people sitting, standing, and crowding the doors separated into groups of fours and tens, delving into the too-slender spaces between the rows of chairs.

An overriding roar of sound made it impossible for Cole to distinguish any distinct conversation. He remained seated, his shoulders drawing tight as the air and the light were momentarily shaved by the bulk of people.

The crowd moved toward Regina as one powerful surging force, boiling like the St. Francis River after a deluge. Chairs scraped the floor, shifting from the strain of too many bodies pressing against the polished wood. Police officers and undercover detectives stood firm at the gate separating the participants in the trial from the onlookers and tried to herd the sweep of humans toward the doors.

Deep commanding voices were lost in the funnel of tornadic noise and slowly penetrated. Like a giant tide, the people gradually ebbed and fell back. The floor creaked in response to the reluctant movement.

Newspapermen elbowed their way through swarms of arms and legs and sturdy bodies to rush up to Regina, clamoring to be the first with the story. Abe brushed them all aside, whereupon several turned to Wendell. Cole wanted to get to Regina, to hold her. At the moment, she was surrounded by Mr. Fletcher,

Abe Grand, one police officer, and a gaggle of news-papermen.

As the courtroom emptied, Cole rose from his seat, his gaze still on Regina. Mr. Fletcher spoke earnestly to her and occasionally patted her hand. Cole tapped one boot on the stone floor, noting idly the scars his hard heels made on the waxed surface. He had to tell her how proud he was, how glad he was for her, how he couldn't let her go.

The clank and rattle of chains drew Cole's atten-tion. Two guards fastened wrist irons on Cross and pulled him to his feet. At least twelve inches of chain dangled between Wendell's thick wrists, not prohib-iting movement, merely inhibiting it.

Cole noted that one guard took the precaution of holding a gun to the outlaw's side. Stories abounded of criminals shackled with the heavy iron who had managed to strangle their guards and escape.

Regina was swept toward the doors in a throng of people. Cole followed.

Behind him, the guards took Wendell and moved along in the wake of bodies. Cross would be taken to jail to await hanging in the morning. Cole walked swiftly through the halls and down the interior stairs, keeping his gaze ever on the silky sheen of Regina's black hair.

After the dimness of the darkly paneled courtroom, the late afternoon sun blazed with blinding brilliance. He squinted and shaded his eyes for a better look.

On the sweeping layers of steps in front of the building, the crowd thinned. People stood in clumps

of threes and fours, staring at the double mahogany
doors behind Cole, waiting. He could see Regina at
the bottom talking to the state's attorney and a petite
auburn-haired woman.

The grinding chink of metal on metal heralded the
approach of the prisoner. The guards escorted Wendell around Cole and down the steps in front of him.

A priest, holding a Bible and fingering a dull silver
cross at his neck, rushed forward to offer his services
only to be glared away. Hisses sounded from a group
of women.

One man, with gray-peppered red hair and beard,
stepped into the guards' way. "They'll be stretchin'
yer neck fer sure, Cross. An' it's no more'n ye deserve."

Wendell raised his fist and lunged at the man, but
the guards managed to pull him away before he
touched him.

Impatience clawed at Cole. He had to see Regina,
talk to her, touch her. He started down the steps. A
distant thrumming sounded in the sky and he looked
east.

Through the fog of thick smoke from the steam-
ships in the harbor, the sky gleamed blue-white, the
sun glared. No sign of rain.

No, the sound wasn't thunder, but hooves. He kept
his gaze on the street, dread uncurling in his belly.

Urgency spurred him. He took the next steps two
at a time. Blood roared in his ears. The steps rushed
beneath his feet, but he felt as though he moved in a
drugged state. His legs were heavy, muscles tight,

edged with a cramp. To his right, someone yelled. He glanced over.

The earth vibrated. Pat Cross galloped by at a dead run, leading a dapple gray mare. Bullets exploded from his gun and Cole crouched. Mr. Fletcher and a guard fell. Abe turned, pulling his gun.

Cole dropped to his knees, rolled down a step, and slid his gun free of the holster in one motion. Holy hell! They should've all expected something like this.

More shots sounded. A woman screamed. A man grunted in pain.

Pat sprayed gunfire at anyone who moved. Wendell turned from the waist and wrapped the chains of his wrist irons around one of the guard's throat. The other guard reached for his gun. A shot cracked the air and the guard fell.

Wendell took the steps backward, dragging the second guard along as a body shield. "Unlock me, damn it. Get out the damn key and unlock me."

Cole sidled closer, sighting a perfect circle right between Wendell's eyes.

Wendell took another step and his head dipped behind the guard. The guard, sweat slicking his face and neck, nodded and reached into his jacket pocket. His hands shook as though he were having a convulsion.

Wendell tightened the chain around the guard's neck. "Hurry up, damn you."

The man choked and clawed at the iron collar, trying to fit the key into the small hole and relieve the pressure around his neck. The lock clicked, strangely loud in between shots. The irons clattered to the ground, metal scraping stone and echoing harshly in the heavy heat.

The acrid odor of smoke scorched the air, filtering into Cole's nostrils. Wendell reached the bottom of the steps and shoved the guard to his knees, then bolted for the horse led by his brother.

Pat circled around Wendell allowing his older brother to mount. A young man dressed in a check- ered suit reached for a fragile white-haired woman next to him. A swift shot from Pat sent the man crum- pling to the ground and a faint cry sounded from the woman.

Grabbing the reins, Wendell vaulted into the saddle and spun his horse around, spurring it straight toward Abe and Regina.

Cold fear clamped Cole's lungs. He squeezed off a shot, cursing when it skimmed Wendell's head and didn't penetrate. Where the hell was Sutter? Double shots staggered each other. Abe fell.

Cole bolted for Regina, flying over steps and prone bodies. Bullets whizzed past him, so close he felt a spurt of wind next to his ear.

Wendell leaned down from his horse and snatched Regina up by the arm, throwing her face down in front of him.

In a flurry of blue skirts, she kicked and slapped at the man, screaming, "Noooo!"

"No!" Cole yelled with her.

She reared up and raked her nails down Wendell's face. He cursed and slammed the side of her head against the sharp edge of the saddle horn.

A cry of fury erupted from Cole. "I'll kill you, Cross."

Regina crumpled like a wilted petal to hang limply across the saddle, arms dangling over Wendell's right leg.

Salty sweat stung Cole's eyes. He blinked it away and his next shot drilled into Wendell's calf.

With Pat in front of him, Wendell tore down the street, spraying dirt and cursing the people who stared after him.

Cole stumbled and went down on one knee in the street, adrenaline shooting through his body, denial twisting through his mind even as he watched. He should've been with her.

From behind him, a gun fired. Wendell's horse lurched sideways, but kept going. *With Regina.* Cole couldn't breathe. He felt as if that horse had landed on him. He aimed and fired. And fired again.

A bloodstain bloomed on Pat Cross's back. He fell forward then slid out of the saddle. One foot twisted in the stirrup and his roan bolted in a zigzag, dragging him down the street.

Wendell Cross jerked his horse around and yanked hard on the reins. Shock mingled with the fury on his dirt-speckled face. The dappled mare rose on powerful hind legs, slamming Regina into Wendell. "The girl dies for this!"

With that bellowed promise, he spurred his horse. Amid a cloud of dust and the glare of the sun, he and Regina disappeared around a winding corner.

She was gone! Cross had taken her!

Cole lurched to his feet, sprinting for the stable down the street where he'd left Horse. A quick glance back showed men already gathered around Abe, who was cursing a blue streak and ordering his own men to follow Wendell Cross.

Sutter—finally!—knelt next to Abe, listening intently. Part of Cole realized his own opportunity to get the man he'd tracked for so many months. An automatic order issued from his brain to his gun hand. *Fire!*

But he knew, true to rights, that he wouldn't shoot. He turned his back on Sutter and kept running. For Regina.

CHAPTER SIXTEEN

Icy fear cramped Cole's gut, but it burned away every peripheral noise, every wasted movement. Each thought, each motion was clear and calculated. He would find Cross and he would kill him.

On his way to the stable, Cole passed the lifeless body of Pat Cross without a second glance. He paused where Wendell had stopped his horse and threatened Regina's life. Cole knelt and ran his index finger lightly around the imprint in the dark earth, looking for some identifying mark to track Wendell's horse.

His breath came in ragged gasps; his heart pounded in his ears, but his mind was cold and lethal, focused only on getting Wendell Cross. He traced three perfect horseshoe prints until he came to the fourth. The right rear print showed a broken piece on the left leg of the upside-down U, leaving a distinct mark in the dirt.

Cole leaped up and bolted for the stable. Throwing six bits at the attendant, he saddled Horse, slapped her on the rear, and swung up onto the mare's moving body. He urged Horse into a steady gallop, taking the corners swiftly but sharply, not wasting time by riding pell-mell down the busy street.

Pounding hooves kept rhythm with a litany in his head. Da dum. Da dum. Kill Cross. Kill Cross. Blood thirst rose up in Cole. The scents of fresh manure and horseflesh wafted through the air. The dust of dry parched earth choked him.

He passed streams of people in the street, scanning all for Cross. Noises of street railcars, steamship bellows, factory whistles dulled in his ears. Fixed on his course, fear funneling through his body, Cole shut out everything except what was in his path.

One thought jerked at the rhythm of his heart—he had to find Regina.

Urgency needled him, but Cole paced himself, avoiding carts and dogs and children. He reached the outskirts of St. Louis, the sun slanting low in the sky, and knew he had only two to three hours of light left. Fear bubbled through him, threatened his self-control, but he fought it back. Regina's life depended on him. He couldn't let fear or anger cloud his judgment.

He kept her sweet face in the forefront of his mind, focusing on her gentle smile and the way her eyes turned to smoky green when he looked at her. All the while he searched the road. The main thoroughfare leading into St. Louis was a jumble of lumbering carts, sleek wagons, and horses.

Wide metal-banded wheel tracks tangled with thin carriage ones. Solid shoe prints were overrun by children's footprints and dog paw prints, all mixed and mangled in the dirt so that Cole could barely distinguish the print of a horse from that of a chicken.

An hour outside of St. Louis, the tracks thinned. Cole easily picked out the heavy marks of a laden wagon, the uneven stride of a limping horse, the shuffled prints of a child. And the faint marks of a horse with a chipped shoe.

Lack of rain had left the ground oak-hard and not prone to taking tracks, but the horse also carried two people, which helped put an imprint in the dirt. Cole was able to make out enough to follow Cross south and east.

Keeping his gaze carefully on the tracks did not keep his mind from Regina. His memory skipped through time with her, back over things she'd said. Things he'd wanted to say to her. He wanted to tell her he loved her. He should've told her earlier except—

Holy hell! He loved her! Cole's breath stuttered then eased out. Why hadn't he realized earlier? Why hadn't he told her the night he'd visited her at Grand's? Because he was a damn fool.

The truth struck him. He hadn't told her because he'd thought that if he admitted it to himself it would somehow make him obligated to give up Sutter.

The trees grew thicker. The fading green of hills loomed. With mechanical inattention, Cole viewed the landscape, counting each step as bringing him closer to Regina. He imagined finally touching her satiny skin then blowing a hole in Cross's head.

Thoughts tumbled through his mind. He replayed the scene outside the courthouse, still hardly able to

believe he'd left Sutter standing in the streets unscathed. But there had been no other choice. Regina
was in danger.

Cole's stomach knotted. He loved her. What if he
never got the chance to tell her?

And if he did, it might still be too late. She'd said
he was like her father, always absent when needed.
He'd tried to prove her wrong by going to the courthouse, but that wasn't enough. She needed to know
she could count on him more than once. He remembered now, her voice playing like soft sighs in his
mind, how she'd reminded him that his vengeance for
Sutter had come between him and his family. How it
would come between him and her.

As though touching a new wound, his mind feathered over the last year and a half. Driven by hate, he'd
lost all but the most minimal contact with his family.

What Regina said was true. The realization scraped
along a rusty conscience, peeling away months of self-
imposed hardness, leaving a wake of regret to throb
under the raw hurt.

So was she right about Sutter too? Cole's mind
shied from the possibility. He'd spent too much time
and effort tracking the traitorous bastard. How could
he give it up?

Yet, for the first time since he'd found Luke and
Sarah together, doubts about killing Luke bombarded
him. Small pangs of regret bit into him.

He didn't want to feel regret about Sutter and tried
to turn his mind to thoughts of Regina. Could he
reach her in time?

But the doubts pelted him, hitting at his conscience like needles of rain and bringing flashes of the past. Like slits through a rickety fence, he glimpsed buried memories of Sutter. Cole didn't want to look, but they suddenly unfolded in front of him.

Their first day at school when they had both beat up the town bully, Johnson Witmer; their race to see who could kiss Billie Sue George first; the day they graduated from university in Iowa.

Cole could still see the pristine starkness of his uniform against the dull brown of Luke's trousers when they had both received their assignments. Years of half-lived days, spent grieving for the friend he had believed dead, rippled through Cole's conscience. His desperate attempts to convince himself that he'd done the right thing by marrying Sarah. And finding her with Luke.

He'd been crazed with rage and hurt because he'd learned that the baby might have belonged to Luke. And even if the baby were Cole's, Sarah and Luke had intended to raise the child.

Other memories, long buried, clawed their way through Cole's thoughts. Luke had been holding Sarah, kissing her, but their clothes weren't disarrayed. Luke insisted that they hadn't been together, but Cole's anger had buzzed in his ears. All he could hear was Sarah's defiant threat that she and the baby were leaving with Luke.

Cole dammed the thoughts, cutting off the memories that he only now realized proved the things Regina had been trying to tell him about his own family, his own life. How had she done it? Without invading his privacy or judging him harshly, she had set all his convictions about Sutter to wobbling.

The tracks he followed suddenly faded and Cole nearly missed the signs. As it was, he had to backtrack almost half a mile and pick up the tracks again. At a fork in the road, picked clear of any grass or tree roots, he went down on one knee. The broken horseshoe print appeared on both roads. The hard ground made it impossible to follow the line of tracks with his eye so he mounted and took the left fork.

He lost the tracks soon after, but covered a little more distance to be certain. He resented spending the time, but couldn't take the chance that he might miss something.

He found no more tracks so he turned back and rode the other fork. Here the tracks continued. The sun hung low in the sky, promising only another hour of light. He had already lost almost an hour, but at least he was on the correct trail.

Darkness finally forced him to stop. As faint as the tracks were in the daylight, Cole would have no luck following them at night. He found an abandoned farmhouse and stopped. Fear urged him to go on, but he couldn't risk losing the tracks. Or wasting any more time by taking the wrong trail. Cole hoped he was closing in. As long as Wendell felt threatened, Regina might live longer.

Cole rubbed down Horse and fed her, ate a cold supper of beans and a hard biscuit he rummaged from his saddlebags, and sat inside the limp and barely hanging door of the cabin counting each minute of darkness.

Wendell headed for the cave.

He pushed the gray as hard as he could, ignoring the flecks of spittle that flew from the horse's mouth, the sides pumping hard against his thighs. He couldn't afford to stop.

Going through town, people had noticed the girl slung over the saddle. A few had even given pursuit, but he'd lost them. Just outside of Carondelet, he'd stopped on the shadowed side of a well house to tie the girl's wrists and stuff a torn strip from his shirt into her mouth.

She hadn't moved or made any noise since he'd knocked her out, but he knew she was alive. He planned to keep her alive to ensure his safe passage out of the state. He knew Abe Grand would follow or send his men; right now they were probably hot on his trail.

His leg burned, tendons shredded and screaming from the bullet shot by the man in black. Wendell couldn't stop until he reached the cave. Maybe someone—Big Bill Waincott or the Daltons or Jameses—would be there to help.

Since Grand's men had joined Pinkerton's on a blood mission for Frank and Jesse, all the outlaws were holed up in various caves or farmhouses throughout the state. Wendell would find safety in the cave.

One of the boys would get this bullet out of his leg. Pat would've already done so if he had made it.

A searing flash of anger clouded his vision for a moment. Pain axed his body as though his arms were being pulled off. Both of his brothers—dead! Part of him was dead now too, and he would kill the man in black for that. Regina Harrison, too. And anyone else who came after them.

So Wendell continued to push the gray. They didn't stop for water, and he allowed the horse to slow to a canter only once. Landscape turned from sheets of flat green to rolling mounds of hills dotted with trees. They traveled southeast, over creeks, around a broken bluff, past a dozen farming communities.

The sky finally doused the sun and still Wendell prodded the mare. They were close. Even blind, he would've known the trail through dense brush and towering woods of oak, juniper, and ash. The clouds fogged the moon, giving only slight wedges of light.

His leg throbbed with an ache that had long ago spread up his thigh. In a clearing, the horse slowed. Twelve paces ahead, the face of a cave yawned. Wendell's eyes, bleary from sun and fatigue, searched for the telltale identifying sign and found it.

At last! He angled his body off the horse, wincing when fresh pain speared up his leg. He pulled the girl off and pushed her, stumbling, in front of him.

They stopped at the mouth of the cave and Wendell called out, "The sign of the cross seeks entrance into No Man's Land."

Silence answered his secret code. The mare snorted and stamped her feet. An animal scurried into the underbrush behind them, but no voice called out in welcome.

Wendell cursed. He was on his own. He snapped his fingers at the horse to follow and walked past the wizened hickory with the split trunk into the welcome darkness.

Thick blackness swallowed them up. Regina's hair, torn from her braid, streamed across her cheeks and tangled in the rag in her mouth. Her back ached, her breasts were tender from the bruising ride, and her shoulder twinged for the first time in days. None of that compared to the shrill pain above her left ear. She remembered hitting the pommel and blacking out.

When she'd come to, she was gagged, her hands tied behind her back with sturdy rope. She and Wendell were alone. Where was his brother?

She forgot her battered body as dank cold air, rancid with the stench of decaying flesh, stung her nose. She choked, desperate for clean air. The gag in her mouth swelled in her throat, suffocating her and thrusting her into panic. She tried to calm herself and take in a small breath around the strip of fabric.

The odor of death was strong enough to bring tears to her eyes. And thoughts of Cole tumbling back.

Please come for me, Cole. Please. She had no idea if he would and knew she shouldn't even want him to, but she did. Abe would certainly send someone, but would they arrive in time?

If Wendell had used her only as a means of getting out of town unscathed, he didn't need her anymore. A chill of fear crawled up her arms, raising the flesh and making her shiver. He shuffled in behind her and coughed.

"Ugh! What is that? Some kind of dead animal?"

He fumbled in the darkness behind her. Something fell to the ground, a hollow tinny sound echoing through the cavern. A scrape, a swift bitter odor then light flared. Regina turned to see Wendell holding a lantern. Faint orange light capered on the sleek walls, casting giant shadows of her and him.

He opened a canteen and guzzled greedily. Regina's mouth and throat ached from thirst, but Cross screwed on the cap and stepped away.

Regina blinked, a shaft of pain spearing her head. Her brief relief at being able to see was quickly squashed as she glanced around. Walls slick with water and moss surrounded her. Deep pockets of black yawned in front of her. With surprise, she registered a table, three chairs—one with a broken leg—the lantern Wendell held, and a small cache of plates and cups stacked in a corner.

He'd brought her to a hideout. For outlaws? She'd heard tales of the James brothers holing up in caves through the state. Had they been here?

"Aaaahh!" Wendell groaned behind her. "James, no! James! James!"

Regina whirled, her heart skipping a beat at his startling cry. He knelt over something close to the entrance and she stepped up to look over his shoulder. Her breath froze in her chest as she gazed at a pair of denim covered legs and boots. A body?

Ripped pants revealed red streaks on the flesh beneath the cloth, the left thigh swollen bigger than the right. Despite the chill in the cave, sweat dappled her forehead and neck. Fear drilled into her. She took a step back. She knew without looking at the face that the body belonged to James Cross. Nausea threatened and she backed up against the table.

Its wooden leg scraped across stone, the harsh noise echoing over Wendell's ragged breath. He leaped up and turned around, his face bulging and discolored even in the amber light. He loosened the gag. "You did this!"

"No!" Regina crowded against the table, ignoring the sharp corner that jabbed her thighs. Wendell looked ready to murder her. She twisted her wrists, heedless of the biting pressure of the rope. "No."

"He was coming after you. And I know he found you. Pat told me." Wendell's eyes were glazed, focused on her, but not seeing her. He stepped toward her, squeezing her against the slick wall of the rocky room. "You killed him."

"He tried to kill me!"

He slapped her. The crack of his palm on her face exploded like a gunshot in the hollow room. Her head jerked back and tears sprang to her eyes. Fear scraped at her, but fury swelled over it. She lifted her chin and glared at him. "It's no more than what you did to my family."

Rage swelled his features until his eyes bulged and his cheeks puffed. He raised his fist and stepped toward her again. She pressed against the wall, cold slime slipping over her tied hands and braced herself for the blow, but his leg buckled. Crying out, he went down on one knee. His hand went to his leg and he pulled himself to a chair.

"This leg is your damn fault, too," he huffed. "But I'm gonna take care of you good and proper."

She hugged the wall, hating the clammy chill that soaked through her dress. Her mind wasn't on the threat, but on escape. Wendell's face was distorted with pain and his eyes were cloudy.

He slid a knife from inside his boot and limped past her to the opening of the cave. The blade was long and distortedly wide in the half-light. Metal gleamed on one side, but the other was shadowed, giving the illusion of a thin, long blade when she could see it was four inches wide at its base. She inched toward one of the chairs. Her shoulder throbbed as did her head. She watched him steadily, waiting for her chance.

Standing between her and freedom, Wendell reached the horse and fumbled with the thongs on a saddlebag before pulling out a half-full bottle of whiskey. His hands shook. Even in the dusky amber light, Regina could see the sheen of sweat on his face.

He took a swallow of whiskey and made his way back to the chair that sat about five feet away from her.

With the knife, he slit the side seam of his pants. A nickel-sized hole pierced his calf. Blood glued the fabric to his skin and he winced as he yanked it free. Fresh blood trickled down his leg.

He dribbled a small amount of liquor on the wound, sucking air in through his teeth at the contact. After pouring a liberal amount on the blade, he set to work. At the first cut into flesh and the free spurt of blood from his leg, Regina inched toward the cave entrance.

He began to talk, his words dogged as though he could keep his mind from the pain. "That man in black, the one who wasn't a stone's throw from you all during the trial, he's the one who killed my brother. He shot Pat."

Cole had also shot James, but she saw no need to tell Wendell. She swung her head toward him, feeling her way along the slimy wall with her fingertips. He dug the knife deeper into his skin. A vein popped out on his neck and blood rolled down his leg, but he determinedly pushed the blade further.

"I'm gonna kill him, you know." His voice leveled out, strangely calm and promising. A serene peace flooded his features as he pushed the blade deeper, not even wincing this time.

She licked her lips, edging along the rock wall toward freedom. Her arms, twisted behind her, ached. The rope burned into her wrists and she cursed her lack of movement. The slick floor concealed the sound of her movements. Her last glimpse of Cole had been of him running down the courthouse steps, firing his gun. Then the world had gone black.

In that instant, she knew. He was coming. She hadn't dared to hope, only to wish. Regardless of what had happened between them, she wanted him.

She believed that he had tried too late to change his plans with Grand, but did that mean he would give up Sutter? She didn't know, but prayed she got the chance to ask him.

The knife protruded from Wendell's leg. His eyes closed to half-slits and Regina glanced at the entrance of the cave then at the stiff body of James Cross. She whirled, bolting for the outside.

The horse shied as she scrambled past, her legs tangled in her skirts. Thrown off balance by having her

arms behind her, she stumbled and slid. She heard a
dull thud and at the same instant fell into the mare's
muscular shoulder. Struggling to steady herself on the
slick floor, she leaned against the horse and glanced
down.

Wendell's knife, still quivering from the throw,
pinned her skirt to the slimy floor, stuffing pieces of
blue fabric deep into red-black clay. Fear choked her
and her knees buckled. She curled her bound hands,
clutching to hold on to the mare's leg or chest.

"I can't kill you yet." Wendell spoke in a slurred,
pain-hazed voice. "Grand probably already has men
on my tail."

Unable to free her skirt, Regina watched as he levered himself out of the scarred chair and limped toward her. Her knees shook like a hollow reed in the
wind.

He jerked the knife out of the ground and held the
mud-smeared blade up to her face, close enough that
she could feel the chill from the steel. "Now, you're
not gonna try that again, are you?"

She swallowed, but didn't answer.

He pulled her back inside and shoved her into a
chair in front of his. Shoving the gag back into her
mouth, he knotted the rope around her wrists even
tighter. With an extra length of dirty rope, he tied her
in the chair. He sank down into his own chair and
resumed his makeshift surgery.

Tension stretched across her belly, drawing the
muscles taut and heavy. Sweat slicked her palms.

"After I kill your man, I'm gonna kill you. Real

slow. So you can remember how I killed your daddy."
He grunted and flicked the blade at the wound. "Ah."

He lifted up the knife to reveal a small dented ball
of lead. Grabbing up the whiskey bottle with an unsteady hand, he tipped it over the seeping wound. He
bound the leg tightly with a strip torn from his shirt
and eased back in the chair.

Through the night, she felt his glacial blue gaze on
her, filled with such hate that she feared he would
change his mind and kill her anyway. She counted the
minutes, praying for light and Cole.

They left the cave when the sky was still velvet gray.
A ragged pink edge of sun peered over the horizon,
sending thin streamers of rose into the passing night.
Again, Wendell threw her face-first over the saddle
and climbed up behind.

Regina's ribs and left shoulder jammed into the
leather-covered wooden pommel. Her head was now
sore only to the touch, but pain pierced her mending
shoulder. The ground swelled before her eyes, seeming to rise closer with each step the mare took. How
could she hope to escape hanging upside down as she
was?

Sharp pain drilled into her head and blood rushed
to her face. Nausea threatened. She closed her eyes,
feeling every step of the horse as a jab to her stomach
and breasts.

Time was measured in the clipping gait of the mare.
The rushed *tch tch tch* pounded into her, driving,
spreading, coursing through her head in a rhythm that
threatened to crescendo with her next breath.

The horse stopped and suddenly she was yanked backward from the saddle. She stumbled, her feet slipping on the ground as though greased with lard. Pain exploded behind her eyes and turned the world black for a moment.

Blood roared in her ears, drowning all sound. Against her head, Wendell's mouth moved, but she couldn't hear. Slowly, she realized they were in a small clearing, marked with the remains of a campfire and surrounded by trees.

He jerked her tight against him and wrapped one arm around her throat. The handle of his knife, strapped to his thigh by a holster, bit into her leg. A gun appeared in front of her face.

"Let her go."

Cole! His voice came from a dense copse of trees in front of her and finally penetrated the ebbing roar in her ears. Cole had come for her!

Relief nearly buckled her knees and Regina searched among the brush for him. Her stomach knotted and sweat dappled her neck and chest. She tried to remain still, her gaze focusing through the deeper shadows of the trees.

Wendell tightened his blood-encrusted sleeve around her throat, pressing against her windpipe. "I'm walkin' outta here or she dies."

She fought down panic, struggling to breathe as Cole stepped out from behind a cedar tree.

Despite the weary eyes, tight lines drawn between his brows, and more than a day's growth of beard, he had never looked so wonderful. She wanted to cry.

Wendell backed away, hauling her limp body with

him. Regina's legs, numb from her long night of sitting, tingled with pain and she moved stiffly. His arm pulled against her throat, arching her neck painfully while she struggled to match his steps.

"Give it up, Cross." Cole stepped fully into the light, leaving the shade of an oak tree. Movement exploded and she wasn't sure what happened first.

Cole cocked his own gun, the sound muffled under the shuffle of Wendell's feet. Wendell pushed Regina straight at Cole and ran. She stumbled, obscuring Cole's vision.

He struggled to catch her without discharging his gun and managed to hook one arm around her. "Hell!"

Knowing Wendell was escaping, Regina fought to right herself, thrown off balance by having her hands tied behind her. Cole steadied her, ran his gaze over her, and bolted for the brush.

In only seconds, Cole returned, folding her in his arms. "He's gone."

He buried his face in her neck and crushed her to him. Wanting to touch him, she squirmed, tears burning her eyes. He released her long enough to slip the gag from her mouth and untie her hands. She wound her arms around his neck and held on, inhaling the welcome scent of warmth, horseflesh, sweat and safety.

"Regina," Cole breathed into her hair.

Her breasts crushed into the rigid wall of his chest. Relief seeped into her. All bruises and aches faded as the essence of Cole soothed them away. She pressed close, reassured by the sound of his heartbeat, soaking in the dark muskiness of him, gaining strength in the power of his arms.

"I love you—"

"I understand why you—"

"What?" They spoke in unison, the shock and blurred edge of hope in Cole's face mirroring Regina's own.

He stared at her with wonder dawning on his face. "I was afraid I wouldn't reach you in time to tell you. I love you."

Regina's head still reeled from all that had happened in a few short seconds. "You do?"

"Yes."

"Oh, Cole." Joy exploded inside her, showering out to tingle in her hands and toes. She leaned into him, meeting him halfway as his head lowered. "I love you, too."

She felt the tension in him, the restraint of not following Cross immediately, but his lips covered hers, devouring as if to prove she was really alive and here in his arms. She understood the desperation, the frantic need to feel the stroke of his tongue on hers, the velvet heat of his breath.

His lips gentled then, savoring the taste of her, buckling her knees. Her eyes burned. Withdrawing slowly, he gazed into her eyes, his own fevered with desire and love. A shiver tripped down her spine.

He drew back and gingerly touched her hair. "Are you okay? Your head?"

"It's sore, but I'm all right." She pressed close again, reluctant to lose the feel of his warmth wrapping around her.

His thighs widened to cradle hers and he hardened against her. She welcomed the familiar fire that stroked her insides and reveled in the feeling of safety.

"I was afraid I'd lost you."

She touched her fingers to his lips, smiling when heat traveled up her arm. "I was afraid I wouldn't be able to tell you—"

"What?" He leaned close for another kiss and another.

Breathless, she curled her fingers into his iron-hewn arms and held on. "I believe you . . . about Grand. And Luke."

His gaze speared her, starting a flame at her toes that worked its way up to her breasts. A muscle flexed in his jaw and his throat worked. "Thank you."

Hoofbeats thundered toward them and Cole spun as Luke Sutter reined his horse to a skidding stop in the clearing.

"Luke!" Regina stepped toward him, smiling.

"Am I too late?" He drew in a deep breath and glanced around. "Did you get him?"

"He's gone." Cole moved around her and panic edged in. An unyielding predatory gleam frosted his eyes and her muscles tensed.

Luke's blue gaze settled on her. "You okay?"

"Yes, thanks."

"Good. I'll go after Cross. How far ahead of me is he?" Luke wheeled his horse around, glancing back at Cole for an answer.

Cole drew his gun.

Regina gasped. "What are you doing?"

CHAPTER SEVENTEEN

Sutter stiffened in the saddle, drilling Cole with a steely blue gaze.

In his concern for Regina, Cole had forgotten Sutter, but seeing him now, Cole couldn't turn away again. The doubts he'd experienced lately only fueled his deep-seated anger and pain.

Fury snapped something deep inside and his gun hand shook. "I've been waitin' for this day a long time."

"Cole, don't do this!" Regina looked from Cole to Luke. "Please."

Her voice tore at him, but Cole forced himself to ignore it. "You're gonna pay for what you did, Sutter."

Sutter threw down the reins and vaulted from the horse. "That's rich! I'm not the one who married my best friend's girl then killed her."

Regina gasped. Hate pulsed in the air, vile and thick as poison.

Cole focused on Sutter, rage driving through him like a rail track spike. "I thought you were dead."

Images of Luke's funeral spun through Cole's mind. Sarah with Cole on one side, her father on the other. The hollow spent feeling that ate Cole's guts inside out. The sting of freezing rain on his face, reminding him that he was alive and Luke was dead. "Hell, we all thought you were dead!"

"And when you learned I wasn't?" Luke tore his hat from his head and threw it to the ground then began rolling back his chambray sleeves.

"It was too late. Why didn't you at least get word to me?"

"You know why. I had to disappear." Sutter stood, hands on hips, eyes burning with blue fire and stubbornness.

"You took my wife, would've taken my child if she'd lived." The words snipped at Cole's conscience and forced him to finally voice the question he'd not dared all these months. "Was that child really mine?"

"Of course she was."

A red haze hemmed in around Cole, jamming his breath, bringing a sting to his eyes. "Then how could you agree to take her from me?"

"Cole, don't do this. He used to be your friend." Regina placed a hand on his arm.

He shook her off. From the corner of his eye, he saw her stiffen and step away. Pain and self-disgust hooked into him. He wanted to reach for her, beg her to believe he was doing this for them, but he wasn't.

He kept his gaze focused on Sutter's icy eyes. His

thumb, slick with sweat, wobbled on the trigger. "If the child was mine, why would you take her?"

Sutter spat a profanity Cole had only heard him utter one other time, the night Cole had found him with Sarah. Sutter threw down his gun and punched Cole in the belly. "You blind stupid bastard!"

Cole doubled over in surprise as much as in pain. Then Sutter was on top of him. A brutal right jab to Cole's jaw sent his head snapping back.

Sutter's heavy weight knocked him to the ground. He shoved his face into Cole's. "Your wife! Your wife! Damn it, what about me? She belonged to me first. Sarah was mine. She loved *me*."

Cole doubled his fist and smashed it into Luke's side then slammed his forehead into Luke's chin. They rolled, fists pummeling flesh, tender skin splitting, blood spattering knuckles and clothes. Balancing one hand on the ground, Cole pushed to his knees and rose on unsteady legs. Luke butted him in the stomach with his head.

Cole's breath *ooomphed* out. He folded to the ground and struggled back up. "Don't try to turn this on me."

They circled each other like trapped animals, desperate to escape, willing to fight since they couldn't. Sweat trickled down Cole's temple, seeped into his eyes and stung.

He drew in shallow drafts of air, fighting to regain his breath. His words were strained and hoarse. "Sarah was legally mine and, if you're telling the truth, the baby was, too."

"I wasn't going to go." Luke faced him, chest heaving in mirror image to Cole's. Blood oozed from cuts at his mouth and eye. "You damn fool. I told Sarah no. I tried to tell you, but all you could see was blood. My blood."

"You were planning to leave when I found you!"

"I wasn't!" Luke's fist slammed into his lower jaw and Cole went down on one knee. "*Sarah* was."

Like an involuntary reflex of muscle, memory jolted him. He remembered Luke swearing that he and Sarah weren't going. Sarah's face had crumpled in disbelief and betrayal, then she had run out. Cole shook his head, trying to staunch the memory. His hand crawled over packed earth and latched on to his revolver, dragging it to him. "No. You were going to run. Because they *both* belonged to you."

Sutter faced him, hunched at the waist and holding his gut, blood dripping from his chin drop by black-scarlet drop onto the parched earth. Fury mottled his bruised face and shook his shoulders. "Sarah would never have betrayed you. I don't know why she said the baby wasn't yours."

"She loved you, not me." Cole's voice was wooden. His aching knuckles wrapped around the butt of his gun. "You said it yourself and I knew it."

"I was never even with her! I never knew what it was to lie with her and you did." Sutter's lips twisted. Hate and sadness carved his face into unrelenting lines. Blue flames burned his eyes as he spat, "My best friend, lying with the woman who was supposed to be *my* wife. I should've been chasing *you* all these years."

"My baby's dead because of you." The rage leveled

out, rushing through Cole's system like a runaway lo- comotive, pumping, gathering icy momentum, screaming for release. He cocked his gun and sighted between Sutter's eyes.

"Cole, please!" Regina sobbed, grabbing for his arm again. "He's not to blame for that. And you know he was never with Sarah in that way."

Regina! Her voice lashed him with guilt. The fin- gers digging into his arm underscored the doubts that had attacked him lately. He slanted a glance at her and flexed his shoulders against the self-loathing that un- curled within him. Doubts at following through with this vendetta stabbed at him.

His gaze swung back to Sutter, wanting to see mockery in his eyes, a challenge, a hint of smug sat- isfaction. Instead, Cole saw pain and hollow loss and the tired blue eyes of a man who had once sworn to die for him.

He passed a dirty stiff hand over his eyes, urging himself to get the deed done.

"I won't beg, Wellington. I've suffered as much as you ever did. Hell, I'd welcome death after this."

"Don't do this, Cole." Regina's voice came low be- hind him.

Her voice was steady now. He noticed because the quiet determination was at odds with the jumbled mass of fury and doubt inside him. Sutter stared right through him, daring him to finish what he'd started.

"He's been good to me, Cole. Please don't do this." Her voice tore at him, stripping little pieces of a con- science he'd cursed for too long and only recently be- gun to hear again.

Tremors shook his body. Anger, hurt, and adrenaline churned inside him. His finger stroked the trigger. *Shoot*, his mind urged. *Don't*, his heart answered.

Sutter spoke the truth. A desperate frantic voice bubbled up inside and shaded the anger. *He's been hurt as much as you have.*

Regina tried one last time. "Isn't it time to let go of the past?"

Torn between listening to his conscience and settling the grudge he'd harbored, Cole lowered his gun. "Go," he growled before he could question himself.

He watched Sutter mount and ride off. Loneliness and guilt and regret pinched his gut. He holstered his gun and looked at Regina.

Tears streaked her cheeks, flowing freely, but she was smiling and her eyes glimmered like washed emeralds. He shifted, uncomfortable with the pride on her face.

He wasn't certain he could really let go of his grudge, but he couldn't have killed Sutter in front of Regina. Cole wouldn't have been able to bear seeing the love in her eyes turn to loathing.

"Oh, Cole. I knew you couldn't kill him."

He wished he were as sure of that. Uncomfortable with the belief in her eyes, he turned away. "Don't, Regina."

With his sleeve, he wiped away the sweat and blood mingling on his face.

"You did the right thing."

So, why didn't he feel relieved? Why didn't he feel any peace?

* * *

Fear sliced through her. Had her interference sev-
ered forever the bond between her and Cole? He
wasn't angry, but even so he was locked away in some
place she couldn't reach.

Around her the sun splashed over gray-silver rock
and bounced off with polished light, over the blades
and clumps of grass that colored from brown-green
to vivid cedar.

The rolling emerald hills, speckled with browns and
gold of the coming fall, dulled as Cole turned away
from her and led Horse out of the trees. Desperation
clawed at her. "Cole, are you angry with me?"

He carefully looped the reins over the saddle horn
and swung up. "Let's just go."

He didn't look relieved as she had hoped. Instead
his eyes were bleak and he appeared to regret sparing
Sutter's life.

Cole set a ruthless, demanding pace. Despite the
Indian summer warmth, Regina's body was numb at
his withdrawal. Cerulean blue sky blurred into misty
purple horizon. The rushing drum of Horse's hooves
tangled with swallows' cries, loose clattering rocks, the
low groan of saddle leather. All normal, everyday
noises echoing in painful throbs through her body.

The sun dipped lower in the powdery sky. Inky
stains of night spread across the horizon and mirrored
the dark mood of the man in front of her.

On and on they rode, hours merging. Their steady
rhythm gathered in her mind as one thought.

They loved each other.

Was that love now null, set aside because she'd
dared to interfere? Or was Cole's withdrawal due to

the fact that he hadn't yet come to terms with the past, despite letting Sutter go?

Uncertain silence loomed between them like the wildly churning waters of a flooding canyon and they stared across the grappling waters with no hope of reaching each other.

A dull ache drilled through the bruise above her ear, striking harder and mushrooming with each pounding step of the horses.

Finally, the night snuffed out the sun and they stopped in a wooded clearing. She ached for Cole and the distance between them eroded her nerves.

She slid to the ground without his help and watched as he tossed the saddlebags and blanket onto the hard earth.

"You wouldn't really have killed him?"

After a second's hesitation, he uncinched the saddle and hefted it off Horse, lowering it to the ground.

She rubbed at a knot in her lower back, watching him carefully, fighting for some response. "It would've been murder."

His shoulders were taut and straining against the black cloth of his shirt. With tight movements, he tore the striped saddle blanket from the mare's sweat-darkened back and threw it by the saddle. Had he heard her at all?

"I know." His voice was terse, throbbing with anger and uncertainty.

"You would've hated yourself." A fine trembling scissored through her body. She fought the urge to wrap her arms around her waist.

Cole grasped a fistful of grass and moved his hand

over the horse's flanks and rounded belly, rubbing down the tired animal. Silence swelled, each long stroking motion layering the air with tension. "Don't try to paint me as something I'm not, Regina."

"I know you." She stepped toward him, reaching out with her heart at the guilt and self-disgust in his voice. "You're hurt, you're angry, but you couldn't have killed him."

He whipped around in a finely honed movement, his eyes burning like lightning-fused midnight. "I spent nearly two years of my life trying to do just that."

"Did you?" Regina fastened her gaze on his. "Or were you trying to escape the only way you knew?"

He stared at her as if he couldn't decide whether to laugh or slap her. "Whatever you want to call it, I'm not sure I can promise you that it's over."

She took a step toward him, fervent to make him know that she did understand the difficulty of getting over the past. "I realized some things about my father, things I couldn't remember because I was too focused on . . . the bad things. I couldn't have done that without you." Her voice faded on a whisper.

Closing his eyes, he shook his head and hopelessness etched his face.

A slow ache spread through her middle. "If you'd killed him, it would always be between us."

"And now, since I haven't, *yet*, what do we have?" Black eyes, masked and frigid, pierced her.

She told herself to look past the pain that caused him to be so scornful. "You wouldn't have been able to live with yourself."

"What are you, my damn conscience? Where were you when I found them together? When Sarah bled to death and lost my baby?" Cole lunged toward her and backed her into a tree.

Her heart fluttered, partly in fear and partly from relief that he was at last talking to her. "Can't you forgive me? Forgive yourself for taking her when she wasn't yours in the first place?"

His head snapped back and a vein throbbed in his neck. "Shut up."

"Isn't that how you feel? That your baby was lost because you took Sarah when she belonged to Luke?" She drew in a deep breath, sobs aching in her chest. Her voice was a bare whisper. "An eye for an eye?"

He stood as still as the trees surrounding them, his face white with pain. His eyes had blanked with fury and now they were half-wild, bordered on the edge of violence.

The struggle was evident on his face, in the convulsive clenching of his fists, the careful draw of breath. She waited. Had she gone too far? Or not far enough?

Impatience snapped inside her. She leaned into his face, anger pulsing through her body, masking the tingle she felt when her breasts teased his chest. "You know Luke was telling the truth."

"I don't know what I believe anymore." The words lacked their usual edge of conviction. He stared at her a long moment, control clearing the violent fire from his eyes. Fatigue and the vestiges of anger deepened the frown between his brows. "Leave it. We'll be home tomorrow."

"And then what? You'll go after him again?"

"Regina." His tone was laced with steel, a threat rather than a warning. He slipped off Horse's bridle and hung it on a sagging tree branch.

"How can you do that? How can you chase a man who's as hurt as you are? A man who lost as much as you did?" She stepped up behind him, hating the words even as they spewed from her mouth, willing to try anything to make him see, to lose the cold hard face of a stranger. *"Who you took from first."*

He wheeled. His arms shot out and hauled her hard against him. Her breasts crushed into the pillar-stiff wall of his chest. His heat, smoky and intense, surrounded her. Jet eyes glittered at her, twin coals of burning fire.

Fear that she had pushed too far unraveled as a cold knot in her belly.

His gaze swept over her. Desire then contempt flared in his eyes and bitterness pinched his mouth. He pushed her away.

Pain stabbed, swift and deep in the heart of her soul. For a moment, she stood there uncertain, wanting to call him back. A quick flash of fury like a sudden summer storm jolted her.

At this moment, he hated her, probably enough to strangle her, but he wanted her, too. She had seen it in his eyes, felt it in the hard lines of his body.

She wanted a life with him, free of the past. To her, it was worth fighting for. But how? He didn't believe in her love.

She, however, believed in his.

He slapped Horse on the rump and sent the dun

mare into the woods. Cole stood staring into the stand
of trees for a moment, veiled in darkness, his black
shirt and britches barely visible in the shadows of
night.

But Regina could make out the broad outline of his
shoulders heaving with silent fury, the blue gleam of
twilight on onyx hair. Before she could change her
mind, she moved up behind him and cinched her
arms tight around his waist.

His belly tensed rock-hard and his back bowed.
"Regina."

She clenched her hands tighter and pressed her
breasts against his back. With her heart clenched in
apprehension, she kissed a spot below his ear. "I'm
here and I'm not going anywhere."

He jerked and swore, his hands bolting over hers
and pulling. She tightened her arms around his waist
and breathed against his skin. "Please, Cole."

"Damn you." The words panted out in a half-
growl, half-plea. He spun and yanked her to him,
slamming his mouth down on hers.

She gasped, the sound lost in his mouth. By no
means was he gentle or even seductive. His lips were
grinding, bruising. Punishing, she realized with a jolt.

No! This wasn't what she wanted. She wanted him
to talk, to yell or break down, but not this.

She struggled in his arms, twisting her head to try
to escape the savage heat of his mouth. One broad
hand cupped her scalp, holding her steady, waylaying
her attempts to escape. Tears swelled in her chest.
Sadness bored into her like a dull spear tip.

His lips bruised, moving over hers with deliberate hardness, not trying to coax a response but to teach a lesson. A sob choked its way past her throat. His arms bit into her ribs. She wedged her hands between them and pushed, to no avail.

Powerful, trunk-hard thighs branded hers through the skirts of her dress and petticoat. Heat and the horse-and-leather scent on his skin wrapped around her, suffocating, stripping, baring.

He lifted his head finally, his breath tearing out in ragged gasps, his chest nudging hers. Black eyes burned into her. "Is this what you wanted?"

"No." She gouged a trembling hand into his chest, a futile but necessary attempt to stop him. Her lips were swollen and aching, both from his assault and the loss of his heat. Her face tingled where the scrape of his day-old beard had rubbed her. "Cole, no."

"Tell me to walk away. Tell me I'm not good enough for you." He said the words against her lips, taunting and supremely confident. Pushing her into the rough trunk of a tree, he jerked her skirt up and pulled her to him. "Tell me you don't want me."

She opened her mouth to tell him to stop, to beg him, but his head swooped down and his lips covered hers again. Panic hooked into her and she twisted away from him, a scream of fury and fear rising in her throat.

Some part of her fogged mind finally realized a change.

His lips were demanding, but not punishing. Pliant and warm, they moved over hers, long drugging kisses that sucked her strength. Slowly, with each caressing stroke of his tongue, the anger became want, the desperation urgent need.

His tongue flirted at the corners of her mouth. She forgot the words she wanted him to say and yearned only for his touch.

Long wicked fingers shimmied up the inside of her thigh and delved under the bunched fabric of her skirt, petticoat, and chemise. He touched the hot pulsing center of her and she cried out, raw with need for him.

Tendrils of heat curled through her arms and legs. The ground shifted beneath her feet and she clamped her arms around his neck, searching for steady support. He lifted her and braced her against the tree. His body welded to hers as he moved his lips over her face. Black eyes glazed with desperation and hunger.

The hard buckle of his gunbelt jabbed her thigh; the rough fabric of his britches scratched the sensitive skin on the back of her knees where they were latched around his waist. Because it matched her own, she felt the ache in him to bond. The need washed through her in honeyed heat. "Please, Cole."

Her words seemed to penetrate the haze. He looked at her with shock, then stared down at the joining of their bodies.

Her skirt was gathered in his hand, shoved around her waist. Her naked thighs gleamed palely in the shadows. He jerked back. "Holy hell, what have I done?"

"Nothing, yet." She licked her lips, muscles tensed and poised for retreat . . . or surrender.

"I'm sorry, Regina. I'm sorry." He eased her legs

from around his waist then slid her body down his. "For being angry. For trying to use you to get to Sutter. Especially for that."

"I know." Even through the gathered folds of her dress, she could feel the warmth of his skin, the rigid definition of his muscles. The ache in her spiraled into a fiery knot. "Cole, please don't go. I need you."

He stared at her, hesitation and uncertainty warring on his face. With a shaking hand, he reached out and stroked her cheek. "Not like this."

"Yes," she whispered fiercely. She curled her arms around his neck, lifting her head for his kiss. "Just like this."

He held back, his eyes dangerous, tinged with reluctant desire. For an instant, she thought he would pull away and turn his back on her. "Even after what I nearly did to Sutter?"

"Yes. You let him walk away and I love you for that."

Hunger and dark fire flared in his eyes. "Even if I can't promise to leave him be?"

"Even then."

CHAPTER EIGHTEEN

His arms locked around her waist, crushing her to him. He pressed frantic kisses over the smoothness of her cheek, his lips trailing fire along her jaw to her ear. Flames licked up her belly. Any triumph she felt at getting a response was quickly doused as her knees turned butter-soft.

His tongue plunged into the moist heat of her mouth. She flattened herself against him, her breasts aching for his touch. Her heartbeat merged with the thunder of his. The rough silk of his tongue scraped her teeth, stroked the dark velvet inside her mouth.

All the hurt and pain of the last few days melted away under the onslaught of his touch, the harsh whisper of her name on his lips.

Fire churned and boiled inside her, crashing, colliding with her reason. This was what she wanted, what they both wanted, but would it solve anything? His fingers trailed down her spine, releasing the buttons of her dress and erasing her thoughts.

Blue serge sagged down around her shoulders.

Never taking his lips from hers, Cole pushed the dress to a puddle at her feet.

His hands, calloused and hot, moved up the bare flesh of her arms. Her breath locked in her lungs. Against the swell of her breasts, she could feel the rough fabric of his shirt, the beckoning heat of his chest.

His kisses grew deeper, more languorous. Regina grabbed a handful of his shirt for balance and thumbed the buttons free, desperate to touch his skin.

He shrugged out of it, keeping one arm curled around her waist. Her breasts met the hard wall of his chest, separated only by the practical linen chemise she wore.

He lifted his head and stared down at her. Need and fierce hunger tightened his features. Despite the bruises and cuts on his face, she thought he'd never looked more handsome.

He shook out the blanket and laid it over a cushion of soft grass under a silver maple tree, reaching out a hand for her. Soft warm air whispered over her skin. She tucked her hand in his and sank to her knees in front of him.

His mouth covered hers, gently pressing, offering himself. Shaking fingers roamed down her jaw to her neck. His thumb pressed lightly into the base of her throat, measuring the rapid shot of her pulse. Her blood steamed; her skin tingled beneath the coarse callouses and smooth valleys of his palm.

She pulled away and gazed into his eyes. They were sharp with desire, burning her with blatant want. She touched his face, wanting to prolong the exquisite agony of his touch. "Go slow this time."

The banked fires in his eyes flared. Jaw tight with control, he gave an almost imperceptible nod. Moonlight filtered through the trees, sheathing half his body in pale light, speckling the ground with silver and shadow.

Branches stretched overhead, dark spindly arms merging with the night and creating a canvas of sky. Stars peeked between the leaves. The curve of a pale moon floated in and out of the branches.

Regina focused on Cole. She studied the play of thick muscle under the supple leather of his flesh, mesmerized by the corded definition of his biceps as he reached for the buttons down the front of her chemise.

Her own hands reached out, gliding over the tempered muscle of his chest and across a flat brown nipple. When his nipple peaked, she smiled and moved her hand to the other one.

He covered her hands with his and stared down at her. A smile, half-wicked, half-tolerant, quirked his lips. "Turn around. I wanna play, too."

Anticipation erupted in a ticklish burst. She did as he asked, facing away from him and looking back. Lean muscular thighs bracketed hers and a thick hard chest cushioned her shoulders. Fever pulsed from the growing arousal pushing against the small of her back. Cole's sultry heat wrapped around her, promising, protecting, luring.

Long familiar fingers burrowed into her hair, unraveling the last of her braid. He pulled his fingers through the silky length then buried his face there. Moist breath caressed her scalp, stirring the hard edge of desire, melting her insides.

Hot lips kissed the tender flesh at the base of her neck and moved around to nibble at the slope of her shoulder. A shudder passed through her. Delicious warmth invaded her limbs, tugged her toward restlessness. She sat on her knees, allowing her eyes to drift shut as heat trickled through her veins.

Her loosened chemise parted easily to bare one shoulder and ivory breast. Cole's hands clasped her around the waist and dragged up her rib cage, stopping just under the curve of her breasts.

She opened her eyes and saw his hands, large and dark against the white of her shift. Her breath came in shallow pants. Fire coiled in a knot between her legs. She sat completely still, focused on the promise of his hands on her breasts.

Moist warm lips kissed her bared shoulder then moved to the puckered scar on her back. His heat soaked into her skin, caressing, healing the jagged wound from James Cross.

She felt whole, cherished, loved. Emotion knotted her throat.

With his lips still pressed to the scar, Cole pushed her chemise down her arms. His hands moved up over her breasts. Teasing at first, just a glancing touch that made her nerves twitch and her back arch for him. He chuckled softly in her ear, his tongue flicking little circles of heat around her lobe.

Need merged with desire. She reached back, no

longer able to keep from touching him. Her palms itched to feel the smooth flow of skin over the corded sinew of his shoulders and arms. Hugged between his legs, she ran one hand up the knotted muscles of a denim-covered thigh. He pressed into her, his arousal stiff and demanding against her back.

He kissed the other ear and whispered wicked words. She shivered, her hands clenching convulsively on the soldered strength of his thighs. One hand stroked her neck, splaying wide fingers to rest just at the swell of her breast, taunting.

The other hand slid her chemise down around her hips. Warm air, light with the scent of fallow earth and bruised grass, flicked her bare skin.

Regina wanted to see him and turned her head, but at that moment, his hands covered her breasts. Desire stabbed deep in her belly, stung in her nipples. She looked down, mesmerized by the sight of Cole's hands kneading her flesh.

His hands, wide and tender, cupped her. He was walnut-dark against the pearl of her skin. His fingers pinched lightly at her nipples, rolling them into hardened wind-sensitive tips.

Her breath came out on a sigh and her fingers squeezed tighter onto his legs.

His tongue flicked and tortured her. He suckled and laved her neck, her shoulder, her back. She ached for his mouth to touch her breasts. A bubble of heat swelled inside her, mushrooming, grazing other nerve endings that ached to be stroked. One hand left her breasts and she moaned, unable to stop pressing into the hardness at her back.

Suddenly she felt his hand curve over her bottom then slip between her legs and delve inside her. A rush of slick wet heat surrounded him and she gasped. Reflexively, she squeezed her legs together to keep him there.

His finger moved in a slow caressing rhythm, stroking her, sliding deeper, reaching ever closer to the bubble of heat low in her belly. Her breath panted out to match the rhythm of his hand. She threw her head back, resting it on his shoulder. His lips moved to her neck, suckling, nipping.

Her hips rocked against his hand, straining toward his fingers and the stroke deep inside her body. Heat rushed through her and a fine trembling seized her.

"Here, honey." He withdrew his hand from between her legs and turned her toward him. She whimpered at the loss of contact and clutched at him, scooting close. The world faded into edges of blue and gray. All she could see was Cole's face, his eyes ignited with the promise of sin.

He faced her on his knees and pushed at his britches. With trembling fingers, she helped. The muscles of his belly were locked, tense with control and desire. She trailed her nails over him and the muscles rippled under her fingers.

Her mouth grew dry and with eager hands she pushed the britches to his knees. Wasting no movement, he shucked off one boot then the other, removing them along with his pants.

Then he knelt before her. Moonlight scattered over him, gilding his hair to midnight and silver, touching the strong body with shadow. There was no spare flesh, no soft angles to the man, even on his face. His features were drawn taut with desire. A muscle ticked in his jaw and fever burned in his eyes. Fever for her.

His shoulders, as wide as a wagon brace, were corded with lean power and thick sinew. His arms were brawny, the bunching muscles sculpted with the sharp definition of a master woodcarver.

Her gaze moved down the slope of his chest to a ridged abdomen, then lower. The proud length of him strained toward her. Heat splintered low, tingling between her legs.

Flames licked up her thighs and clawed in her belly. She twisted against him, unable to get close enough. He hooked an arm around her waist and pulled her to him, slowly dragging her closer to his heat.

She was doeskin soft against the smoothness of his body. Dark crisp hair on his chest teased her breasts. Her nipples puckered and she rubbed against him, delighting in the feel of his skin on hers.

He leaned back against the tree and cupped her bottom to lift her over him. The chemise stayed in a pool on the blanket. With his gaze on hers, Cole guided her toward his arousal.

"Not yet," she panted, trying to hold herself away from him.

He tugged her lower. "Shhh. Trust me."

The slight pressure of his bluntness against her most sensitive part made her want to scream. She felt poised between agony and fulfillment, but she relaxed in his arms and shifted her thighs wider.

His throbbing length slid into her. Sleek slow heat streamed through her body and snatched her breath.

Wondrous sensation sparked her skin. Her nerve endings opened up, feeling the velvet hardness inside, the minute pulse of his body, the rub of calloused hands on her hips.

Her legs quivered with the effort to go down slow, to prolong the feel of him sliding into her. Panting, she braced her hands on either side of his head, the tree bark biting into her palms.

His hands stroked up from her bottom to the curve of her waist. Fire tickled up her spine. He held her steady for a moment then his length filled her, pulsing with warmth, chasing the loneliness from her body.

His hands tightened on her waist and he began to move. Slowly at first, showing her how to match him, how to meet his slow withdrawal with the opposite stroke of her body.

Need coiled inside her, tighter, quivering like a drawn bowstring, plucking her nerves into one focused center. The need swelled and burst, squelching her last hold on control. She moved faster and met the hard thrusts of his body with her own, led toward an unspoken promise.

Silken fire pushed into her, funneling through her body. She struggled to keep her eyes on Cole, but the urgency drove her, reaching, reaching for release. Yearning layered with want, building higher, probing deeper, sweeping her mind. His body pumped into hers. She flexed her thighs tight around his and threw back her head.

She cried out and his mouth stilled on her breasts. Tension shattered then released in a burst of showering light. Her body seized up then relaxed in a series of small convulsions.

He drove into her hard, once, twice, three times and cried her name in a low guttural moan. She bowed her head against his shoulder, eyes heavy and her body sated.

"I love you." He mouthed the words against her hair.

She snuggled against him, stroking her hand over his belly. "Mmmm, me too."

He looked up at her and brushed away a damp strand of hair, mumbling sleepily, "I would like, at least once, to have a bed when we do this."

She laughed quietly, storing the moment in her mind.

They lay there together, wrapped in each other's heat and the scent of their loving. Against her ear, Cole's heart slowly thudded back to normal. She pressed close, her legs tangled with his, toes touching.

Night settled around them, black and soft, with brilliant stars winking from a slate sky. Like an insidious infection, thoughts tumbled back of what had happened with Sutter. Cole hadn't said he would give up his vendetta.

She held on to the memory of their lovemaking with bittersweet desperation, wanting to wash away the uncertainty with the warmth of his touch and the hard edges of his body against hers.

Nothing had changed.

Making love with Regina tripped the doors to Cole's past. As they left camp the next morning, voices, harsh and gentle, rained through his mind.

I never knew what it was to lie with her and you did.

I'd rather kill you myself than watch you waste any more of your life.

I'm glad my children can't see what their uncle has become.

It's time to let go, Cole. I'm here. I'll help.

The voices flicked through his head, stinging his conscience.

He wanted a life with Regina. He saw that clearly, simple and direct.

He also saw the searing pain on Luke's face yesterday as they'd fought.

Feathery memories exploded like mortars. He and Luke behind the schoolhouse taking licks in the third grade. The twin sorrels they had raised and trained together then raced. The first dead man they'd seen when they were twelve. They had shared utter trust, utter secrecy. Until the war.

Other memories pushed at Cole, bringing the bite of regret. The times he'd missed with his family, the nights he'd slept outside and ached with the pain of hating his best friend only to wake more determined than ever to find him.

Behind him on Horse, Regina sat with her cheek cushioned on his back, arms around him, her breasts full against him, her legs straddled on either side of his. A sense of long-forgotten peace shifted through him. For the rest of his life, he wanted to feel her next to him, wake up and see her green eyes smiling and cloudy with sleep just as he had this morning.

Oh yes, he knew he wanted that. And just the knowledge gave him a feeling of being unfettered, a sudden swell in his chest as though he'd been freed from a giant vise.

Regina was the one who'd made Cole see past the pain of losing his baby, into the promise of another future. She'd also made him see that Sutter had lost the woman he loved and to his best friend at that.

Cole realized, with a sharp stabbing in his gut, exactly what Luke and Sarah had shared. And lost.

Since he and Regina had left the campsite, she'd been quiet, withdrawn. Plagued by memories of his harshness last night? Raw mind-burning need for her had consumed him and he hadn't been able to tell her what she wanted to hear.

Sunlight drenched the rolling hills around them. White light glinted off the grass in blue-green prisms. To the east he could see the dark smudge of roofs and the white spire of a church pinpointing the small town of Advance. They weren't far from Calcutta now.

Horse moved with an impatient abbreviated version of her longer stride. Cole kept the reins tight on her, wanting to prolong the trip as long as possible. His gut was pinched with regret and confusion. Was it really as easy as Regina said? Could he simply let go of Sutter and the past?

You believe him, don't you?

Yes, he did. Cole had been a blind fool, run by hate and anger. His hands gripped the reins tighter, leather burning between his fingers. He loved Regina and tried to imagine what it would have done to him if Luke had married her, conceived a child with her, as Cole had done with Sarah.

Regina shifted, cuddling closer to him. His back

perspired lightly with the added heat of her body on his. Their physical bond had produced a deeper, emotional one. He knew she would always feel about him the way he felt about her. Cole knew now exactly what Sutter had felt for Sarah.

He wanted to shed his desire for revenge. The admission, one he'd shied from for months, coursed through his body. It softened the hate and vengeance and blind anger that had driven him for almost two years. It left him feeling as though he'd been knocked to the ground by a bolt of lightning. Winded, amazed, incredibly lucky to be alive and have a second chance.

"Do you think Luke will find Wendell?" Regina's voice came low over his left shoulder. She raised her head from his back.

Despite the way he'd lashed at her last night, she didn't dance around the subject of Sutter. Cole's hand caressed hers where it curved onto his belly. "Yes."

She sighed. "Good. I hope . . ."

"What is it?" His senses pulled to her through an invisible connection. He recognized the worry under her words and the hint of a fear that had nothing to do with guns or knives or Wendell Cross.

"What if they don't want me to stay?"

For a brief instant, he didn't understand. Then he did. The town. His hand curled over hers and squeezed. "You'll always have Leah. Once you explain, she'll understand."

"What about the others?" Her words were shadowed with pain and uncertainty. "What about Elliot?"

"I don't know, honey." He wondered how the

townspeople would react to her now and decided he would gladly strangle anyone who treated her badly. He said fiercely, "All I know is, I'll be there for you and so will Leah and the rest of my family."

"You can't force them, Cole," she said with a small laugh.

He glanced at her over his shoulder and grinned. "Sure I can."

She nuzzled his cheek and tightened her arms around his waist.

They rode in peaceful silence for a moment. Cole tried to draw her mind from the problem of town and Cross. "What will you do with the money Abe gave you?"

"I'd like to buy some land. What about your part?"

"It's not my money."

"Of course it is. You helped me get there, alive."

"Nope, I'm not touching it."

"What *will* you do?" Then low-pitched and laced with dread. "After we get home?"

Cole swallowed, studying the glimmer of golden light on the green hills beyond, the sparkling silver of a bluff face, the dark twist of the Mississippi off to his left. He swallowed hard and felt a surge of release. "I'm gonna settle with Luke."

Her body grew tight. At his waist, her hands relaxed then fell away. Despite the warmth of the sun, he felt a loss as cold as a winter night burrow between them.

"Not the way you think," he said quietly. For the first time, he realized exactly what he was giving up. And what he was gaining. A life free of secrets, free of guilt and hate, the promise of a future with the woman he loved. "I need to see him face to face, tell him I was wrong—"

He broke off, feeling her gaze swerve to him. For a moment, there was only the whisper of stirrup-high grass brushing the horse's legs and belly, the muffled thud of hoofbeats, the charging rhythm of his heart.

"You're giving it up? You're sure?"

"Yes. Partly for you, but for me, too." He half-turned in the saddle, caught her green eyes shimmering with hope and disbelief. "This thing between us, this love . . . I never thought I'd find something like that, like you."

"Cole."

"You showed me there were things other than hate, like light and happiness and strength." He scraped a thumb across the dewy skin of her cheek. "You made me see what I was missing, but mainly what I took from another man." He leaned toward her, brushing his lips over hers.

Her gaze held his, heating with pleasure. "Really?"

"Yes. It's time to let go. I knew it yesterday, but—" He paused and exhaled a deep bitter breath. "I was a fool, blinded by anger. And guilt. I haven't done right by him and I've been trying to justify it by repaying him for what I thought he did to me."

"Oh, Cole."

"He did nothing more than love a woman. I'm the one who took her."

"You can't shoulder all the blame for that," Regina pointed out quietly. "She married you, too."

"I know, and it was wrong. On both our parts. I knew I didn't love her in the way I should've when I married her. I suspect she felt the same, but Luke was gone. I thought I could keep some part of him that way. It was a mistake. For a long time, I felt it was the one mistake that cost Sarah's life."

Silence dragged between them, peppered with the scrape of the bit against Horse's teeth, the overhead cry of a hawk. Relief rushed dark and healing through his soul, dredging up old pain, washing it through his body and releasing it in one last gushing torrent.

"What will you tell him about her?" Regina rested her head on his shoulder, her breath tickling his ear.

Cole exhaled slowly, filled with melded images of an innocent blond girl laughing up at Luke, a broken woman crying at his funeral, pale and dying in Cole's arms. "I'll tell him the good things. She never stopped loving him, wanting him. We were friends at first, she and I, drawn together out of grief. But we married for the wrong reasons."

His breath came in halting jerks just like his words. Purifying, releasing the past and tucking it away in a newer, more forgiving part of him. "It drove us both to do things, *say* damnable things. I felt trapped and now I see she did, too.

"She wouldn't have betrayed me. He was right about that. I know he wouldn't, *didn't*, either," he corrected. "He needs to know that."

"So you're going to find him?"

"I have to." He heard the uncertainty in her voice and turned to reassure her. "I won't let it drag on for years. I'm not turning it into another mission, but I have to try."

Her gaze met his, searching. After a moment, she

nodded. Her arms tightened around him and she was quiet for so long Cole held his breath. *Did she believe him? Could she trust him?*

She edged up onto the saddle until even the slight wind couldn't squeeze between their bodies. Her voice was a choked whisper. "I love you, Cole Wellington. I don't know if I'll ever love you more than I do at this moment."

His throat burned and he gripped her hand hard. "I love you too, Regina."

"Why don't you stop this horse and show me? Right now."

With a slow grin and a quick jerk on the reins, he did.

They entered Calcutta on the north end of town. Shadows stretched down Main Street, painting everything in the muted red-gold light of sunset. Regina felt the same uncertainty and fright she had the day she had first arrived.

She'd come then on a steamer, rather than the back of a horse. But then, as now, she was uncertain of her reception. And once again she had escaped Wendell Cross.

Tensed against the security of Cole's back, her gaze scooted over the town and rested on familiar things. Late day sun glared off the sparkling windows of Stern's Mercantile and polished to buff the brass door plaque announcing Clemma's Restaurant and Boarding house. The familiar carefully carved wooden sign above the door boasted the best apple pie in the state of Missouri.

The climbing chime of a steamboat floated from the docks. A barge bumped the pier and the tip-tap of footsteps was interrupted by the clatter of a dropping plank.

Scattered groups of people littered the streets. Couples strolled from Clemma's. An elderly man hobbled out of Stern's. From the Blue China came the loose clatter of the piano and the hooting of card players.

Two boys darted across the street in front of Horse and disappeared down the alley leading to the docks. Nostalgia bloomed inside Regina. The town was unchanged, welcoming, sheltering.

Cole gave Horse a sharp kick and the mare took the last few steps into town. Regina closed her eyes for a moment and savored the security of being home. Would the town take her back? Uncertainty drew tight across her shoulders.

Cole squeezed her hand. "We're here."

She opened her eyes and finally allowed her gaze to rest on the orphanage. Golden lamplight, faint in the last rays of the sun, gilded the gleaming double windows. The weathered gray-brown wood drew as much pride from Regina as a brand-new home would have. The old straight-backed chair hadn't moved from its place by the front door, still guarded by the cracked churn.

Regina held on to the slat-hard muscle of Cole's arm and slid to the ground. She stood for a moment, soaking in the warmth of the place, garnering strength from it.

Cole dismounted behind her and laid a hand on her shoulder. "They'll be glad to see you."

She glanced at him and bit her lip. The front door opened abruptly, making her jerk around. For a frozen instant, she stared at Leah.

A smile broke through the shock in Leah's gray eyes. "Regina, Cole! Oh, my goodness. Welcome home."

She hurried off the porch to be caught up in Cole's arms. Regina thought Leah looked surprised at her brother's greeting, but pleased, too. She hugged Cole, reaching out her other hand for Regina.

Regina grasped it gratefully, her words caught in her throat. Long seconds passed before Cole lowered his sister to the ground.

Tears sheened her eyes when she opened her arms to Regina and hugged her. "We've all been so worried. Are you all right?" She glanced from one to the other, her gaze pausing for an instant on Cole's arm, now around Regina's shoulders. "We got your wire, but that was a week ago."

"We're fine," Cole assured her, still keeping his arm wrapped around Regina. "Got a lot to tell you."

"I'd say so." A teasing warmth lit her gray eyes.

"I must apologize right up front. I'm not a nun. I had to lie about that. Oh, Leah, I'm so sorry." Apology and dread and excitement pushed through Regina. The words tumbled out. "I should've told you what I was doing here, but I couldn't. It was too dangerous."

"Don't worry. Cole told me a little bit in his wire, but I still expect a full explanation."

"You'll get one." Regina smiled at her friend, overwhelmed with wanting to tell everything, including about her and Cole. She stepped up to the porch with Leah.

"Regina?"

She turned to find Cole regarding her with that familiar heat in his eyes. Along with an unease she hadn't seen before. "I'm gonna let you talk to Leah Beth alone."

"Are you leaving?" Surely he wasn't going after Luke now?

He jerked his head in the direction of the saloon down the street where Gage and Emmett stood. "I'm due a long talk with my brothers. That's where I'll be, okay?"

"Okay."

He leaned over and brushed a soft kiss on her lips then walked away.

Regina stood looking after him, feeling an aching warmth at the sight of his loose-hipped saunter. Love swelled in her heart, a piercing deep stab. She hoped everything would work out for him, for them.

Beside her, Leah gawked. Looping an arm through Regina's, she whispered, "Do tell."

Regina laughed, a slight blush warming her face as they stepped up on the porch. "I will, I promise. But first, how are the children?"

"They're fine, except for missing you. They didn't really understand."

Regina shook her head, hurting at all the pain and confusion she had caused the children. She still hadn't forgotten the wounded look on Elliot's face and hoped it wasn't too late to regain his friendship and trust.

"Miss Leah, I've finished the potatoes." Elliot

rounded the corner of the orphanage and came to a dead stop. "Sister—"

The word broke like a brittle twig as memory and anger flooded his face. For a brief unguarded instant, joy and relief flushed his newly shaved cheeks then were masked. With a stiff nod, he spun and marched back behind the orphanage and toward the field beyond.

"Elliot, wait!" Regina started after him then turned to Leah. "I owe you an explanation, too."

"I can wait. Go."

"But—"

"Go." Leah gave Regina a gentle shove and opened the door to the orphanage.

"Who's that, Miss Leah? Is someone here?"

Regina recognized Laura's voice and her heart clenched.

"Yes, Laura. A surprise for later." Leah gave Regina one last commanding look before she shut the door with a firm click.

Regina took a deep breath and hurried to catch Elliot.

CHAPTER NINETEEN

Wendell shifted his weight from his injured leg, staring through the crack in the warehouse door. Regina Harrison disappeared around the corner of a small mouse-gray building across the street. Wellington had hightailed it to the saloon and gone inside with two other men.

Wendell had been holed up here for almost a whole day and he was hungry. His leg, where Wellington had shot him, was healing slowly, but there was no infection.

Uncaring of the few people in the street, Wendell pulled his hat low over his eyes and stepped outside. He walked across the street as though he were going to Stern's Mercantile. At the porch, he sidestepped into the alley that separated the store from the building where he'd seen Regina Harrison disappear.

He could hear her voice, low and impassioned. And at odd intervals, a young male. He caught back a chuckle, leaning down to slip the knife from his boot.

She wouldn't get away this time.

*   *   *

Regina reached the back corner of the orphanage, her gaze scanning the stand of trees beyond, the hoe and shovel leaning against the back door of the kitchen, a freshly curled pile of potato shavings with browning edges, stacked branches and twigs in the woodpile.

"Elliot!" she called, turning for the lean-to.

Orange-red sunlight cast long shadows. Through the half-open door, she saw a movement. She walked forward, praying she would know what to say and that he would forgive her.

"Elliot, please." She stepped inside, assaulted by cool air and deep pockets of shadow. "Won't you at least talk to me? Let me explain."

"I've got work to do. Haven't got time for any talking." His voice was gruff and he pushed past her, his arms loaded with a burlap bag of potatoes.

Squaring her shoulders, she followed him. She noticed the dark hair, longer now and curling over the collar of his work shirt, a tiny nick in his neck attesting to the fact that he had started to shave while she'd been gone. "We were friends once, Elliot. I hope you'll remember that and give me a chance."

"Friends don't lie to each other." He dumped the bag and potatoes rolled onto the ground, thudding into the weathered base of the orphanage. He leveled an angry hazel gaze on her. "Friends don't leave without saying anything. They don't just disappear."

"I didn't run off and abandon you and the others. There were reasons, very good ones. Mainly though I was concerned about your safety."

"I can take care of myself."

"That's not what I meant." She sighed, praying for patience. She couldn't really blame him for acting more like a boy than a man. After all, he was hurt and angry and she had left him with no explanation. "Remember on the steamer, how you wanted to protect Joel?"

He didn't acknowledge that he'd heard, just picked up a potato and wiped it on his grimy pants. His jaw tightened.

She forged on. "You knew you couldn't protect him from the disease, but you tried. You kept him warm and covered, stole food for him, kept people away from him."

He stared intently at the potato as if he'd never seen one before. "It's not the same thing at all."

"No, it's not, but I'm trying to tell you I was protecting you the only way I knew. Just the way you protected your brother. If I'd told you the truth, you could've been killed just as easily as I could've."

"We don't need you anymore." He didn't look at her when he spoke, just stared angrily at the vegetable in his fist. "We have Clemma and Reverend Holly. Clemma wants us, the little ones at least."

"I'm sorry, Elliot. I never meant to hurt you. If you change your mind, I'd like to explain." Regina turned away, dejected.

Though she couldn't have done anything differently, she blamed herself for the secrecy. She walked to the corner, hoping he would stop her, but there was only silence and the rustle of a gentle wind in the trees.

"I-I thought you were dead. When I saw that man

in the lean-to—" Elliot's voice cracked. "And then you disappeared."

Slowly she turned and saw the anger and fear and hurt in his eyes. Her heart squeezed for him, caused her words to come out raw and hoarse. "I didn't leave on purpose. I had to. The man who killed Lance tried to kill me, too."

"Tried to kill you? Why? Does the man who tried to kill you know you're not really a nun?"

"Yes." Emotion burned her throat. "That man's name was James Cross, but he came after me as a favor to his brother, Wendell."

"Why?" His rawboned hands clenched then unclenched. He stepped toward her. "Why would they want to kill you?"

She swallowed, somehow more desperate for him to believe her than she had been about the jury. Of course, at the trial she'd had Abe and the evidence he'd gathered. Now it was only her word for Elliot. "Wendell killed my father and I saw him do it. I've been in St. Louis, testifying at his trial."

"I'm sorry." A flush crawled up Elliot's neck and sheepish tortured eyes met Regina's. He sucked in a deep breath. "So it's over? You're home to stay?"

Regina gave a tremulous smile and plunged in, telling him of Cole's help, the trip, and the shock of Wendell's escape. She left out nothing.

In the saloon, Cole sat across the table from his brothers. Gage flicked one card then another from the top of the deck onto the middle of the table. Emmett leaned forward in his chair, his hands wrapped around a double shot of scotch. Cole had explained about Regina and how Sutter was connected to her and Cross.

"I'm glad to hear you're staying for good, Cole." Emmett sipped at his scotch. "Mama and Papa will be, too."

Gage sat silently, tossing cards with a quick flick of his wrist.

Cole judged his younger brother's stoic silence. "You don't believe I'm staying."

"It's not because I don't want to. I'm just skeptical."

"How about if I asked to join your horse operation?"

A wide grin split Emmett's face and he glanced from Cole to Gage.

Gage's hand froze, a card balanced between his first two fingers. "You mean it? You're that serious?"

"I'm damn serious. If you want me, I think I could be of use to you."

"You know I've wanted your help since I started, but what about Sutter? Are you gonna be here all the time or only when you don't have the itch?"

"I still have some things to settle with him—"

"That's what I thought." Gage pitched the card through the air to flick Cole's chest.

"No. It's not like that. It's strictly to apologize, try to mend some fences." The saloon doors banged open behind Cole. "I figure I owe him at least as much of an explanation as I gave all of you."

"Well, looks like your chance just walked in the door," Gage drawled, his voice terse.

Emmett sputtered into his scotch. "Great day! I never thought I'd see him again."

Cole frowned and turned.

Sutter, his chin scabbed and swollen from his fight with Cole, strode over. "I'm glad I found you." He bobbed his head at the others. "H'llo, Gage. Emmett."

"What's going on?" Cole rose from the table, uncertainty and apprehension tangling in his body. Alarm bumped his chest. "I thought you were after Cross."

"I am."

"What is it?" Dread clamored and Cole's hand closed over his gun.

Gage and Emmett immediately bucked away from their chairs.

Gage crowded into Cole's elbow, bumping the table across the floor. "Don't pull that gun."

Cole noticed the pinched mouths, the wary gazes fixed on his revolver, and realized with a stab of disappointment that his brothers still weren't sure of him. He couldn't blame them. It would take more than a chat to show them he meant what he said.

A wry smile curved Sutter's mouth as his gaze skimmed over the other Wellingtons. "I've been following him since I left you."

"He came through here?"

"No. He came *straight* here."

"Regina." Cole said her name on a gut-squeezing breath, launching for the swinging doors. "She's at the orphanage."

Luke pivoted. "Let's go."

"Leah's over there, too." Emmett followed Cole and Luke with Gage one step behind.

The four of them filed through the saloon doors and Emmett turned the opposite way. "I'm going for the sheriff. Don't do anything stupid. Just check it out."

"Right." Cole nodded. He glanced at Luke, already stepping off the planked porch. "How far behind him were you?"

"I've been here since last night, watching for some sign of him. So far, nothing."

Cole nodded, his heart starting the slow gathering rush of a well pump. "We'll check inside first, make sure they're okay."

The three men walked abreast on one side of the street, stirring up anemic whorls of dust, their boots making hollow scraping sounds on the hard earth.

Cole's gaze roved from one side of the street to the other, taking in the spanking white porch of Doc Warren's house and office, the clump of people gathering in front of Clemma's. Eyes slitted against the last blood-red rays of daylight, he studied the warehouse that belonged to his brother-in-law, but saw no movement.

More people streamed outside Clemma's to stand on the porch. Their voices buzzed like a stirred nest of hornets. Above the hum, he could hear one voice clearly, but only drifts of the conversation.

"She's here . . . no nun . . . not staying."

They passed Stern's Mercantile and slowed. Cole shut out the noises of the people, the calls from the docks, the squeal of children, and focused on the orphanage.

Like the corners of a separating triangle, the men

fanned out to bracket the building. Cole listened closely, focusing on a point of rusty light that slanted onto the weathered porch.

"It's too quiet," he murmured in a bare whisper.

Gage and Luke nodded. With one finger, Cole motioned Gage behind him. Sutter waited at the left corner, gun at the ready. Cole slipped up to the door then kicked. The door crashed open, splinters chipping off and spewing into the air.

He knelt, gun drawn, and stared into the startled gray eyes of his sister. A small girl with dark hair, clutching a handful of Leah's skirt, peeked around from behind her. Two small boys froze in the act of rising from their place on the floor. An older girl peered around the corner of the hallway.

"Cole! For heaven's sake!" Leah pressed a hand to her throat, eyeing him with exasperation.

With a quick scan of the room, Cole judged they were alone. "Where's Regina?"

Leah frowned and gestured toward the door. "She's outside. Looking for Elliot. He was in the back—" She broke off, her eyes going wide as Sutter stepped up to the door. "Luke Sutter? Lord!" Her gaze sliced to Cole. "What's going on here, Cole?"

He didn't answer, but whirled and bolted out the door. Sutter followed.

Leah's voice echoed behind Cole. "Somebody tell me what's going on."

"Later," Gage promised, following Cole outside.

Cole faced Luke. "Let's split up."

Luke nodded sharply. "I'll go around back. One shot if you find something."

"Right." Cole stepped off the small porch and halted, turning back as Sutter strode to the opposite end of the porch. "Sutter?"

"Yeah?" Luke halted mid-stride, glancing over his shoulder.

"Thanks."

"I'm not doing it for you. I'm doing it for her."

"I know. If he's back there—"

"I'll get his attention. You kill the bastard." He glanced down the alley. "Don't miss, soldier."

Don't miss, soldier. From the time they were ten until they were fourteen, Cole and Luke had pretended they were fighting the British and King George. They took turns issuing orders as the commanding officer. Cole felt an answering smile before he could stop it. "No, sir."

At the word, Luke looked shocked. A flash of memory warmed his eyes then he turned away. His shoulders disappeared around the corner between the orphanage and Stern's.

Cole started down the building-length alley toward the lean-to, searching the dirt, his ears straining for any telltale noise.

He picked out partial footprints, wide-spaced ones then some that might be Regina's. Was she behind the orphanage? He could feel no watchful eyes, hear no voices. Nerves stretched taut. His gaze rose and scanned the edge of trees at the north end of town, the barely visible corner of the lean-to.

A scream shattered the quiet and raised hackles over Cole's back.

*   *   *

Sweat trickled between her shoulder blades, down the side of her face. Regina gripped the thick piece of blunt wood she'd snatched from the woodpile and faced Wendell Cross.

Elliot, pale and unmoving, lay sprawled facedown on the ground behind Wendell. Blood seeped from his mouth. He'd tried to overtake Cross, who'd knocked him unconscious with two well-placed blows.

She eyed the bandage on Wendell's leg where Cole had shot him and noted that Wendell moved with only slight stiffness. He advanced on her, shifting his knife from one hand to the other in a careful rhythm. Back and forth. Back and forth. Taunting, stalking, closing in.

Fading sunlight glared off the metal, striking silver-red shards of light over the ground. The blade, sleek and newly whetted, winked at her, coveting her skin.

Cross stepped closer, triumph and avaricious confidence gleaming in his blue eyes. The threat of losing her future with Cole struck a savage blow. Rage erupted and showered through her like expelled gunpowder. Raising the wood above her head, Regina screamed in fury and brought the stick down, aiming for Wendell's head.

He blocked her, the blade ringing hollowly against the wood. She swung for his belly. He jabbed, ripping a hole in the material of her skirt.

He was close enough that she could smell his unwashed skin and his breath, musty like old water. "I'm gonna carve you into little pieces." He edged closer.

She swung straight and true, slamming wood into his injured leg. He screamed, an animal cry of fury and pain. Momentarily he faltered, his knee buckling, one hand reaching for his leg. Pain wrenched his face into deep distorted lines.

She whirled and ran.

A hand tangled in her skirt and yanked. She toppled back into his chest. One thick arm circled her waist and hot breath seared her ear. "I've waited a long time for this. You're gonna pay for everything you did to me and my brothers."

Before she could move, cool steel caressed her neck. Panic wedged into her lungs, fluttered at the edges of her mind. She stood without moving. *Think*, she ordered. *Be calm.*

Wendell's shirt buttons dug into her back and moist heat soaked from him through her clothes. Fear roiled in her belly, churning until she felt nauseated. Air became sparse, tight. Her head spun and her eyes blurred.

The sleek edge of the knife pressed into her throat. A pain stretched across her chest and she realized she wasn't breathing. *Cole. Oh, Cole, help me.*

"Let her go!"

"Drop the knife, Cross!"

Regina gasped. Cole *and* Luke!

Wendell jerked, shifting the flat side of the blade against her windpipe. He turned so that he and Regina stood between Cole and Luke. "Lose you guns or she dies *now*."

"Let her go, damn it!"

"I said back off!"

"Drop it!"

"Cole!"

The voices butted, colliding, raspy and brutal, threaded with hysteria. Cole's deep baritone and Luke's resonant voice meshed with Cross's cracked, angry words and Regina's shrill call, joining in a seething mass of frenzied noise.

Cross cursed and pressed the knife into her throat.

She cried out and the voices aborted immediately.

Thick silence pressed the air, weighted, deadly. Wendell's voice rasped. "Drop your weapons."

A polished Winchester rifle slid across the ground in front of Regina. Then an ivory-handled Smith & Wesson revolver.

Wendell wheezed in a deep tone, "Get over here where I can see you."

Luke walked slowly in front of them, anger pinching his face, drawing white lines around his mouth and eyes. Skin stretched taut over high cheekbones.

Regina shifted her gaze to Cole. A vein throbbed in his temple. Fury darkened his face, sharpened his eyes to murderous points.

"Go!" Wendell tipped his head toward the alley and town. When Cole hesitated, Wendell tightened his arm around Regina. With a subtle movement of his wrist, he pointed the blade tip at her throat.

Blood rushed from her head in a dizzying spin. She kept her gaze on Cole, away from the wide silver blade pinching her skin. Every second pulsed with dread, scraping across her raw nerves.

With impotent rage creasing their features, Cole and Luke moved backward toward town. Wendell followed, shoving Regina along with his body. She couldn't feel her arms or legs, only the promise of the blade against her flesh, and her vision blurred.

The alley spread and gave way to trees and the north end of Main Street. Cole and Luke backed past the orphanage and stopped beneath a monstrous elm. Wendell nudged Regina forward and past the porch of the orphanage.

She gasped.

Cross stiffened in alarm.

The entire town was gathered in a knot in the middle of the street. To her right, Leah and Gage stood with the children on the porch. The adults wore a look of startled fury; the children's eyes were wide with horror.

"Damnation," Wendell breathed, but kept walking. "Anybody moves, she gets it."

"You can't get us all, Cross." Cole's voice, strong and sure, bounced from under the tree.

"Give it up." She recognized Luke's voice.

"Turn yourself in. You haven't got a chance." Was that Marshal Sanders?

"I mean it. Get back or she dies." Wendell shifted the knife until the wicked edge nipped at her throat.

"If she does, we'll torture you slow and let the vultures finish you off." Cole's voice shook with anger.

Fear bubbled in her throat. She struggled not to panic and skimmed her gaze over the crowd. Paden Stern, owner of the mercantile, looked angry and confused. Clemma stood next to Reverend Holly, both their faces pale.

Marshal Sanders spoke again. "You're outnumbered, Cross, and you know it."

"I'm gettin' on that horse and we're leavin'."

Regina felt Wendell's lips move against her hair, though the words sounded distant and thick. Revulsion shuddered through her. Like the roll of a giant tide, gradual and testing, the crowd moved forward.

Wendell tensed and tightened his grip on the knife. Regina felt a tremor rattle through his hand. A sharp pain pierced the left side of her neck.

She sucked in her breath as she realized he had pricked her. Her knees buckled and she dug her heels into the hard ground, afraid she would cut herself if she collapsed.

Abrupt silence webbed the town, shrouding the sound of breathing, the squawk of birds, the more distant noises of feet and planks from the docks.

From the corner of her eye, Regina saw a blur of movement in the trees next to Cole. Wendell must have seen it, too.

The next few seconds jammed together in Regina's mind. Wendell flicked his wrist to slide the knife across her throat.

"Now!" Cole yelled.

Luke lunged for Wendell, feigned then rolled to the right.

The knife flew from Wendell's hand and flipped end over end, spinning through the air with deadly precision. The blade buried itself in Luke's leg. Regina screamed and elbowed Wendell in the stomach. A shot cracked the air.

As though pulled by a heavy force, Regina turned. Smoke curled from a gun in Cole's hand. A gun? How had he gotten a gun?

She saw Elliot then, standing next to him, staring with wide horror-filled eyes at Wendell. Wendell's arm around her waist went limp then locked. He toppled to the ground, pulling her with him.

Hysteria and fear erupted inside her. She scrambled and rolled away, yanking her dress from his hold with short, jerky movements.

Turning, she balanced on her hands and knees, seeing the small round hole between his eyes. Blood seeped from the back of his head and soaked the hard ground. Whimpers echoed in her ears. She realized they came from her.

A chill funneled through her and her teeth chattered. On her knees, she backed away, digging her hands into the earth, ignoring the small pebbles and hard dirt scraping at her palms. "Cole? C-Cole?"

"I'm here, honey. I'm here." He fell to his knees and scooped her up in his arms. Holding her close to his chest, he rocked her, crooning sweet words she didn't understand. "Are you all right? Regina, look at me."

"Y-yes." She raised her gaze to his, belief seeping through the shock. A trembling hand stroked his face, tapering gently over the worried frown between his brows, the deep creases around his mouth. "Oh, Cole. How did you do that?"

He laughed and hugged her to him. She looped her arms around his waist, soaking in the strength and warmth of him, squeezing her eyes shut.

It's over. It's over. She let the thought circle her mind, resounding until it calmed her shaking. She was safe. Cole was here. Luke— "Luke? And Elliot?" She pushed away from Cole's chest. "How are they?"

"Here's Elliot." Cole tightened his arms around her and turned so she could look up at the boy. "He's the one who got the gun to me."

He stood behind Cole, the glare of the sun masking his face. Marshal Sanders, Clemma, Reverend Holly, and Paden Stern gathered in a small clump beside him.

Elliot knelt beside her, his right cheek puffy and swollen. Blood caked at the cut on his mouth, but his eyes were bright. "Are you all right?"

"Yes." The words hurt her throat. A knot of love and relief tangled there and she reached out to him. "Oh, Elliot, thank you. My dear, dear friend."

He ducked his head as though embarrassed, but squeezed her hand. "You're welcome."

Regina looked up at Cole. "And Luke?"

He glanced over his shoulder. "Gage and Emmett are takin' him to Doc Warren's. Let's go see."

He set her on her feet and steadied her, then rose, holding her close.

She peered at Elliot's bruised face. "Are you sure you're okay?"

"I'm fine. Go ahead."

Regina took a step away from him. "I'll be back."

Clemma and Reverend Holly spoke at once. "Regina, are you all right?"

She smiled and assured them she was.

The children rushed up along with Leah, who raised her voice above the din of concern. "Regina?"

Her gray eyes were wet, her sooty lashes spiked with tears.

Regina felt her own eyes fill. "I'm fine."

"Thanks to Luke," Cole added somberly.

"Can you take care of Elliot?" she asked Leah, turning to gaze at the boy behind her.

"Yes." Leah hugged the younger man. "He'll be fine."

Elliot walked to the orphanage porch with Leah, then turned. "Sis—I mean, Regina?"

She turned, her heart stuttering at the old title. "Yes?"

"I'm glad you're back," he said simply, his hazel gaze holding hers.

In his voice, she heard forgiveness. Joy choked her for a moment. "Me, too, Elliot. Me, too."

"So are we." Reverend Holly took her hand in both of his and squeezed. Clemma nodded, dabbing at the corner of her eye.

Regina realized that the townspeople had rallied to save her from Wendell and emotion lumped in her chest.

Marshal Sanders clapped Cole on the back. "That was some fancy shooting, Wellington. I could sure use a deputy with an aim like that."

"Thanks, Ted, but I'll be workin' horses from now on with my brother."

"Well, if you change your mind, there's a place for you."

Cole glanced at Regina, who was staring at him with emotion knotting her throat. "I was gonna tell you later."

"Everything went okay?"

He smiled, wide and full of hope. "Yeah, it did."

She squeezed his hand. "Let's go check on Luke."

With Cole's arm tight around her, they walked down Main Street toward Doc Warren's Victorian-style house, which also served as his office. She and Cole walked through the sitting room with its burgundy wingback chairs and lacy curtains into the small examining room where everyone stood gathered around Luke.

A pair of torn bloody pants lay in a heap on the floor. Luke rested on a table in the middle of the room, his lower half covered by a sheet. Doc stood to one side, threading a needle.

Luke was pale, but his eyes gleamed at Regina as she neared the table where he lay. "Glad to see you're all right."

"Yes, thanks to you." She dashed the edge of one hand under her eyes. "I don't know what to say. You took an awful chance."

He squinted over her shoulder and up at Cole. "I told you it'd work."

"Yeah. Just like when we were kids."

Regina held her breath, hardly daring to hope, as Cole moved up beside her. Would Luke accept Cole's apology?

Luke's eyes fluttered shut for a moment then opened. "Yeah. That was a pretty good plan."

Cole leaned over him. "I can never repay you for what you've given me. For saving her life. After everything I've done—" His voice cracked into silence and he bowed his head.

Regina's heart swelled with love and with the hurt he felt. She slipped her hand into his and he gripped it tight.

Anger, pain, deep fondness shifted through Luke's eyes. "You'll have to owe me. I like the sound of that." He grunted in pain as the doctor lifted the sheet and peered closer.

Cole's lips flattened. "If words are worth anything, I'm sorry. About you . . . and Sarah. About everything."

"You've got—" Luke hauled in a breath as Doc Warren drove the needle through his skin. Sweat pebbled his upper lip and forehead. ". . . lousy timing, Wellington."

"Always did." Cole's admission trailed off.

Tension arced between them. Both waited, uncertain, still proud, steeped in the old anger that stood between them like a shrine.

Their gazes locked. Cole's jaw clenched tight.

A muscle flexed under the bronzed skin of Luke's cheek.

Regina ached for both men.

With an effort, Luke spoke. "You're through . . . chasin' me?"

"Forever. I'm stayin' here. Workin' with Gage."

"And the baby?" Luke squeezed his eyes shut as Doc tied off a knot.

"I believe you, that she was mine." Cole's voice cracked, soft and rusty. "And I finally understand what I took from you all those years ago."

"About damn time." Relief skittered through Luke's eyes, then they clouded with pain. His gaze went past Cole to Regina. "You gonna make an honest woman out of her?"

"If she'll have me."

"Ask . . . her."

Doc chuckled and pulled another stitch through. Behind them, Gage and Emmett chortled.

Cole grinned, the movement erasing some of the deep worry lines that had carved his cheeks and forehead. He turned to her. "What about it, Regina Suzanne Harrison? Will you marry me?"

"So, that's her name," Gage murmured.

A wide grin split Emmett's face. "We can't rescue you if you say yes, Regina."

She laughed and moved into Cole's arms. "Yes, I'll marry you."

From the table, Luke watched through eyes that were alert, but glazed with pain. "Good." He made a feeble motion with his right hand. "We've still got some things to settle."

"I'd welcome the chance."

Everyone in the room was silent, witnessing the death of bitterness and the resurrection of friendship.

Cole turned and pressed a tender kiss on Regina's lips. She clung to him, not caring that they stood over the patient's bed in Doc's office. She and Cole had a new beginning. Maybe Cole and Luke did, too.

"I love you," he whispered against her lips.

"I love you." She smiled up at him. "No more secrets?"

"Never again."

EPILOGUE

Noon sunshine slanted through the front door of Gage's house and glinted off the freshly polished windows. From her vantage point at the top of stairs, Regina could see people milling about waiting for the wedding to begin.

In the month since Cole's proposal, preparations had been made in a whirlwind and her impatience had only been heightened. She felt a sense of security she hadn't known since childhood and wished her parents could see her today. The thought brought a catch to her throat.

It seemed everyone from town was here. Cole's mother and father had arrived earlier from their home in Farrell, a few hours' ride away.

Cole's shoulder and the left side of his dark head were visible just outside the door jamb. Also on the porch, Leah and her husband talked with Gage, who'd agreed to stand up for Cole. Reverend Holly gave her a gentle smile from the door and turned to the crowd outside, raising a hand in a signal to begin.

A hush fell over the audience then the sweet slow strains of "The Blue Danube Waltz" trickled up to Regina. Cole played the song slowly, but not with the loneliness she'd heard the first time. Instead, he dragged long pauses and fanned notes that reminded her of his hands on her body, his lips caressing hers. A shiver of anticipation stroked up her spine.

She closed her eyes, savoring the sound for a moment, the security it invoked, the love that swelled her heart. Cole and a new life were waiting for her. A life free of secrets and vengeance, full of hope and promise.

She opened her eyes and smiled at Abe. He'd agreed, with slack-jawed amazement, to give her away. She was relieved that his arm, shot by Cross, was healing nicely.

Emily pressed a kiss to Regina's cheek then one on Abe's lips. Tears gathered in her eyes and she dabbed at them with a dainty kerchief. "You're both stunning, my dears."

Regina returned the kiss and smiled as Emily hurried down the stairs and outside. The children stood outside with Clemma and Elliot.

Reverend Holly had invited Regina back to manage the orphanage, but she had seen how attached Clemma had grown to the children while caring for them in Regina's absence. And the children had grown close to her.

The decision to turn over the care and management of the orphanage to Clemma had been a difficult one. Regina felt a bond with each of the children, but Elliot was now old enough to fend for himself. He had, in fact, already approached Cole about working the horses with him.

She would never stop caring for the children, but she also understood what it was to need them as Clemma did. In the end, she had given them over to the tall, willowy blonde.

Abe tucked Regina's hand in his and croaked, "Ready?"

"Yes." Her eyes stung as she looked at him.

Brown eyes danced at her. With careful steps, he led her down the stairs and to Cole.

She wore a taffeta gown of blush pink, which brought her eyes to vivid green and contrasted the jet black of her hair. Leah had given her the gown as a wedding gift, for which Regina was both grateful and moved.

Cole's gaze branded her, from the tips of her white kid shoes to the fall of hair draped over her right shoulder. His eyes smoldered with love and sinful promises and her heart lurched.

He took her hand in his, looking dangerous and handsome in a black suit with a crisp white shirt. She'd never seen him in any color but black. The shirt deepened his skin to mahogany. The bruise at his cheek and eye had turned purple-green, reminding her again of Sutter. Cole's smile was dazed and his eyes gleamed like black diamonds, hungry for her. Together, they faced Reverend Holly.

The only flaw on an otherwise perfect day was the absence of Luke Sutter. Cole and he had talked until late last night, but Cole had warned Regina not to expect any great changes.

"I ruined a deep friendship, honey. He may never forgive that. Lord knows if I could."

Regina wished Luke could have at least attended the ceremony, but she understood how difficult it must be for him.

Reverend Holly's gentle voice penetrated her musings.

Cole's rumbled, "I do," drew her gaze to him.

She listened to Reverend Holly, answering his questions about love, honor, and cherish. "I do."

A sudden spurt of noise at the back of the crowd drew their attention. Cole turned first and he stiffened. With a thud of alarm, Regina turned.

Luke sat his horse at the edge of the crowd. A smile bloomed on Regina's face and she glanced at Cole. His hand found hers and squeezed.

Luke's penetrating gaze cleaved a path through the crowd and straight to Cole. Blue eyes met black. The crowd glanced from Luke to Cole, but Regina kept her gaze on Luke, waiting, hoping.

With two fingers on the brim of his hat, he saluted.

Cole returned the salute, a smile curving his lips.

Luke grinned, a mix of fondness and nostalgia flitting across his face. He wheeled his horse and disappeared over the rise.

Luke's gesture laced the air with a sense of goodwill. After a short pause, the crowd turned back to Cole and Regina.

She laid a hand on Cole's chest and smiled up at him. "Well, what do you think of that, Mr. Wellington?"

His smile was the first genuinely tender smile she'd

seen on him. "Things won't ever be the way they were, but at least I've got some peace now." He dipped his head, whispering on the way to her lips. "Thank you for that, Mrs. Wellington."

Cole's lips covered hers in a searing kiss, telling of promises made and yet to be made, of places unexplored, of secrets never again kept.

Behind them, Reverend Holly cleared his throat. "You may now kiss the bride."